Growing Jewish Minds, Growing Jewish Souls

PROMOTING SPIRITUAL, SOCIAL, AND EMOTIONAL GROWTH IN JEWISH EDUCATION

EDITED BY
Jeffrey S. Kress

URJ Press • New York

For permission to reprint, please contact:

URJ Press
633 Third Avenue
New York, NY 10017-6778
212-650-4120
press@urj.org

Library of Congress Cataloging-in-Publication Data

Growing Jewish Minds, Growing Jewish Souls : promoting spiritual, social, and emotional growth in Jewish education / edited by Jeffrey S. Kress.
    p. cm.
Includes bibliographical references.
ISBN 978-0-8074-1169-8 (pbk. : alk. paper) 1. Jews--Education. 2. Jewish religious education. 3. Moral education. 4. Spirituality--Study and teaching. I. Kress, Jeffrey S.
    LC3557.W57 2012
    371.829'924--dc23

                                                                          2012031541

Printed on acid-free paper

Book design and composition by John Reinhardt Book Design
Manufactured in the United States of America
10 9 8 7 6 5 4 3 2 1

Contents

Foreword

WHAT IS THE PURPOSE of Jewish education? For the past fifty years or so, it's likely that most Jewish educators and supporters of Jewish education in North America would have answered this question with some variant on the theme of "strengthening Jewish identity." Jewish education has been valued as a bulwark against assimilation, a vehicle for instilling a sense of Jewish pride and belonging, and a means of socializing and enculturating young Jews into a Jewish community and a people with a shared history and textual tradition, characteristic values and behaviors, and a collective identity threatened by corrosive forces in the modern world. Partly as a result of this focus on strengthening "Jewishness," Jewish education in practice has emphasized the acquisition of knowledge and skills that are seen as central to preserving Jewish distinctiveness and solidarity.

There has always been, however, a second strand of thought running through the fabric of American Jewish education, one that has viewed the purpose of Jewish education more broadly. In the last few years, the number and volume of voices proposing an alternative framing of Jewish education's goal and potential impact have increased. Here, for

vi   GROWING JEWISH MINDS, GROWING JEWISH SOULS

example, is how a young Jewish educational innovator, Anna Fuchs, put it recently in a blog post:

> What is the job we want Jewish education to get done? When I ask teachers this, they tell me, the job of Jewish education is to engender Jewish identity, ensure the continuity of the Jewish people, have our students feel proud of Israel, teach Hebrew, guarantee Jewish textual literacy, and more. These are good, noble, *hamish* answers.
>
> But, they are totally irrelevant to our students....
>
> Wonderful! If our goal is not relevant, we can unshackle ourselves from the often stated job of Jewish education and harness our energy and resources toward a meaningful, relevant Jewish education. *Nu?* So? What's the job of Jewish education?
>
> The job of Jewish education is the same as it has always been! The job of Jewish education is to help people be more human, more humane.[1]

The claim being made here, I would suggest, is not that Jewish identity per se is irrelevant, either to our students, educators, or the world, but that seeing it as the purpose or "job" of Jewish education sets our sights too narrowly. Jewish tradition and culture do not aim to make us more Jewish. They aim to make us better human beings, more like the "images of God" we have been created to be.

In this context, the subject of this book—spiritual, social, and emotional learning—is, in reality, the very heart of what Jewish education must be about today. This is so first and foremost for the sake of our students, who, research confirms, are already quite comfortable with their Jewishness and do not feel threatened by a too hostile or too hospitable world, but who are earnestly seeking answers to the critical questions of their lives: How should I behave? What should I believe? How can I do something meaningful with my life?

The good news, as amply illustrated in this volume, is that Jewish education *can* be an effective setting and vehicle for nurturing and guiding the growth of young people in their wholeness and complexity. Today we are seeing a new openness and eagerness among Jewish educators to engage with the wider world, with ethical, social, aesthetic, and environmental issues. Questions of meaning and purpose—not just what the text says, but how we wrestle with its implications for our lives—are moving to the forefront; our learners are demanding it. When Jewish education embraces the job of providing holistic learning that addresses both the intra- and the interpersonal realms, it actually helps foster a fuller and richer Jewish identity, one that has real value in a world of near-infinite choices.

The paradigms of Jewish education are shifting today on many fronts. Technology is empowering learners in new ways. Formal and experiential learning are increasingly intertwined. Teachers are learning new roles as guides and mentors. Silos are being broken down so that individuals and families can embark upon true lifelong Jewish learning journeys. All these shifts reflect the same realization that underlies the case studies and reflections that comprise this book: the measure of Jewish education's success today is its ability to inspire passionate lifelong Jewish learning, learning that actually helps us to live satisfying, meaningful, and purposeful lives.

Without vibrant spiritual, social, and emotional learning, there is no possibility for Jewish education to reach this goal. The authors of the chapters of this book chart new pathways to educating Jewish human beings who will be ethically sensitive, morally steadfast, spiritually alive, and socially committed. The programs and methodologies they describe are often new, but the purpose behind them is ancient. Jewish education is returning to its roots, and that makes it as relevant to twenty-first-century Jews and the challenges of the contemporary world as we could ever hope it to be.

Introduction

Jeffrey S. Kress

IN MY YEARS OF RESEARCH, teaching, and consulting, I have repeatedly found that Jewish educators articulate a consistent range of themes when asked about their goals for their students and their biggest hopes for success. While relative emphasis on particular outcomes may vary, the similarities outweigh the differences. Day school and supplemental school teachers, camp and youth group educators, and educators in settings across denominations as well as in non-denominational institutions frame their goals broadly, envisioning not just a student possessing a particular body of knowledge (though that is an important part of the picture), but a type of person with particular traits and proclivities. They describe a person grounded in and engaged with their community and society (Jewishly speaking and beyond), whose actions are guided not by transient trends but rather by a lasting value system based on a vision of meaning and purpose. As you read through the following list, based on phrases I have encountered throughout my work, think about how your goals fit within this spectrum:

- To feel connected to the Jewish people, historically and across contemporary geographic boundaries

- To see Judaism and Jewish texts as relevant in their lives
- To want to make the world a better place (through acts of *tikkun olam*)
- To experience moments of awe, mystery, and awareness of something greater than themselves in the world
- To make decisions based on Jewish values even when these may not coincide with what is popular
- To exhibit *derech eretz* (positive interpersonal behavior) and *menschlichkeit* (being a good person)
- To be able to respectfully disagree with others about important topics
- To feel a link to Israel and to the Hebrew language
- To feel a love of God
- To want and be able to participate in Jewish communal and life-cycle events
- To have Jewish friends
- To want to pass Judaism on to their own children

I have used the term "Jewish developmental education" to describe efforts to promote holistic outcomes in multiple Jewish realms.[1] These realms can be understood as the inter- and intrapersonal; the cognitive, affective, and behavioral; or knowing, doing, and feeling. Regardless of one's preferred terminology, the basic idea remains the same: *a Jewish education that fails to address any of these elements is incomplete.*

These broad, all-encompassing themes are echoed by Jewish educational theorists as well. For example, Rosenak describes three categories of goals of Jewish education:

(1) [To] effect the socialization of the child into a religious community . . . ;
(2) [to] foster the child's individuation as an implicitly religious person; and
(3) [to] negotiate the tension between religious belonging and reliability, on the one hand, and religious "becoming" and spiritual autonomy, on the other.[2]

Rosenak's "ideal is of a Jew who is animated by love of his language yet open to others, loyal to his community yet critical of its shortcomings, involved with its problems yet sensitive to ultimate concerns and responsive to the universal, proud of his identity yet secure enough not to trumpet his pride."[3] The goals of Jewish education, such as those articulated as part of the groundbreaking collection *Visions of Jewish Education*,[4] repeatedly reference a broad range of outcomes that span the inter- and intrapersonal realms. Twersky, for example, sees the goal of Jewish education as "achiev[ing] both an overriding love of God and a genuine worship of God—both a deep understanding and a true piety."[5] For Moshe Greenberg, this is expressed as "[1] love of learning Torah and love of the fulfillment of the commandments between man and God . . . ; [2] acceptance of the Torah as a moral guide . . . ; [3] a way of life that creates a community . . . ; [4] a relationship to the Jewish people in all the lands of their dispersion."[6] Every day, Jewish educators actualize these visions as they help students achieve individual and group identities, negotiate adherence to religious norms while at the same time living in a pluralistic society, and connect with history while recognizing the divine in the present. Interestingly, many of these educators work toward these ends as they themselves navigate these same tensions and seek the same range of outcomes for themselves and their families.

A focus on developmental-educational outcomes in the inter- and intrapersonal realms is not unique to Jewish education or even to religious education. Many educators in secular (public and private) schools have embraced the notion that their role in student learning, traditionally defined as development of cognitive skills and competence with subject matter, can be enhanced by attending to broader developmental needs of students, and research has supported these linkages.[7] In fact, state education standards, often seen as the blueprints for a strictly content-oriented education, are infused with elements in the social and emotional realms.[8] Many teachers lament that a retreat on the part of nonacademic influences (e.g., family, religious institutions) has resulted in a reduction of allies for schools as agents of personal growth and transmission of pro-social values, not just academic learning. Concern remains among educational leaders that the current test-driven environment detracts from the focus on such outcomes.[9]

Further, the issue of spirituality, while perhaps more controversial, is also entering the discourse of secular educators. While acknowledging the need to separate church and state and to avoid promoting any specific religious form, educational leaders are increasingly embracing the idea that "by not welcoming the sacred . . . our schools run the risk of raising a whole generation of young people who will be bereft of the wisdom and connectedness they need to live a fully human life."[10] Developmental research supports the interconnection of issues of religiosity and spirituality with what the researchers term "thriving," including having a moral compass, maintaining a positive future orientation, and holding various pro-social attitudes.[11]

The Challenges of Jewish Education in the Spiritual, Social, and Emotional Realms

The earth was a chaos, unformed, and on the chaotic waters' face there was darkness. Then God's spirit [ruach] glided over the face of the waters. (Genesis 1:2)

We've got spirit [ruach], yes we do! We've got spirit [ruach], how 'bout you? (Popular camp cheer)

The second verse of Genesis is a familiar one, part of the opening section of the Torah, imprinted by the learning and repetition of the Creation story. This rich description of an unfathomable vista prompts us to imagine the scene, to impose a familiar image based on our own interpretive framework. Rashi, for example, describes God's throne hovering above the water. The above-quoted cheer is also a familiar refrain, pulling on the memories of Jews who have spent time at a camp, youth group convention, or Shabbaton. The memory brings its own images of energetic children screaming and banging on tables in crowded dining halls.

These two quotations are linked in their use of the term *ruach*, "spirit," and provide a stark illustration of the multiple meanings of this term. In particular, they highlight two tensions in the understanding of spirituality—the nature of its relation to the emotional and the social spheres. At the risk of opening a can of metaphysical worms, I think it is reasonable to suggest that the image of *ruach Elohim*, "the spirit of God," does not involve hoarse vocal cords or tables and chairs used as drums. To me (and, I think, inherent in Rashi's comment) the term, as used in the creation story, invokes a sense of reverence, a counterpoint to the unformed and void chaos of *tohu vavohu*. The emotional tone is a quiet one; the social dimension is one solitary point of spirit existing amid the void. On the other hand, the chaos of *tohu vavohu* is an apt categorization of moments of *ruach* in a camp dining hall! Here, emotion is pouring forth, and the nature and context of the chant (the emphasis of "we" compared to "you") emerge from and further build a sense of group and community and connectedness.

The discussion of spirit has a parallel in the discussion of emotions; the two terms are overlapping though, importantly, are not synonymous. To start with, there are emotional elements inherent in both the contemplative and exuberant connotations of spirit. Researchers have even used the term "sacred emotions" to describe affect often associated with religious or spiritual experiences—for example, awe, reverence, and gratitude.[12] To George Vaillant, a Harvard psychiatrist who has written extensively on the topic, "spirituality is all about positive emotions. These emotions include *love, hope, joy, forgiveness, compassion, trust, gratitude* and *awe*. Of enormous importance is the fact that none of the eight are 'all about me.'"[13]

Further, a parallel tension exists between an emphasis on emotional control and a focus on emotional awareness and expression. Scheindlin sees educational efforts too often aiming toward the former.[14] Both psychology and Judaism have had complicated relationships with emotions. Both have conceptualized emotions alternatively (or even simultaneously) as potentially dangerous forces to be controlled and as aspects of experience to be embraced. While acknowledging an interplay of affect, cognition, and behavior, educators and psychologists often start from a standpoint of cognitive hegemony. Sheffler's often cited work on the "cognitive emotions" is an example of looking at the latter through the lens of the former.[15] Contemporary research in neuropsychology, however, points to "hardwired" emotional pathways subject to change and learning in ways similar to those of cognition.

One might characterize spirituality and emotion as having both centripetal (inward or central) and centrifugal (outward) elements. Spirituality and emotions can ground us internally, giving us a strong sense of who we are and what we believe most strongly. They can serve as an internal compass as we interact in the world. The centripetal element encompasses issues of reflectiveness, sense of wonder, emotional awareness, dealing with frustration and challenges, goal orientation, creativity, empathy, and appreciation of one's strengths.

Spirit and emotion can also serve to mediate and motivate our engagement with others, providing meaningful connections with friends, communities, nature, and so on. These centrifugal elements have to do with pro-social activities such as social justice and social action as well as positive everyday social interactions. Likewise, we see heightened spiritual and emotional awareness emerging from both social disconnection (think about the prototypical meditator sitting on the mountain) and social engagement (imagine an emotional song session at camp). Paradoxically, these two elements are often described as intertwined, with solitary meditation leading to feelings of connectedness. Judaism sees an interplay between the individual and the collective, which results in "individual responsibility coming together for the sake of community."[16] "Spirituality" and "emotion" are marked by ambivalence in Judaism at least as old as the rise of Hasidism and the opposition that accompanied that movement. We still draw a distinction between *keva*, the fixed elements of ritual, and *kavanah*, the elements involving intentionality. We stereotype spiritual practitioners alternatively as individuals who live lives of deep religious meaning and those who focus on surface elements of rituals, the equivalent of singing "Kumbaya" around the campfire.

Perhaps it is because of this breadth of meaning that Judaism has struggled with the idea of spirituality. Empirically, Jews were found to score lower than other Americans on a broad range of spiritual indexes.[17] Data also point to denominational differences, with Conservative and Reform Jews reporting lower rates than Orthodox on spiritual indexes having to do with transcendent experiences (such as prayer) and feelings of "oneness of nature and the universe."[18] Over a decade ago, researchers found that while adolescents value a search for meaning, "Judaism is often seen as irrelevant to this search."[19] There have been Jewish communal leaders who have expressed pointed concern about Judaism's limitations in doing "the one thing Judaism is supposed to do best," namely, helping "to create a personal intimate relationship with God; a life of cosmic meaning and purpose; a life of soul satisfaction, true inner happiness, and deep-felt joy and fulfillment."[20]

However, there are indications that the language of spirituality, of finding meaning (even in idiosyncratic ways), is entering into the Jewish, and Jewish educational, mainstream. A recent edition of RAVSAK's publication *HaYidion*, for example, focuses on the topic in the context of Jewish day schools.[21] Cohen and Hoffman report what they call a "closing [of] the spirituality gap."[22] That is, the younger generation of Jews report higher levels of spiritual engagement than older Jews, counter to trends among Americans in general. As these respondents raise families and enroll their own children in Jewish educational venues, they will bring this set of expectations with them. Reactions to this finding are again marked by ambivalence. While the authors of the study note the potential for the blossoming of Jewish learning and other manifestations of the quest for Jewish meaning, others are less sanguine. For example, Dr. Jack Wertheimer, reacting to the study (and reflecting the spirituality-as-individual versus spirituality-as-collective dialectic discussed earlier) notes that he "would not want to see spirituality come at the expense of Jewish collective action."[23]

Though spirituality is a difficult construct to define, it can be seen as sharing elements of the social and emotional domains: self-awareness, a sense of (or a seeking of) meaning and purpose in one's life, an appreciation of the interconnectedness among living things and between living things and their environment, and sense of transcendence and of the sacred. The ambiguity surrounding the term is a challenge to educators, but not one that should stymie efforts to promote elements of spirituality.

Rather than indicating lack of clarity, the multiple uses of the term *spirit* may reflect ambiguity in the literal sense of having multiple meanings. The various manifestations of both "spirit" and "emotion" are reflective of the realities of the human experience. Think about the educational settings with which you are most familiar, be it a school, a summer camp, a synagogue, or even a family dinner table. Do you want, ideally, to see at this setting the quiet soothing manifestation of *ruach* as in Genesis? The boisterousness *ruach* of a camp dining hall? Intensive emotional introspection? The exuberant outpouring of emotion? If you—like many educators—find yourself answering, "Yes, all of the above," this is an indication that the language of "spirit" and "emotion" may be insufficient to capture the broad range of outcomes we associate with these terms. Rather than being constrained by the limits of language, we would do well to live with linguistic ambiguity while we work toward a broad range of inter- and intrapersonal outcomes.

Educators in Jewish and secular settings alike face considerable challenges to their efforts to address outcomes in the inter- and intrapersonal domains. The issue of "finding room in the curriculum," already heightened by the environment of assessment and accountability, is compounded in Jewish day schools by the rigors of a dual curriculum and in Jewish supplemental schools by the limited number of hours of attendance. Educators are concerned that their students' parents and the communities in which they live have diminished in their will or in their capacity, or both, to serve as allies in achieving these ends. They see the media, long suspected of undermining attempts to build values and community, as becoming ever more invasive and ubiquitous. And, though they may lag behind their students in technological know-how, they are aware that social interactions are becoming both faster-paced (with texting, IM'ing, and social networking) and more interpersonally distant (with electronically mediated interactions replacing face-to-face dialogue).

In the spiritual realm, educators may be unsure about their own beliefs or struggle with their relationship with God. The range of approaches to God and spirituality within the Jewish tradition[24] may provide multiple access points for belief but can also cause educators to try to juggle multiple expressions of belief among themselves, their co-workers, their students, and their communities.

Educators are increasingly being called upon to help students develop the skills needed for social, emotional, and spiritual development as well as to provide opportunities for students to practice the use of these skills and to integrate them into a sense of self. Educators in Jewish educational settings have some particular advantages in meeting these challenges. Jewish educational settings generally embrace their role in promoting values and spiritual growth. Many Jewish educators are comfortable with values language and embrace the holistic nature of their work. While far from perfect agreement, there is at least a general consensus about the scope of these values. Jewish schools exist within a network of Jewish communal organizations in which many students and families already participate, though the connections among these may be tenuous. These educational and communal settings are, to varying extents, communities of choice for which a degree of shared values and goals is asked in exchange for membership.

Innovative efforts have been undertaken by Jewish educators to promote outcomes in the intra- and interpersonal realms. The goal of this volume is to bring these efforts together to provide an overview of what is happening, what is possible, and what might be learned from the experiences of these educators. Lessons from these efforts would inform not only those engaged in Jewish educational research, practice, and policy making, but also their counterparts working in general education.

Addressing an Elusive Construct: Origins of This Book

This book is rooted in two set discussions. In 2004, I became involved in a research endeavor that became known informally as the "Happiness Project" supported in part by the funding from the Steinhardt Foundation for Jewish Life.[25] Our leadership team (Dr. Michael Ben-Avie, Audrey Lichter, Alan Mendelson, and myself) focused on four core central constructs that emerged from the existing literature and from conversations with Jewish educational leaders as key goals of Jewish education:

1. Connectedness to family, peers, and community
2. Successful intelligence, including critical and analytical creative problem-solving skills
3. Social and emotional competence
4. Sense of meaning and purpose

While each area brought methodological challenges, "sense of meaning and purpose," and its associated dimensions of spirituality, proved to be particularly vexing. In order to help define the construct and to consider research methodologies, we convened a group comprising Jewish thinkers[26] and behavioral researchers[27] who have studied related phenomena. The conversation took place at the Jewish Theological Seminary during the fall of 2007. Aside from issues of research methodology (which are less germane to this book), our team learned much about issues of spirituality, meaning, and purpose, much of which frames the ideas discussed above.

Not long after the Meaning and Purpose Symposium, the Covenant Foundation convened a group of practitioners involved in issues of spirituality and social-emotional learning in Jewish education.[28] The purpose of this symposium was to generate dialogue among practitioners with a common interest and to think about how best to advance the field. Participants discussed the need to address the spiritual, social, and emotional needs of Jewish youth and the great interest in doing so that they have encountered among educators. This was consistent with the findings of the Happiness Project team. The practitioners in this consultation discussed their own work in this area as well as other initiatives with which they were familiar. As is often the case with educators, there had been little contact or dialogue among those working in this area. Among the recommendations of that group was to create a product that would highlight some of the work in the arena of spirituality and social-emotional learning.

This book is meant in the spirit of that recommendation. It is not an exhaustive survey of efforts to achieve spiritual, social, and emotional goals, nor is it a report of best practices (although I will draw out some general recommendations in the Conclusion) or a "how-to" manual for change. Rather, these chapters are the product of thoughtful educators who discuss their work with spiritual, social, and emotional issues. The chapters are meant to touch on a diverse range of approaches to the topic and to illustrate what can become the spiritual, social, and emotional organizing frameworks for our work.

A few editorial notes are in order. The contributors to this book might identify themselves as practitioners, educators, researchers, academics, or any and all of the above. I have tried to balance consistency of tone across chapters with maintaining each author's voice. I have aimed for consistency of transliteration across chapters but have opted to include translations for Hebrew terms in individual chapters rather than in a general glossary. The terms used in this book generally have to do with social-emotional or spiritual issues, and, as such, translating them without applying an interpretive framework is particularly tricky. Rather than imposing an overall interpretive framework, I opt for leaving room for individual nuances when needed.

The chapters in this book are not divided into formal sections. This decision was made to reflect what I believe to be the fundamentally interconnected nature of the various efforts to address spiritual, social, and emotional issues. There is no one program, approach, or idea that holds *the* answer. Rather, these chapters, taken together, are meant to represent a variety of approaches to the topic. The chapters, however, are not organized randomly.

- Chapters 1–4 set the stage by offering an overview and a discussion of key terminology and concepts. Shire provides a developmental overview as well as the framework of an educational approach. Ingall focuses on the idea of transcendence. Scheindlin discusses sensitivity in the spiritual and emotional realms, while Levingston delves into the interconnections of spiritual and moral education.

- Chapters 5–7 emerge from work done through three groundbreaking programs to address holistic student outcomes. These programs originated in general education; the chapters here demonstrate their deep connection to Jewish education. The programs discussed demonstrate that a structured approach to promoting spiritual, social, and emotional outcomes need not imply rigidity and constraints but can be geared toward deeply rooted changes in a system. Weaver, Hirschberg, and Greenwald write about the late Rachael Kessler and the PassageWorks approach that she developed; Simons and Gafni describe implementation of the Open Circle Program in a Jewish day school; and Darsa and Sleeper discuss the Facing History and Ourselves approach.

- Chapters 8–10 each explore an initiative that uses a specific focus area as an entry point to the discussion of promoting outcomes in the spiritual, social, and emotional realms. Novick discusses her work addressing bullying in Jewish schools, Wachs and Schatz describe the lessons from an intervention to enhance the *t'filah* (prayer) experience in one school, and Epstein discusses her work on *Evaded Issues*, such as those related to gender. As with the previous three chapters, the authors show how addressing their particular focal element requires a deep engagement within a setting.

- Though schools are the primary focus of the early chapters, chapters 11–14 expand the context (I will say more about non-school settings in my concluding section of this book). Aaron, Feigelson, and Libenson describe two initiatives geared toward college students through Hillel, and Winer and Sheanin discuss a variety of contexts with the Union for Reform Judaism's youth-related work. The final two chapters deal with adult education, though quite differently. Levites and Stone discuss an adult learning series based on *musar*, while Elias and Gootman talk about spiritual, social, and emotional elements of parenting.

1

Nurturing the Spiritual in Jewish Education

MICHAEL SHIRE

J EWISH EDUCATION TODAY is mainly concerned with the transmission of knowledge, the development of ritual skills, the formation and strengthening of Jewish identity, and the affirmation of values. It deals very little with the nature of religious experience, the development of religious growth, or the general field of spirituality. Jewish education has found this area of religious education difficult to promote in a modern secular society, with teachers and parents ambivalent about their own religiosity, let alone about transmitting it to others.

Dimensions of Jewish Education

Jewish education has primarily been concerned with the outer dimensions of religion: the historical, social, and theological forms of religious expression. Those elements of religion that are expressed through verbal or tactile components of religious practice or expressed ideas about God include prayer and liturgy. Jewish education has been less concerned with elements of spiritual and religious experience such as trust, awe, wonder, reverence, and love of God—factors that have been deemed inner or implicit domains of religion.[1] These dimensions of outer and inner are reflected in the eleventh-century writings of medieval Jewish philosopher Bachya ibn Pakuda in which he distinguishes between the "duties of the limbs," those commandments enshrined in halachah (Jewish law) that involve the various parts of the body, and the "duties of the heart," which comprise inner intentions and emotional responses to religious experience.[2]

Where Jewish education has focused on inner dimensions, particularly in early childhood or informal education, it has not considered the nature of the relationship between inner and outer. Aspirations for graduates of Jewish educational programs often focus on evidence of knowledge, pride of association, and expression of moral values. Where spirituality is included, it is often regarded as a separate entity. This might be expressed in music or experiences removed from the home and synagogue and include activities such as camping or Jewish travel.

RELIGIOSITY

Jews have generally been uncomfortable with the use of the word "spiritual" when it has related merely to a series of inner spiritual virtues. For Jews, spiritual awareness without explicit religious expression is incomplete. Martin Buber used the word "religiosity" to describe a spiritual openness within a prescribed religious tradition.[3] Succinctly put by Rabbi Arthur Green, Jewish religiosity is described as "striving for the presence of God and fashioning a life of holiness appropriate to such striving."[4] Jewish spiritual life is thus a continual task of striving to create holiness even in the most mundane of daily acts as Jews seek to build a life of holiness for communities and for individuals.

Religiosity defined in this way is a vital component of Jewish life and experience and needs to be integrated into the very fabric of Jewish education. Many Jewish educators are uncertain as to how it can be translated into educational objectives incorporated into the curriculum of Jewish educational settings. One of the key issues for Jewish education is how to make spiritual development an explicit objective of educational programming.

FAITH

Since the establishment of the field of faith development in the 1980s, there has spawned a vast array of research and studies in the area of children's spirituality, religious development, theologies of childhood, and educational approaches to religious growth. For Jewish educators, however, questions and concerns abound about defining children's spirituality in a Jewish context as well as understanding the roles of the Jewish educator in enhancing it. Critiques of both the definition of spirituality and its intended outcomes have been expressed by Jewish educators. The universalistic approach to spiritual development expressed in a definition of "making meaning" is seen to blur distinctions between religious traditions. This is felt to ignore the particular Jewish notion of religiosity in favor of a generalized definition. The linear nature of spiritual development as expressed by Fowler's stages of faith results in a defined "spiritual maturity" that negates an iterative process or indeed a change in structuring faith that is reversible.[5] Spiritual development, however, has become a normative feature of state children's education in the United Kingdom. This has further resulted in its assessment of attainment in British schools by the Office of Standards in Education.[6] Prompted by this newly developed field of educational development, Jewish educators need to ask questions about the nature of educating for religious growth and spirituality, and the relationship of religious development to religious learning and practice. How will the faith of the child be characterized and expressed in Jewish terms? What conceptual tools can be used to best understand the nature of the spiritual child? How can faith be formed and nurtured authentically in Judaism, and how can young people be personally enriched and their faith enhanced through Jewish religious education?

What is meant by spiritual development? Is it different from spirituality, religious development, or religiosity? There is little consensus about the nature and scope of this particular dimension of life. Where there is research, it has situated itself within the field of the psychology of religion. The originator of this field of study combining theological inquiry with psychological development is Professor James Fowler of

Emory University in Atlanta. Fowler's theory of faith development is summarized as follows:

> Faith may be characterized as an integral, centering process underlying the formation of beliefs, values and meanings that (1) gives coherence and direction to people's lives, (2) links them in shared trust and loyalties with others, (3) grounds their personal stance and loyalties in relation to a larger frame of reference and (4) enables them to face and deal with the conditions of human life. The stages of faith aim to describe patterned operations of knowing and valuing that underlie our consciousness.[7]

Fowler uses a broad definition of the word "faith." Rather than limiting faith to religious belief, Fowler denotes a process of making meaning that is shared by all human beings. Faith, therefore, is a process of trusting and structuring meaning making, which incorporates belief and goes beyond it.

Fowler conducted research interviews with hundreds of people from a variety of different backgrounds, ages, sexes, and religious affiliations. From these interviews, he derived six stages of faith through which an individual passes. These stages are structural; they characterize the inner operations by which a person makes meaning of the world. These stages are claimed to be common to all people. Though the content of each stage will vary from individual to individual, Fowler suggests that all people at the same stage compose meaning in a structurally similar manner. The stages are sequentially ordered, with each stage incorporating the processes of the one before while adding to it in a new dimension. Each stage has its own integrity, so that stage 4 is not categorized as more faith full than stage 3; rather, it has developed in a qualitatively new way. The transition from stage to stage becomes apparent when individuals are no longer able to make meaning using their familiar processes and seek to move beyond them. These transitions are often triggered by life crises where new ways are sought to understand painful and difficult circumstances.

STAGES OF FAITH

Stage 1: Intuitive-Projective Faith
The faith of the young child is one in which meaning is made intuitively and by imitation. Knowledge and feeling are fused and formed by

significant people in the child's life. Here sensitive and caring teachers who foster trust in the child are important, as are the images, stories, and symbols that are formative at this stage. Fact and fantasy may be undifferentiated, leading to imaginative and creative images of God. Religious meaning is associated with concrete images and symbols.

Stage 2: Mythic-Literal Faith

At the stage of schooling, children are conscious of being part of a larger group, more than just their family, as they engage with the stories, myths, and values of a religious tradition. These can be particularly understood in very literal terms as God is portrayed as the ultimate powerful being or force.

Stage 3: Synthetic-Conventional Faith

According to Fowler, stage 3 is conventional in that individuals are anxious to respond to the expectations of significant others. There is a strong tendency to rely on institutional authority as the holder of religious authority. Symbols become more deeply understood, allowing for symbolic meaning to become important. A personal relationship with God can be expressed, and a sense of community is valued. Religious feelings are deeply felt but tacitly held before they become examined more critically later on. This is the time for confirming a religious identification and belonging to a community or religious heritage.

Stage 4: Individuative-Reflective

As the congruence of this position breaks down in the adolescent who questions authority, there comes more of a position of individual choice with regard to meaning making, authority, and belief. Fowler characterizes this next stage as coinciding with Piaget's formal operational thinking; it is more inner dependent and involves a way of making meaning that is more personally chosen and self-consciously different from the religious identity of others. Prayer and spiritual feelings can take place in any location, not necessarily connected to a religious institution. Ritual shared with like-minded individuals is preferred over a large community. Stage 4 faith diminishes the power of the concrete symbol in favor of the central idea it represents. Individuals ready for transition in young adulthood find that their faith is excessively reliant on their individual consciousness. This leads to an awareness of the purely personal perspective of truth and meaning without regard for a historical or community-based conception.

Stage 5: Conjunctive Faith
Stage 5 faith combines what one knows and trusts from within with the perspectives of others even from outside one's own community of faith. In this stage, there is a universal perspective to one's faith as well as a return to ritual and symbol as sacred roles and objects. The symbols of a religious tradition have deep meaning resonant in their historical and contemporary identification. Often individuals can infer new meaning in the role of these symbols and rituals.

Stage 6: Universalizing Faith
The final and most comprehensive stage, according to Fowler, is exemplified by those who can perceive paradoxes in life and yet create unity in their spiritual life by combining a particularistic religious tradition with a universal humanitarian outlook. Fowler suggests that this is rare in human beings and only some exceptional individuals achieve it.

Spirituality in Education

The work of faith development in the United States and Switzerland, coupled with the work of spiritual development in the United Kingdom as part of the Religious Education National Curriculum, has prompted much debate about the nature of spirituality in education. This has resulted in philosophical reflections on spirituality and psychological approaches to learning for the development of spirituality. This bringing together of theology and developmental psychology marked the innovative uniqueness of the faith development school. The approaches of James Fowler of the United States[8] and Fritz Oser of Switzerland,[9] Canadian scholar Clive Beck,[10] and British scholar Kevin Mott-Thornton,[11] however, all attempt to forge a universalistic approach to the nature of spirituality. This approach widens the definition of spirituality so as to allow those without a religious heritage or affiliation to accept the notion that one can be spiritual without being religious. Such a universalistic and syncretistic approach blurs the significant differences between religious traditions and often assumes a Western rationalist position where the cognitive predominates over the affective.

Critiques of these developmental theories take issue with the normative linear structure of the stage theory that leads to an endpoint that is highly rationalist and universalistic. In addition, the theory focuses on the way in which individuals structure their faith in line with the faith stage paradigm. The predominant feature of Jewish religious life is the increasing nature of one's obligation to community and the ways in which community impacts upon an individual's religious life.

There is no normative outcome of Jewish religious maturity. There are at least three distinctive paths toward religious maturation in Judaism that incorporate intellectual accomplishment (*chacham*), a devout piety (*chasid*), and/or moral leadership (*tzaddik*). Where faith is defined as leading to a universal norm, it does not take into account the specific nature of differing religious traditions. For Judaism, the corresponding Hebrew term for faith, *emunah*, denotes a relationship of trust between God and humankind, one in which we put our trust in a transcendent reality and expect a covenantal relationship in return. However, *emunah* is not merely an idea. It is expressed in Judaism through the performance of mitzvot. These mitzvot become the ways in which we act out *emunah* in the world. Our relationship to God is intensified by the deepening consciousness of the mitzvot. Mere performance, however, will not necessarily engender a spiritual awareness. Medieval philosophers such as Bachya ibn Pakuda in eleventh-century Spain had already warned of a life based on mitzvot that had no inner significance. He called for a priority to be given to what he labeled "duties of the heart" that underpin and make meaningful the traditional practices of faith. If the inner dimension is not nurtured, then the external commandments cannot be properly fulfilled. It is necessary, therefore, to have intention (*kavanah*) in carrying out the mitzvot.

Development of Religiosity

My research with early adolescents resulted in an ability to evaluate the impact of different educational programming on their explicit and implicit religiosity. Students enrolled in Jewish day schools, congregational schools, Jewish summer camps, and Israel experiences were interviewed with a view to investigating both their religious commitment and their spiritual awareness. Through projective picture interviews as well as participant observations, students generated notions of their spirituality through projective associations and connections to their religious experiences. A series of categories could be developed from the data and correlated with each educational setting. From this research into the enhancement of religious development, I have proposed an approach to educational programming that enables educators to explicitly take into account religious development in Jewish educational programming. Three elements of curriculum design have been identified as contributing to religious development in Jewish education: *encounter, reflection,* and *instruction.* These are components of both planned curriculum by educators and experienced curriculum by students. They can be identified as distinct in both the planning and experienced curriculum but do not necessarily occur sequentially. The three phases are not so much a curriculum design as elements to be found in environments that promote spiritual growth.

ENCOUNTER

Promoting experiences for encounter involves providing supportive times and spaces that evoke an emotional response in an educational setting. These responses can be intense feelings, moments of contemplation or peacefulness, and expressions of wonderment or awe. The intensity of the experience marks the encounter as students express a closeness to God or a sense of God's presence. A participant in a Jewish educational program describes this phase of the curriculum:

> Being spiritual should be a feeling of contentment. It's like opening a door of perception. It can be a road to somewhere else, another way of thinking, another plane of awareness.[12]

The opportunity for spiritual encounter is paramount in nurturing religious development, and the experience of it leads to motivation to learn more about the nature of a religious life. Music, ritual, the creative arts, prayer, and meditation are all catalysts for such experiences of encounter. Encounter can be an experience with the self, others, a text, an idea, a location, or God. It prompts questions in students, enabling them to verbalize spiritual feelings and awareness. Group experiences can heighten the sense of encounter, particularly in adolescence as the group becomes the shared locus of making meaning. During this phase, educators act largely as facilitators, structuring experiences and framing perceptions.

REFLECTION

A second phase of program design involves reflection, an activity that prompts students to question and review perspectives. Reflection provides the opportunity to deliberate on religious questions of meaning and is often evident in personal meditation, prayer, and dialogue. It can also be a component of creative writing, adult-led or peer discussion, and debate. Reflection is an intimate, imaginative, and highly personal activity that allows for speculation, exploration, and personal discovery. The connections made during this phase bring deep consciousness and realization to new meanings personally held. Educators facilitate reflection through questioning at the highest forms of Bloom's taxonomy with questions of analysis and judgment.

Reflection, therefore, allows students to translate their spiritual encounters into Jewish religious language. It aids in naming and understanding the experiences of students and provides critical reflection on their encounters in educational settings. In this mode of reflection, educators act in a counseling role, offering encouragement and active listening and sharing experiences. It is evoked when there is a strong relationship between educator and student. However, it is often the presence of supportive peers that allows for the most significant opportunities for reflection. This support is fostered where spiritual experience is seen as normative for human development.

INSTRUCTION

Instruction for religiosity is the third phase and includes the use of creativity, knowledge, and acquisition of skills. It provides the theological underpinnings for students' spiritual experiences and forms a critical consciousness in the student. This phase includes a connection to Jewish history and tradition, as well as engagement with the texts of our tradition. Instruction is a phase that encompasses elements of multiple modes of learning, including the affective and cognitive dimensions of learning, as well as knowledge and skills. Teaching varying concepts of God allows students to place their experience in personal meaning understood at its fullest depth; what makes truth religious is not that it relates to some abnormal field of thought and feeling, but that it goes to the roots of experience, which it interprets.

THE THREE PHASES

The spiritual awareness found in encounter and the verbalizations that emerge from it can lead to articulation of questions in reflection. These questions are responded to by the Jewish context offered in instruction. The three phases of encounter, reflection, and instruction for religiosity are not sequential, but operate concurrently. All three influence each other, as instruction for religiosity opens up students to new encounters. Reflection is a crucial phase, however, in that it allows articulation of spiritual awareness to be connected to explicit religiosity in instruction. Reflection allows others to hear experiences and encourages a future disposition to such encounters or a questioning attitude that places the encounter in a religious context. The sharing of reflections is as important for the individual as it is for the educational group. As Buber has posited, it is in the asking of questions by students and the subsequent learning by the teacher that a mutuality of education takes place.[13] The identification of the three phases of encounter, reflection, and instruction for religiosity allows Jewish educators to understand the processes at work in enhancing religiosity in any educational environment. All three phases are needed, and educators will need to plan for them when formulating their programs. In each phase the role of the educator changes, making it important to understand these differing roles and to develop a repertoire of skills to be used in differing phases. The enhancement of religiosity is promoted through the presence of all three phases in the curriculum. The challenge of educating for religious experience is to help learners identify spiritual experience as Jewish religious experience.

2

Teaching for Transcendence

CAROL K. INGALL

Introduction

THE *OXFORD ENGLISH DICTIONARY* defines "transcendence" as, "the act or fact of surmounting or rising above, elevation (obs.); excelling, surpassing or the condition or quality of being transcendent, surpassing eminence or excellence." I propose that transcendence includes both spirituality and social and emotional intelligence, and is an essential ingredient in building community as well as enriching students' inner lives. Like spirituality, transcendence can be approached from both a secular and a religious perspective. The secular aspect is universal (i.e., not specifically Jewish) and not connected to a specific religious tradition, neither in its creed nor in its practice.

Its goal is to produce what Rachael Kessler called a "soul-welcoming" classroom.[1] The push for community building, for learners to aim high, for appreciating the beauty of nature—all examples of secular transcendence—are unlikely to elicit controversy, whereas "spirituality" may generate concerns for parents who are skittish about New Age faddism.

I prefer the term "transcendence" to "spirituality" because it allows for a religious, particularistic, specifically Jewish dimension, as well as a secular, universal one. A religious perspective is theistic; it assumes a God who transcends the natural world, the world that God brought into being. Jewish transcendence is capacious enough to include Jewish mysticism throughout history (like the *merkavah* mystics, Isaac Luria, and Chabad) and a more normative, Rabbinic, everyday mysticism, as expressed in the *Amidah*, also known as *HaT'filah* (The Prayer). In it we thank God for God's "miracles that we experience every day." This aspect of transcendence, through which learners recognize the sacred in everyday life, as they move from the realm of the commonplace to the divine, is the essence of religious transcendence.

Our task as Jewish educators is to combine both the universalistic aspects of transcendence and the particularistic. Our students need models of how to live in two worlds, and teaching about the secular and universal, as well as teaching the religious and particularistic, helps them to integrate those worlds. Teaching for transcendence can include the mundane (in its original sense of worldly), garden-variety transcendence like classic Deweyan community improvement projects. This might include cleaning up public parks and petitioning for more funds for embattled public libraries, and it surely includes the building of community. Another secular manifestation of transcendence is striving for achievement. Schools are hardwired for this kind of transcendence. They all profess that they promote excellence (has anyone ever read a mission statement that aims to create a mediocre school?). All schools want students (and teachers) to stretch their capacities, both intellectual and interpersonal. Teachers routinely ask students to better their academic performance and to push for excellence; coaches and gym teachers preach, "There's no I in TEAM."

But Jewish educational institutions, be they schools, camps, or nature centers, must also teach Jewish perspectives on transcendence. Some of them could be universalistic in nature, like *derech eretz* initiatives in the classroom and caring for animals and plants. Who doesn't agree that Jewish schools must teach *mitzvot bein adam lachaveiro* (the obligations we have to each other and to our communities)? But lest we forget, most Jewish schools, although some might find the terminology challenging, are *religious* schools. As such they must also teach *mitzvot bein adam LaMakom*, the tougher mitzvot that deal with one's relationship to the Divine. A commitment to transcendence in Jewish educational venues integrates the universal with the particular and requires that we be as attentive of one as the other. It means that we must attend to the distinctly Jewish elements of transcendence: preparing learners for prayer and for appreciating the power of ritual, and encouraging a religious sensibility based on awe and mystery.

Transcendence as an Antidote for Entitlement

At one time or another we have all wrung our hands over our self-centered learners, whether we teach in elementary schools or graduate schools, in camps or adult learning initiatives. The individualism exhibited by Bellah et al.'s Sheila[2] or by those interviewed by Cohen and Eisen,[3] espousing what the authors dubbed the "sovereign self" ideology, or by the lone bowler popularized by Putnam[4] has become the deeply rooted entitlement that suffuses so many contemporary social interactions, not an issue for children alone.

The self-esteem movement has done its work all too well. How can we reverse its excesses and rescue youngsters from what Walker Percy called "the great suck of self"?[5] How can we teach teachers to create environments in which students connect with something larger than themselves? The question is one for all educators; how much more so for those who are involved in religious education. Abraham Joshua Heschel reminds us, "The self gains when it loses itself in the contemplation of the nonself. . . . Self-expression depends on self-attachment to what is greater than the self."[6] We teach the contemplation of the nonself when we teach transcendence.

One aspect of universalistic transcendence, involving oneself in a bigger entity, is what Parker Palmer calls "radical communalism."[7] He links radical communalism to spirituality, which he defines as "the eternal human yearning to be connected with something larger than our own egos."[8] (Personally, I prefer transcendence for reasons I explained above.) Addressing the question of excellence in higher education, Palmer highlights the importance of service learning to break down the isolation of intellect from action and thought from feeling. Joel Westheimer is one of the leading researchers in the field of social studies education. He is the university research professor in the Pedagogy of Collective Action and Reflection at the University of Ottawa. The trajectory of Westheimer's academic career is instructive for those of us in Jewish education. He has widened his lens from the local to the national, by moving away from studying service learning[9] and moving toward teaching of democratic citizenship and what it means to be an informed member of a community.[10] Today's most popular *tikkun olam* projects have similarly sought a wider arc of social engagement or, at least, a more exotic locale. Working in the Jewish community for social justice now seems ho-hum. The appeal to young Jews of the Darfur protest, of American Jewish World Service projects in Mexico, Guatemala, and Rwanda, their embrace of ecological change and small-scale projects like Heifer or Kiva, indicate a hunger for something bigger than the vapid one-shot programs that have been passing as mitzvah projects.

IMPLEMENTING RADICAL COMMUNALISM IN THE CLASSROOM: UNIVERSALISTIC TRANSCENDENCE

What do we need to create a community that nourishes its members, to have children lose themselves in the ethics of action? First, we need teachers who are committed to best practices in contemporary pedagogy: to making room in their professional repertoire for cooperative learning, to valuing the many skills that students bring with them to the classroom, and to embracing differentiated instruction. Good citizenship must be taught explicitly as well as implicitly. Regardless of the venue, Jewish education has to address the question of what is community and how one takes on the responsibilities, as well as the benefits, of membership in a community. The father of moral education, Émile Durkheim noted, "If man is to be a moral being, he must be devoted to something other than himself; he must feel at one with a society."[11] Feeling "at one with a society" does not mean feeling at home in a society; it means taking an active part in the workings of a society and trying to fix what is awry, whether by putting away toys in a kindergarten classroom, mobilizing others for change in local government, or discussing current events in Israel and North America in light of their impact on the Jewish community.

In a healthy community, bullying and name-calling are taboo. The norm must be calling one's sick classmates, making sure they get their assignments, and welcoming them back upon their return. One of my most vivid memories of Camp Yavneh was how the entire camp, staff and campers, would line up Friday mornings, led by our director, Walter Ackerman, *z"l*, to clean up the grounds. Responsibility for the classroom and the school should play a significant role in a curriculum for transcendence, fundamental to what Noddings calls a caring curriculum.[12]

The examples I've listed above are universalistic; we would expect to find them in any educational setting, not only in a Jewish venue. What would characterize "radical communalism" in its particularistic, Jewish embodiment? During prayer services, students who have just celebrated their *b'nei mitzvah* would receive *aliyot*, extending the bar or bat mitzvah celebration to the school, not only the synagogue. Older students would be called upon regularly to make up a minyan so that a member of the camp community could recite *Kaddish*. Taking advantage of the teachable moment, students would learn how to behave while making a shivah visit to a mourning family. As soon as students became *b'nei mitzvah*, their name would be put on a call list to help to make up shivah minyanim in the future. They would acknowledge seeing rainbows, experiencing thunder and lightning, eating the first cherries of the season, and donning a new pair of shoes with the traditional *b'rachot*. The teaching of Jewish social studies would include the linkage of American Jews with Jews in other Diaspora communities; twinning initiatives with Israeli communities and schools; working to provide relief for the Jews in communities hit by natural disasters like floods, hurricanes, and tornadoes; as well as helping what Noddings calls "the distant other."[13]

Transcendence as Spiritual Elevation

If Buddhism is posited on an escape from this world, Judaism is posited on the obligation to sacralize the world, for example, by making the ordinary act of eating a meal an opportunity to thank God and those who helped to bring food to our tables. Rabbinic literature promotes the potential of elevation, part of the *OED* definition of transcendence, in everyday life: *Maalin b'kodesh v'lo moridin*, "We raise in holiness and not lower" (*M'gilah* 26). Donated scraps of velvet from worn dresses and waistcoats from medieval and early modern Jewish communities made for handsome Torah covers, Torah curtains, and cloths to cover the reader's lectern.[14] Mundane objects, like clothing, were elevated to beautify the public reading of the Torah. This is what Kadushin refers to as "normal mysticism":

> We can perhaps now begin to recognize why the rabbinic experience of God can be thought of as normal mysticism. The ordinary, familiar, everyday things and occurrences, we have observed, constitute occasions for the experience of God. Such things as one's daily sustenance, the very day itself, are felt as manifestations of God's loving-kindness, calling forth *Berakhot*. *Kedushah*, holiness, which is nothing else than the imitation of God, is concerned with daily conduct.[15]

Gillman elaborates, "The food we consume, the normal functions of our bodies, sunrise and sunset, the cycles of the seasons—all of these become infused with a sense of the mystical that makes us aware of God's immediate presence in the world."[16]

Designing a Pedagogy for Religious Transcendence in Jewish Settings

There is an abundance of useful material to help teachers and educational leaders create what I have referred to as secular or universalistic transcendence. Best practices include a commitment to nurturing social and emotional intelligence, downplaying competition and promoting cooperative learning opportunities, considering multiple intelligences theory and differentiated instruction in the planning of learning experiences and assessment, and making sure that the school bus and the playground—as well as the classroom—are no-bullying zones. In reflecting on a pedagogy of religious transcendence, there are other dimensions to consider. The work of Laurence Sheindlin and Kathleen Talvacchia, two religious educators, has influenced my thinking about the preconditions for effective religious education.

Scheindlin has written thoughtfully about our need to prepare the ground if we expect to sow the seeds of religious awareness and readiness for prayer experiences.[17] A first step is to make room for emotions in Jewish schools, camps, and other learning experiences. In discussing the work of Israel Scheffler on cognitive emotions, Scheindlin notes, "Emotions...serve as forces which enable us to perceive the world, to form our vision of it and to define its characteristics."[18] If we are to teach our students to see through Jewish eyes, we must begin by tapping into their emotions and giving them the language to express those emotions. But those emotions must be in the service of *talmud Torah*. "The goal is to incorporate emotional goals and strategies within a rigorous, content-rich Judaica curriculum."[19]

Like Scheindlin, Talvacchia also has much to teach us about a pedagogy that deals with heart as well as mind. She asks religious educators to teach for a transcendence (although she does not specifically use the term) that expands the minds of students by adopting "a spirituality of multicultural teaching" that includes an emotional as well as intellectual valence.[20] Such a pedagogy requires educators to integrate several different types of content in learning: academic content knowledge (from subject disciplines), social location knowledge (from an understanding of the reality of difference in an unjust society), and experiential content knowledge from the student's wisdom of life experience. Her definition of multiculturalism is one of the most expansive I know, including gender, that is, learners who come from lesbian or gay families or who may be themselves lesbian, gay, or bisexual; children who learn differently and who display diverse talents or multiple intelligences; as well as ethnicity and race, that is, understanding and honoring the customs, ideas, and behaviors from different kinds of cultures.

On the simplest curricular level, we Jewish educators can begin by rethinking how we teach Jewish history and holidays. We do so from an almost universal Ashkenazi viewpoint. However, merely adding a unit about the Golden Age of Spain and the expulsion will not give us a pass on our obligations to open the eyes of our students to Jewish diversity. A discussion of holiday customs, Jewish history, or Jewish current events should reflect the stories of Jews from North Africa, Ethiopia, and communities in Syria, Iran, Iraq, India, and China.

The challenge to create critical minds and caring hearts is not only about adding more multicultural content to the curriculum, but is about rethinking pedagogy. Talvacchia's challenge to her Christian readers is ours as well. She asks them to reconsider their teaching in order to push their students to

- Understand their own experiences of marginalization, or lack of it, in relation to the experiences of others
- Think about the marginalization experiences of others empathetically
- See their own and others' experiences of marginalization in perspective from the context of social structural power and the privilege of some groups over other groups in a hegemonic society

This is a pedagogy of transcendence, a teaching for listening and understanding in the hope of creating students who realize they are not the center of the universe. Talvacchia asks that all religious educators teach their students to read texts with a hermeneutic of suspicion: What questions are not being asked? Which groups are not asking questions? Whose perspective is being left out? Whose perspective dominates? Who is the "audience?"[21] Surely such critical thinking skills would be welcome in the study of Jewish texts, be they from Torah, Rabbinic literature, or contemporary Jewish newspapers.

CREATING A RELIGIOUS SENSIBILITY

Heschel noted that for the Jewish community to flourish in America, we must foster "reverence for learning and the learning of reverence."[22] Most Jewish school leaders believe *talmud Torah k'neged kulam* (literally, "Torah study is the equivalent [of all the commandments]"; Babylonian Talmud, *Shabbat* 127a)—reverence for Jewish learning—is a fundamental goal of their institutions. With well-chosen, happy teachers and engaging instruction, this is a goal many schools attain. But where are the schools in the liberal Jewish community that achieve Heschel's goal of learning reverence?

Reverence contains many dimensions. One is aesthetic and is rooted in the arts. If a school is committed to the principle of preparing students for reverence, and here I borrow Scheindlin's language of *preparation* rather than direct instruction,[23] we can build on what the fine arts are supposed to teach: "heightened consciousness and esthetic experience."[24] The arts must be a part of Jewish education, not as an accessory, but as an essential role of the life of a Jewish school.[25] Scheindlin repeats a well-known but still powerful story of a teacher who understood how to create a heightened consciousness, the first step in preparing children for reverence:

> A group of children once walked into a room where a meeting was to take place. It was an early spring morning, and an enormous vase of lilacs had been placed on a table at the front of the room. The children entered, it was apparent, with eyes that did not see the lilacs, and with noses that did not smell them.
>
> The adult in charge, noticing these, said, "Did you realize that the lilacs opened this week? Have you stopped and really looked at them? Have you taken a deep, deep smell of them?" She walked over and inhaled their fragrance deeply.
>
> "Did you ever stop to think that you can only see the lilacs open about seventy-five times in your whole life? You have only one chance a year. I have already used up quite a few of my chances."
>
> The effect of the few remarks on the group was startling. Many of the children spontaneously came forward to see and smell the lilacs. They acted as though they truly felt that here was something that they had better not miss.[26]

In analyzing this vignette, Scheindlin notes that this teacher helped her students to recognize that they had inner lives. She called upon their innate sense of curiosity and evoked a sense of wonder. She helped them find the language for articulating feelings and developed their social and emotional intelligences around an aesthetic experience.[27]

TALKING GOD-TALK

Having an appropriate vocabulary for the discussion of religious matters is an important element in learning reverence. Goldmintz refers to the need for articulacy.[28] Language is key to understanding. He quotes from Christian Smith's study, *The Religious and Spiritual Lives of American Teenagers*, "Religious faith, practice, and commitment can be no more than vaguely real when people cannot talk much about them. Articulacy fosters reality."[29] Jewish educators must be willing to engage in God-talk. Just as moral questions cannot be ducked or shuttled off to the rabbi,[30] religious questions must be addressed or run the risk of being considered irrelevant.

Teaching Virtues

A sense of awe and wonder emanates from a sense of how grand the cosmos is and how small we really are. The traditional Jewish response to the daily miracles is to thank God who provides both the majestic, like the great ocean or high mountains, and the ordinary, like the bread on our tables. The *birchot hanehenin*, the blessings we recite on these occasions, are opportunities for the *midah*, or virtue, of *hakarat hatov*, gratitude. God created the world by setting up boundaries and limits: creating different species, giving Adam and Eve free rein to eat everything in the Garden of Eden but the Tree of Knowledge, and establishing the Shabbat that separates the days of work from the day of rest. A religious sensibility must acknowledge limitations. It is the antidote to unbounded self-centeredness, acquisition, gluttony, and greed. And it may offer benefits in real-world terms. A recent issue of the *New Yorker* caused a buzz by analyzing the famous marshmallow experiment that correlated self-control and the willingness to delay gratification with greater achievement in adulthood.[31]

As anyone who has spent any time with a two- or three-year-old can attest, *hakarat hatov* doesn't come naturally. To borrow a phrase from the musical *South Pacific*, "it has to be carefully taught" (as in, "Say the magic word"). Along with *hakarat hatov*, we should be explicitly teaching another virtue, *anavah*, often translated as "modesty" but more accurately defined as "humility." Just as *hakarat hatov* represents a religious attitude, not merely an Emily Post prescription, so does *anavah*. Like gratitude, humility is a much-needed corrective to self-centeredness and entitlement. The response to the majesty of Yosemite or the Grand Teton is not only awe and wonder, but also an unmistakable awareness of what a tiny part of the cosmos we are. A true *anav* knows that his or her success is due to more than a congeries of personal attributes; the prophets in our tradition responded to God's call with the equivalent of "Who, me? You must have dialed the wrong number." In a classroom discussion, *anavah* expresses itself as listening to others and exhibiting intellectual humility, being able to back off from a position when it doesn't stand up to scrutiny.

In the *Birchot HaShachar*, the morning prayers, we must emphasize the function of a *b'rachah* as an opportunity for experiencing thankfulness and humility. Our response to the bounty of God's gifts is to imitate the God who gave them to us. Kadushin writes that Rabbinic value concepts lead to action, that is, mitzvot.[32] In imitation, we practice another Rabbinic value concept, that of *g'milut chasadim*, taking care of the needs of others less fortunate. We do this by clothing the naked, feeding the hungry, and helping to break the shackles of poverty and illness.

Although these are virtues that stem from a relationship to a transcendent God, they also help to create a more civil society. The qualities of thankfulness, humility, and practicing deeds of kindness are the building blocks of community. Here is where the boundary between the *mitzvot bein adam LaMakom* and the *mizvot bein adam lachaveiro* blur. One of our leading contemporary theologians, Harold Kushner, muses about the role of the mitzvot:

> *Mitzvot* are spiritual calisthenics, designed to teach us to control the most basic instincts of our lives—hunger, sex, anger, acquisitiveness, and so on. In Jewish tradition, the performance of a mitzvah is an opportunity— *l'tzaref et ha-beriyyot*—to refine a person's character.
>
> Refinement of character—through the mitzvot and character education—also has instrumental value. Its end product, the creation of a *goy kadosh* (holy nation) and *mamlechet kohanim* (kingdom of priests) is what the secular transcendentalists like Parker and Durkheim call *communitas*.[33]

TEACHING ABOUT HEROES

Heroes hold a community together. They link the generations through their stories and the moral messages those stories convey. They are the embodiments of the virtues that the community holds dear. I still remember learning as a child the story of the Spartan boy and the fox, just as I remember when I first learned about Rabbi Akiva, who preferred to die a grisly death at the hands of the Romans rather than give up learning Torah. After the American Civil War, when the fractured Republic desperately needed healing, stories about George Washington, the noble patriot who did his duty and then quietly and humbly returned to his farm, as well as the fable about young George and the cherry tree, were purposefully included in every child's public school reader. In providing the glue for community, heroes act as agents of transcendence. The stories of classic heroes, the embodiments of communal virtues, inspire their audience to imitate heroic behaviors. Thus we tell the story of how Abraham greeted his angel-messengers to teach the virtue of *hachnasat orchim*, hospitality. We tell the story of how Abraham demanded that God do justice in the case of the innocent in Sodom and Gomorrah to teach the virtue of *tzedek* (justice), and the story of *Akeidat Yitzchak*, the Binding of Isaac, to teach the virtue of *emunah*, faith. *Midot*, or virtues, remain inert abstractions unless they are embodied in the narrative of a hero.

Besides their place in the Bible and holiday curriculum, heroes have a role to play in the teaching of history, whether it is Jewish history, the history of Israel, or American history. Heroes unlock the imagination: Asher Levy insisted on doing his civic duty like anybody else in New Amsterdam, Theodor Herzl dreamed of a Jewish state in the face of relentless anti-Semitism, and Sarah Aaronsohn spied for the British against the Turks in World War I.

I prefer to distinguish between heroes and role models.[34] Both help build community and inspire others, but some heroes have a capital *H* and some a small *h*. Classic heroes have been around for a considerable amount of time; they are the stuff of legend. The ordinary, everyday, local hero is more akin to Danny Siegel's mitzvah heroes.[35] These are the people who shovel the snowy walks of the elderly, provide gently used tutus and ballet slippers for poor girls who want to study dance, and collect toiletries for men in shelters. We need both if we are to teach for transcendence: the classic particularistic hero, whose story has been told for generations by Jews all over the world because of its connection with core Jewish virtues, and the universalistic mitzvah heroes, who are the kinds of citizens to which we aspire. If we use mitzvah heroes to inspire our students to participate in *tikkun olam*, how much more powerful the undertaking when contextualized in the siddur and in *Tanach*. Providing toys for children awaiting cardiac surgery reaches another level of meaning when framed in the language of Psalm 147, which is recited during the daily *Shacharit* service. In it, God is described as *harofei lishvurei lev,* um'chabeish l'atzvotam, "the healer of the broken-hearted and the bandager of their wounds" (v. 3). Taking care of the sick is ratcheted up to an act of *imitatio dei* (imitating God). Collecting canned food for the poor when bracketed with the legends of Elijah, who made sure that the hungry would have enough to eat, adds a level of transcendent Jewish meaning to a food drive.

We are all aware of the calls for integration in our schools. This includes content integration, like using the arts to teach texts, and introducing technology into our pedagogy; and skills integration, like critical thinking across the disciplines. I am calling for teaching transcendence across the curriculum. The language of awe and wonder can be found in the siddur and in the science lab; I know of a school that called its science fair *Nissim u-Niflaot* (Miracles and Wonders). The language of responsibility and duty not only describes the undertaking of mitzvot but also civic responsibilities like voting and paying taxes. A soul-welcoming classroom is ramped up in holiness when the teacher stops class to point out the first crocus of the season. A soul-welcoming classroom is all about transcendence, both in universalistic and particularistic terms. It addresses what Kessler calls "the soul in education": to attend to the yearning for deep connection, to find meaning and purpose, to express and explore the emotions, and to respond to the need to belong to a community.[36] Students are not only part of a community in which they feel valued and cared for, where they have rights as well as responsibilities, where their emotions as well as their intellects are challenged, but they are also initiated into an "imagined community," one set in Jewish time and space, one that embraces the opportunity of transforming ordinary events into glimpses of the Divine.

3

Seeing Is Caring, Seeing Is Believing:
Teaching Sensitivity in the Classroom

LAURENCE SCHEINDLIN

W E TEACH MORALITY, but people aren't always moral. When we teach mitzvot and *t'filah*, our students, both children and adults, often give every appearance of minds and hearts having been touched, yet outside of the classroom and synagogue they often seem oblivious to everyday moral and spiritual issues. Education in a tradition so suffused with concern for the *ger, yatom, v'almanah* (stranger, orphan, and widow), and so committed to *din* (law) and *rachamim* (compassion) should sensitize its students to their daily encounters so that they become alert to the needs and rights of others even while pursuing their own legitimate desires. Similarly, education in a tradition whose Psalmist writes, "When I see Your heavens, the work of Your fingers...what are humans that You attend to them?" (Psalm 8:4–5), and which expects us to thank God every day "for Your miracles that we experience every day...evening, morning and noon," should heighten its students' spiritual awareness, helping them to see, breaking through the clouds of everyday life, the light of something transcendent.

Excellent teachers have always tried to foster the sensitivities that might mature into a rich spiritual and moral life. How can we adjust our instructional practice to be more certain of building such sensitivity? This educational question is, of necessity, also a psychological and philosophical one, because the key to answering it, I believe, lies in acknowledging that emotions play a much larger role than is often recognized in our rational functioning, including in our moral and spiritual lives. And if emotions are essential to our rational, moral, and spiritual functioning, then education, particularly religious education, needs to adapt its practice without loosening its commitment to the life of the intellect. This chapter is therefore a psychological, philosophical, Jewish, and educational exploration of these issues.

I begin by illustrating why the development of emotional sensitivity is indispensable for moral education and will then make a parallel argument about education for spiritual and religious life, because *sensitivity* seems to me to be a structurally essential, common element in these two distinct but overlapping domains. Since my goal is to answer the question of how our educational practice can be sharpened to enhance moral and spiritual development, I will conclude with concrete recommendations for how to do that without giving up any of the cognitive learning that is so important to us.

Moral Reasoning and Emotions

Lawrence Kohlberg's groundbreaking stage theory of moral development set the agenda for moral psychology in the past half-century, but its shortcomings ultimately served to make more acute the question of why moral reasoning does not always lead to moral behavior. Kohlberg claimed that moral reasoning develops in all people in a series of identifiable and invariant stages. Kohlberg's contribution was vital. At a time when behaviorism was dominant and relativism in vogue, his theory reoriented moral psychology to the interior life, showing how moral reasoning developed along with intellectual maturation. Just as important, his theory made a strong claim for a set of abiding moral standards. No longer could one think that human moral development was a series of responses conditioned by the particular society in which a child grew. The mind mattered and, just as important, Kohlberg showed that certain standards of moral thinking were universal.

But it did not take long before other scholars criticized Kohlberg's work, which richly described how people *thought* when presented with moral dilemmas, for inadequately answering the question of why people would choose to *act* morally. The problem was not, as he himself showed, that many people did not attain the fifth stage and that only a select group of unique souls attained the sixth. The problem rather was that some studies showed that his model accounted for only 10 percent of the variability in individuals' moral *behavior* as opposed to their ability to *respond rationally*; that is, presented in a research setting with descriptions of moral dilemmas, people "solved" them at higher moral levels than they seemed to *act* upon in real life.[1] Furthermore, Carol Gilligan initiated a set of important criticisms that, broadly stated, claimed Kohlberg's theory was grounded in a male orientation of rationality and justice and that it overlooked the possibility that caring was at least as important to morality as justice, and emotion as important as rationality.[2]

Given a clearly defined moral dilemma, people may give verbal responses that demonstrate high levels of moral reasoning. But why act on those judgments? Would these individuals react similarly in real life? Would they intervene in the presence of an injustice? Would they recognize the situation as one calling for action? When confronted with a conflict between egoism and altruism, how might they behave? How sensitive to injustice and need would they be?

Take the following example: A physician has purchased an expensive piece of equipment, a standard elective treatment for a condition that is not life-threatening. The treatment causes moderate discomfort and will limit some of the patient's activities for a week to ten days. The physician has only the one technology she has purchased. Other technologies address similar conditions, each technology having its own benefits and disadvantages. Although this machine will not cause harm, some patients may not benefit sufficiently. If after several treatments it is not fully successful, these patients will need to seek treatment elsewhere—a loss of time and money for the patient and the insurance company. The machine and its maintenance must pay for itself, something that happens only if patients pay for procedures with it. Do all doctors in this situation fully explain the different technologies to all of their patients? Do they provide full information on the relative benefits and disadvantages? Over time, counseling patient after patient, do they sustain awareness of their conflict of interest?[3]

Take another example: A group of fourth-grade boys, good friends, have a regular handball game at lunchtime. Popular and usually a positive influence on classroom climate, these boys are respectful, engaged, high-performing students. One day as they are finishing lunch and heading to their game, one of them says, "I always see Michael playing by himself at lunchtime. Let's invite him into the game." The others shrug their shoulders in unenthusiastic agreement. In fact, Michael has sat by himself at lunch and played alone for weeks. Why did only this one student notice? If the others did notice, why is it that only this one seemed to care? If some of them cared, why did only this one act?

In the example of the physician, she cares enough about her patients that she does not want to cause unnecessary pain or expenditures of their time and money. Additionally, her view of herself as a professional reminds her to be aware of conflicts of interest. Her self-image, together with her concern for others, sustains her awareness as she counsels her patients.

In the case of the student, it is empathy and compassion that enable him to see what the others do not and to act. Surely it is not logic that opens his eyes to the moral situation. Reason or logic, as usually understood acting alone, can only analyze the situation. This might bring the student to say to Michael, "My friends are all good handball players and that's what we need for a good game. Adding a poor player will make it less fun."[4] The physician's situation is more complex. On the one hand, logic might say, "Treating the patient with this machine may benefit him and will certainly help pay for it." On the other hand, logic might say, "Treating this patient may give him no benefit at all." If the physician hears both voices, how does she decide which to listen to? It is either a value—an emotionally held idea, such as, "I want to be fair," "I want to be a good professional"—or an emotional judgment, such as "I don't want to feel guilty afterward." Or it is an active emotion of caring about the patient's overall welfare that will enable the physician to hear and then to act on the second voice.[5] Similarly, it is emotion that would lead the student either to maximize his enjoyment in play with his friends or to identify with the need of the solitary classmate.

Emotion is not always rooting for the good; far from it. Emotions lead to immoral choices as well as moral ones. Let us complicate the physician's situation. Let us say that she is in financial trouble. Let us imagine that she has a child with special needs requiring expensive treatment and specialized schooling. The child's needs, together with other unavoidable family pressures, threaten the comfortable but decidedly moderate lifestyle she has only recently achieved. Her emotions—her concern for her family, her determination[6] to rise above her financial concerns—could lead the physician to make a self-serving decision. On the other hand, empathy for her patient and concern for her own professional identity might also lead her to the more altruistic choice.

Alternatively, let us imagine that she is affluent, has three offices, and has set for herself a personal goal of retiring early and comfortably so that she might devote herself to travel, including spending time in her second home in southern France. It is an emotional commitment that might (but not necessarily) lead her to an unjustified moral choice. Although we all know that emotions are not always oriented toward the welfare of others, we have already begun to see how moral emotions contribute to moral reasoning and action.

If logic functioned on its own, at best it would give us running totals of costs and benefits of proposed decisions but by itself would offer little guidance about how to act. In reality, such decisions are the joint product of logic and emotion in an integrated cognitive process. As the student example suggests, and as we will see in greater detail further along, it is the emotional component of cognition that allows us to notice many of the relevant criteria that we then subject to both logical and emotional analysis. It is that integrated cognitive process that guides us to both moral and immoral choices.

It is false that emotions are selfish and militantly egocentric and that reason must take control if a person is to participate constructively, cooperatively, or morally in society. It is easy to contrast the robustness of our selfish motives for emotion—a child's anger at someone taking her toy, an adult's happiness at undercutting a rival, the avarice that blinds a businessperson to risk—with the often fragile nature of altruistic feelings. But that contrast between emotional motives does nothing to certify reason alone as a more reliable moral motive than emotion, its supposed opposite number. In fact, we have already seen that moral reasoning alone does not predict actual moral functioning. That everyone's emotions, like Raskolnikov's in *Crime and Punishment*, can "cut both ways," only heightens the importance for educators in understanding how moral emotions can be stimulated, nurtured, valued, and developed as part a single, integrated process of rationality.

Moral Emotions

Fortunately, research in recent decades has embraced the role of emotions in moral psychology. It recognizes that from early ages children experience significant moral emotions, such as shame, empathy, and guilt, and that they evince concern when social standards are violated by others.[7] Martin Hoffman, recognizing that the rational processes described by Kohlberg could not explain what would "lead children to take the other's claims seriously and be willing to negotiate and compromise,"[8] has demonstrated at length the role of empathy and sympathy on moral development and performance. He has also described the course of evolving empathy from infancy to adulthood.

Before the end of their first year, infants act distressed when other children get hurt. Because these infants are not yet able to differentiate fully between themselves and others, Hoffman calls these reactions "egocentric empathic distress." Though they are egocentric, they are early and important precursors to moral emotions. At eighteen months and older, children reach a new milestone as they begin to realize that someone else may have different feelings from their own in any given situation. Six- or seven-year-olds not only display distress for others but become aware of their own empathic distress. Before then, a child might be saddened on seeing another child act sad, but now he begins to understand that he is sad because he is witnessing someone *else's* sadness. Hoffman says this is the beginning of true sympathetic distress. He states that this can mature in adulthood into true sympathy, compassion, and caring, in which one acts on behalf of the other rather than on behalf of oneself.

Recent neuroscientific research lends support to the role of emotions in moral functioning. For example, in a study of interest to both educators and fund-raisers, individuals were subjected to MRI scans as they received money and as they donated money to a charity. Researchers observed subjects while they were given money, while making voluntary responses to a charitable appeal, and also while making "contributions" that were exacted from them as a kind of tax.[9] When a participant donated voluntarily, the parts of the brain that are typically activated when eating a fine dessert became active. This also happened when the subject received money. More surprisingly, even when subjects were forced to give to the charity, the same "reward network" was activated, though to a lesser extent. Most people find it rewarding to give.

Emotions and intuition have surely come into their own in moral psychology. At the far end, "social intuitionists," such as Jonathan Haidt, have staked out extremist positions, virtually rejecting any role for rationality in moral psychology.[10] Marc Hauser claims that an innate moral grammar (akin to Chomsky's notion of an innate linguistic grammar) functions both intuitively and rationally in all humans[11]—a claim no less ambitious than Haidt's but more moderate in that it assigns roles to both reason and emotion. At best, Hauser's and Haidt's claims are interesting hypotheses waiting to be evaluated, and given the tender age of neuropsychology, MRI research must be read with extreme caution.[12] It would be premature to conclude from a study like the one above that compassion or its rewards are hardwired in the brain, as has been suggested. Nevertheless, it is difficult to resist the claim of the growing volume of research supporting the significant role that emotions need to play in a comprehensive moral theory. Moral activity is not just about justice and does not spring from cold analysis.

A first step in the direction of a comprehensive theory is James Rest's categorization of four components of moral functioning: moral sensitivity, moral judgment, moral motivation, and moral character.[13] Without in any way diminishing the importance of the last three components, I will primarily discuss Rest's first component, sensitivity, from this point on because it comprises several of the critical steps that might lead toward moral action when we confront a real-life situation. First, we must have an awareness that a moral problem does exist, for failing to recognize one, we are incapable of engaging in moral decision-making activity to address it. We must also quickly determine how various actions and perceptions fit together, and we need to imagine how events might unfold. These are the components Rest describes as "sensitivity." The other *equally* important components leading to moral action—moral judgment, moral motivation, and moral character—refer respectively to the weighing and judging of possible actions. These include the degree of commitment to act and such matters as courage and persistence.

While the order is *logically* sequential, Rest insists that in reality each component influences the other and that the whole is an interactive process.[14] Still, in practice one who does not *recognize* the existence of a moral problem or moral need cannot be motivated to reason or act morally. And as I have suggested, it is not primarily reason, but rather emotion that enables us to notice when a moral issue is at hand. Similarly, in spiritual activity, emotional perception is a first logical step, as we will see. However, we first need briefly to broaden the scope of discussion before circling back to moral perception and spiritual activity.

Emotional Perception

Every moment of existence surrounds us with a greater variety of potential information than any of us can consciously attend to. In large part, it is the emotional force of our values, goals, and desires that guides our perception, leading us to pick out some things and not others from amidst the welter of available information. Our emotions preoccupy us, to use Keith Oatley's term,[15] so that we become conscious of some things and not others. In a real sense, then, we choose what to notice, with our emotions focusing our attention and transmitting to consciousness that which we consider worth attending to.

Our values, goals, and desires lead us to make these choices of perception at both deep and superficial levels: a walk on the beach can be an opportunity for some to notice the varying shades of blue water and sky, for others to notice whether the height of the waves and wind are good for surfing, for others to notice lithe sunbathing bodies, and for still others to notice real estate opportunities on the beach. One person can walk past a homeless person and not notice, while another sees filth and another sees hunger. The fourth-grade student noticed that another student was probably in psychic pain. The doctor perceived the potential to cause unnecessary trouble.[16] Far from being passive, reactive, and unpredictable, emotions guide us toward fulfillment of our goals and guard us from harm. Fear of a threatening individual or situation is the classic example of the rationality of emotions. Alone in my home, hearing footsteps and voices on the stairs in the middle of the night, I am afraid. Experiencing fear, I can take action: grab a heavy object, quickly dial 911, or lock myself in a bathroom. While it is true that excessive fear can incapacitate, in this situation it is the *absence* of fear that would be truly irrational.

Israel Scheffler uses the term "perceptive feelings" to describe how emotions construct our vision of the external world and define its features.[17] However emotions have evolved, he argues that they have come to serve as cues for interpreting situations. Scheffler quotes Nelson Goodman's formulation:

> In daily life, classification of things by feeling is often more vital than classification by other properties: we are likely to be better off if we are skilled in fearing, wanting, braving, or distrusting the right things...than if we perceive only their shapes, sizes, weights, etc.[18]

But Goodman takes the argument even further, to his own subject, art:

> The work of art is apprehended through the feelings as well as through the senses. Emotional numbness disables here as definitely if not as completely as blindness or deafness. Nor are the feelings used exclusively for exploring the *emotional* content of a work....Emotion in aesthetic experience is a means of *discerning* what *properties* a work has and expresses....[19] [emphases mine]

Not only do we experience emotions in *response* to a work of art. In fact, our emotions *guide* us to notice what matters. Even in intellectual and theoretical inquiry, Scheffler points to the emotional life as a "rich source of substantive ideas....Drawing from the obscure wellsprings of this life, the mind's free play casts up novel patterns and images, exotic figures and analogies that, in an investigative context, may serve to place old facts in a new light."[20] This role of emotions and imaginative play in the development of new scientific and theoretical hypotheses is widely acknowledged. But Scheffler goes beyond that, to the stage we normally think of as strictly analytical and coldly objective—the weighing of *evidence,* where, he points out, emotions help us once again to see what is relevant:

They fulfill also a *selective* function, facilitating choice among these patterns, defining their salient features, focusing attention accordingly. The patterns developed in imagination, that is, carry their own emotive values; these values guide selection and emphasis..., highlighting factual features of interest to further inquiry.[21]

The role of perception in the religious life and, implicitly, in morality has been amply articulated in Michael Fishbane's *Spiritual Attunement: A Jewish Theology*,[22] to which I will turn later.

Moral Perception and the Perils of Indifference

Let us return to moral perception. What induces one fourth-grader to *notice* a classmate's distress in the first place? Why is it that some can walk past the homeless person and not notice, while others see filth and failure and feel revulsion, and still others see poverty and feel compassion? We have seen how emotion *guides* what we see, leading us to pick out from all of the available data that which is compelling to us individually and which we therefore consciously notice. In picking out for notice the moral dimension of a situation, we exercise those faculties that Rest characterized as moral sensitivity. As Arne Vetlesen has compellingly written, that empathetic act of *perception* needs to be nurtured.[23]

By way of negative example, Vetlesen cites the Eichmann case and the response of the German public to *Kristallnacht*. In an extended and compelling critique of Hannah Arendt's eyewitness reporting and reflections on the Eichmann trial, he concludes that it was Eichmann's inability to see the Jews as human beings that enabled him to engage in no moral reflection—not before, during, or long after the genocide in which he was an active participant. While Vetlesen agrees with Arendt that Eichmann was motivated not so much by active hatred (unlike the Nazi leadership, who certainly hated), he differs from Arendt by identifying the root of Eichmann's sin in an emotional, rather than a rational, failure: it was, he demonstrates, a failure of the most elementary form of empathy. A complete whiteout of all ability to experience the Jews' reality made it possible for Eichmann to carry out his tasks with complete commitment—he was more than a cog in the mechanism, but less than an evil visionary—and relative effectiveness.

Conversely, when German soldiers began evidencing psychological strain from perpetrating mass shootings, Himmler devised new means of murder. He used gas, the nefarious virtue of which was to increase the distance between murderer and victim, thus reducing the likelihood of empathy and guilt. In this way, he ensured the continued efficiency of the killing operations. In his autobiography, Höss explicitly articulated this motive.[24] In fact, Vetlesen suggests that significant elements of the Holocaust did not require the active hatred of the German populace at large, but their indifference. In a fascinating footnote, he points out that, in a sense, *Kristallnacht* was a failure for the Nazis, teaching them not to rely on the populace at large, who had no love for the Jews, but mostly wanted not to be involved. He cites Ian Kershaw, who summarized the general population's mainstream response as, "Anti-Semitism—o.k., but not like that."[25] The point here is not, of course, to deny the worst kind of hatred among the Nazis and their followers, but to display in full color the destructive potential of a widespread popular failure to perceive the existence of a moral issue and to feel.

In our multicultural and global society, there are many calls for tolerance across racial and cultural divides. But tolerance and even respect are cool, rational, somewhat passive dispositions or emotions. Tolerance will keep me calm when I see people acting in ways I do not understand and that might even elicit my initial disapproval. Respect may lead me to stand back and display deference. But neither tolerance nor respect will take me out of my comfort zone. Neither of them induces me to feel what the other feels, to endure what the other endures, to strive for the other's goals. Neither tolerance nor respect help me notice that my actions have shamed another person, nor do they bestir me to befriend the lonely or devote my time to issues of justice for minorities. *Chesed* (compassion) requires sensitivity.

From among the many lessons to be drawn from the Holocaust, we learn from Vetlesen's analysis the need to cultivate not *tolerance*, but rather *active perception* of others' needs. Indifference happens daily, resulting not, perhaps, in the slaughter of innocent millions, but in inattention to the homeless, the uninsured, and the minority—today's *ger, yatom, v'almanah*—and in the needless hurt occasioned by our own quotidian insensitivities. Only when the empathic imagination—informed by an attitude of caring—opens the eyes, allowing us to "see" the presence of a moral issue or need, can the full process of moral judgment, motivation, and character be mobilized.[26] The ability and inclination to see are the ability and inclination to care. By contrast, Vetlesen writes, "indifference is a prime threat to morality, even more destructive than hatred or resentment, because the logic of indifference sets no limits to its spread."[27]

Fortunately, there is as much good moral news as bad. William Damon provides extensive descriptions of the lives of extraordinarily caring individuals and defines their common characteristics (one of which is that they do not consider themselves extraordinary).[28] More unexceptionally, we regularly read of extraordinary acts by ordinary people: the fireman who has saved three people's lives, each time ignoring ways that could have exposed him to less risk; the writer who took a homeless musician under his wing and restored his life; and the simple but shining acts of kindness that every school principal and teacher witness among children of every age virtually every day. Against the standard charge that emotions are volatile and egocentric, we can agree with Lawrence Blum that "as a motive to beneficence, compassion can have the strength, stability and reliability that Kant thought only the sense of duty could have."[29]

Sensitivity, Spiritual Perception, and Judaism

Judaism's worthy emphasis on the *maaseh* (the act), both ritual and ethical, and its rich intellectualism, together with the pressing importance of teaching skills and knowledge—Hebrew, textual sophistication, the whole array of Jewish knowledge that is in such short supply in American Jewish life—and the urgency of attempting to ensure the continuation of Jewish peoplehood, all tend to preoccupy the curriculum of both formal and informal Jewish education. Yet it very well might be that the most certain way of bringing students back to the well of richness that is Jewish religious life and culture when they are adults is to engage their early sense of religious wonder as they learn to make sense of the world around them. The obverse might also be true: if we inadequately attend to students' emotional and spiritual development when they are young, we increase the probability of their seeking that richness elsewhere as they grow up.

Rest's four-component model of moral functioning offers an interesting heuristic for thinking about spiritual and religious education.

Through the lens of his model, we can think of Jewish education needing to provide for comprehensive development of four components: students' sensitivity, reasoning, motivation, and character. As in the moral domain, it is sensitivity that I discuss in this chapter, while embracing the other three elements as of equal importance.

No one has more effectively explicated the importance of sensitivity, or spiritual perception, than Michael Fishbane. All of us are met with moments, often in response to natural events, when the everyday opens up to the presence of something beyond. These "caesural" moments, as Fishbane calls them, bring to awareness a dimension of life that can easily be overlooked except when such awareness bursts upon us.[30] Valuing these moments, we try to extend and re-create them. Art is one means of intentionally disrupting our normal habits and promoting these more elemental perceptions. And theology goes a step further, trying "to transform this perception of elementariness into a sustained way of life and thought."[31] Fishbane does not mean by this a permanent state of mystical ecstasy, but rather of living in the everyday world, experiencing "all its happenings as points of crossing" because the elemental is brought to our immediate perception. [32] Our *perception* of the "great vastness" transforms our thinking and acting.[33]

Attentiveness is the beginning: "Attentiveness to the double dimension, at the crossing point, is a first prefiguration of theology."[34] Allowing oneself to see, being inclined to see, is to be inclined to believe:

> If we have eyes but do not see and ears without hearing, would we really be ready "to do" and "to hear" what needs to be heard and done? And would we be ready to see and do the unexpected, or deal with all the futilities that haunt us here in the vastness?[35]

If I understand Fishbane correctly, the Jewish theology that emerges from Judaism's unique ways of reading texts is not the goal but a means. "It is not life itself; it is rather a preparation for it: an attunement for attunement," by enabling us to see more immediately and more deeply.[36]

Theology so defined becomes, in Daniel Marom's words, "not a specific area within a religious education, but rather its organizing principle... whose aim is the cultivation, through reflection and experience, of the bimodal consciousness of the routine and the elemental."[37] Just as significantly, he says, rather than attempting to impose something on the student or searching about for a formula for sustaining children's Jewish identity and continuity, "such a Jewish education feeds off of its own authenticity and nothing else."[38] I will return to this point later.

The abstractness of Fishbane's language about spiritual perception might lead us to imagine that such perception is entirely beyond the reach of children. Therefore, a crucial question does need to be answered: To what extent can children be spiritually sensitive?

Children and Spiritual Sensitivity

Just as it has been demonstrated that even young children experience empathy, guilt, and concern when social standards are violated by others,[39] there is evidence that children experience spiritual emotions. The research base is slim, since most studies until recently have concentrated on children's *cognitive* understanding of religious concepts. Furthermore, the difficulty of disentangling spiritual experiences from specific religious traditions complicates such research and makes it controversial. Still, the attempt to identify the psychological underpinnings of spiritual experience need not, by its very essence, threaten or promote any particular religious tradition or orientation. Nor need it invalidate spiritual experience any more than understanding the psychology of music would invalidate our pleasure in listening to it.

In his book *Solitude*, the psychoanalyst Anthony Storr gives examples of accounts of remembered childhood states of heightened awareness or mystical experience left by creative adults. For example, the twentieth-century art connoisseur Bernard Berenson wrote of losing himself in "some instant of perfect harmony":

> In childhood and boyhood this ecstasy overtook me when I was happy out of doors. Was I five or six? Certainly not seven. It was a morning in early summer. A silver haze shimmered and trembled over the lime trees. The air was laden with their fragrance. The temperature was like a caress. I remember—I need not recall—that I climbed up a tree stump and felt suddenly immersed in Itness. I did not call it by that name. I had no need for words. It and I were one.[40]

Other studies support the notion that children may engage in true spiritual experience.[41] Edward Robinson analyzed responses to Alister Hardy's invitation for people to describe if they had ever felt that their lives had been influenced by a transcendent experience. In doing so, he discovered that six hundred of the four thousand responses referred to childhood experiences.[42]

While it might be argued that some of this research is undoubtedly influenced by the researchers' religious orientation, it is more difficult to level the same charge against David Hay and Rebecca Nye's description of "relational consciousness" as the core concept of children's spirituality that has emerged from their research.[43] If anything, their research has come under criticism for being too free of the influence of any religious orientation and thus promoting a secular form of spirituality.

Hay and Nye define relational consciousness as "a distinctive property of mental activity, profound and intricate enough to be termed 'consciousness,' and remarkable for its confinement to a broadly relational, inter- and intra-personal domain."[44] This consciousness, arising within the context of a relationship with someone or something, is one of "unusual awareness," which often entails a "meta-consciousness."[45] One six-year-old in their study, for example, spoke metaphorically of "waking up" and "noticing" the natural world in a moment of special awareness. A ten-year-old described an usual consciousness about his own body and thought. Another ten-year-old expressed a "vivid self-consciousness" that she described as "shocking," relating to thoughts of her personal identity and morality.

The unusual and profound quality of this awareness accords with the type of spiritual perception I have spoken about. This hyperawareness—"attunement" seems like the right word for it—is more than self-awareness. It has nothing directly to do with emotional or psychological health and well-being or with an individual's sense of wholeness (things that other researchers often confound with spiritual matters). Rather, relational consciousness is the profound awareness of a qualitatively deep connection and relationship with another. Hay and Nye's description of the associated "meta-consciousness"—the children's awareness *of* their own acute awareness and closeness to that which is external to them—skirts close to Heschel's description of radical amazement. This is not a coincidence. Hay and Nye seem to have identified among children a capacity for spiritual perception that, *if nurtured*, may be the precursor to a developed and embracing spirituality. In this capacity for spiritual perception and its inclination to see a depth of connection, we have the spiritual parallel to what I have described as sensitivity in the moral domain. There, sensitivity, moral seeing, leads a person to realize, amid the welter of available information at any given moment, that in the scene before him or her lies a moral issue. Similarly, in the realm of spirituality, sensitivity (which I have referred to as spiritual perception) permits awareness of a depth beneath the surface of existence.

Sensitivity, therefore, seems to be an inescapable objective for religious education, especially Jewish education, with its equally inescapable commitment to texts, interpretation, and beliefs. So how to foster spiritual perception in children needs to be a prime question for religious educators.

Wonder: The Door to Spiritual Perception

Radical amazement and spiritual awe are complex emotions and, like all complex emotions, have earlier precedents in simpler emotions from the same family of feelings. Anyone who experiences awe must already have experienced the more common feelings we know as amazement, curiosity, and wonder: childlike amazement at novel objects or events; simple curiosity at how things work; and wonder, in the way that children express a delightful combination of confusion and pleasure toward things they do not understand but which they enjoy.

Some believe that only unusual phenomena—new experiences, infrequent occurrences, or sensational events—induce wonder and that wonder naturally fades with repetition and experience.[46] To be sure, wonder *can* dwindle with repetition, but not necessarily so. In fact, wonder is multidirectional. Confronted with the inexplicable, I might become curious, and that is why curiosity that starts in wonder often drives scientific inquiry and learning. Of course, under the influence of curiosity, I might also experience frustration in my attempts to understand and explain. Frustration of that kind may lead to failure, disappointment, and loss of interest or, with renewed energy, to further attempts to unravel the unexplained. Success at understanding often is heralded by feelings of exhilaration and elevation. The tingling, broadening feelings that often accompany a confrontation with the inexplicably wondrous might also lead to contemplation, aesthetic expression, or a sense of the mystery and awe of creation.

Curiosity, as Thomas Green points out, is wondering *how* something works or comes about. Wondering *at,* on the other hand, "is not to propose an investigation but to be amazed. . . . One may wonder *at* long after one has ceased to wonder *why* or *how.*"[47] The reason this is true, he says, is that we wonder *at* that which *is,* but *need not be.* The world has a regularity that it need not have. What makes fairy tales speak even to adults is that they remind us that the world could be radically different from the way it is. The world's regularity and reliability may be inexplicable. Standing before a wondrous phenomenon, small or large, the inexplicability of its existence amazing us, we become even more aware of our surroundings. Wonder then feeds us with broadened and heightened feelings and attractions, not only for the immediate object of our wonder, but often for all phenomena, and not only for them but for the fact of their existence. It is worth quoting Green directly, for his words' aptness to our concerns:

> To say this is simply to take seriously what is perhaps the most fundamental philosophic contribution of the Hebraic tradition—the claim that though the order of the world is dependable, it is nonetheless contingent. It exists, though it need not exist. Its order is dependable only because its creator is dependable. It is precisely the combination of these two things— contingency and dependability—which, held in proper balance, makes wonder possible.[48]

Wonder differs from other elevating emotions such as joy or happiness. In joy, I typically revel in an object's, event's, or person's high value in achieving one of my more important and, usually, commendable life goals. Thus, I have joy in the birth of a child, the completion of an important project, the acquisition of and dwelling in a particular house. In wonder, on the other hand, I am drawn to something that is, in a significant way, not mine and may never be. Wonder emerges from the distance, at least from the distance in understanding, between me and the object of wonder.[49] Something about that object is of value and worth attending to, even though it is not mine and may never be mine.

Wondering *at* a phenomenon is to see beyond its physical explanation to its ultimate inexplicability, such that wonder spurs further wonder.

To be attuned to the cause of wonder is to be attuned to the presence of what is larger than ourselves. It is a perception of elimentariness, an inclination to see existence in its spiritual dimension.

The other-directedness of wonder leads Martha Nussbaum to the enormously helpful insight that wonder and awe are among the least self-involved of emotions. Because this is so, "children whose capacity for [wonder] is strengthened through imaginative play have a more ro-bust capacity for nonpossessive love," and therefore for compassion.[50] Experiencing the attraction of otherness prepares a person to care about others because one is inclined to "see" them fully—to notice their needs, joys, and sorrows. In seeing lies the capacity for caring.

Perception, Wonder, Reliability, and Morality: The Rainbow

The Bible and the Rabbis made similar connections between wonder, re-liability, and morality. The Noah story is a meditation on violence, that of people toward each other and toward animals, and on the potential for God's violence against the world. The rainbow explicitly symbolizes God's promise never to destroy the world again. Existence, God prom-ises, will henceforth be reliable. But God couples this promise with a demand for a basic moral order: people will be held responsible for the lives of other people, and that moral demand is itself to be symbolized and remembered through the prohibition against consuming blood. The rainbow arching down from heaven touches earth in two places— with God's promise to us and with God's demand—and connects them. Unlike Jacob's ladder, which bridges the distance between heaven and earth, the rainbow brings them tantalizingly close. Its inexplicability reinforces the difference and distance between heaven and earth. Its intangibility reminds us of the fleetingness by which their connection could be severed but is not.

Perhaps no other natural phenomenon is more commonly associated with wonder than the rainbow. Mythologies variously interpret its ap-pearance, for good or for ill, as a sign of transcendence. For almost anyone of any age, seeing a rainbow is a moment of excitement. Its unexpected and transient appearance and the illusoriness of its band of colors dazzle and entice. Even those who understand the rainbow's optics and geometry are stirred at the moment of its appearance. All of us are impelled to look, to try to discriminate one color from the other more clearly, to find, if we can, its ending and beginning points. Here is an event before which wonder never ceases.

Centuries of philosophers, astronomers, and mathematicians, ancient and medieval, devoted themselves to careful analysis, attempting scientific understandings of the rainbow. They developed intricate mathematical explications of its angles of refraction, explaining the phenomenon of double rainbows and so on.[51] The Rabbis, by contrast, seemed unconcerned about the rainbow's physical origins. A reading of the compiled midrashim (interpretations) on *Parashat Noach* in *Midrash Tanchuma* quickly reveals the preoccupation of the Rabbis:

> Our rabbis taught us, one who sees a rainbow in the sky should say a blessing. What blessing? "Blessed is the One who remembers the covenant, is true to God's covenant, and carries out God's word." (*Midrash Tanchuma, Noach* 7).

The midrashim proceed to explain: God's love endures, even beyond death. Unlike a philanthropic person who may provide a poor person with sustenance for days or weeks or even a year, God always provides. God cares about all life, animal and human.

Colors? Water droplets? Angles of refraction? Wrong book. The physical properties of the rainbow fail to attract the Rabbis' interest. Rather, the fascination of the rainbow for the Rabbis is its reminder that there is no reason for the world and life to endure except for the fact that God makes them reliable. But beyond the wonder of physical existence the Rabbis discern in the Noah story something even deeper that engrosses their attention, something that is illustrated by a set of midrashim on the Noah story, grouped around the following verse:

> Your beneficence [*tzidkat'cha*] is like the high mountains;
> Your justice [*mishpatecha*] like the great depths;
> man and beast You preserve, O *Adonai*.[52]
> (Psalm 36:7)

Above all, it is the reliability of the *moral* order that absorbs the Rabbis:

Rabbi Shimon bar Yochai said, "Just as the mountains restrain the depths so that they do not rise up and flood the world, so does beneficence [tzedakah] restrain the attribute of justice [din] and punishment, so that it not come to the world. 'Your beneficence' controls [literally, 'is over'] 'Your judgments' as 'the high mountains' control 'the deep.'"
(Midrash Tanchuma, Noach 8)

The moral order itself is complex and contingent. Strict justice is one of God's attributes, but so is compassion. The Rabbis' object of wonder is not so much the contingency-yet-reliability of the *physical world*, but of the *moral order*. Knowing that an excess of compassion or of strictness can bring chaos, the Rabbis here seem more impressed with the world's physical survival, and less with the delicate balance of its moral foundation. The wonder of the rainbow, in their eyes, is the promise of the *moral* order of the universe. To wonder at the rainbow is to see and be reminded of the world's moral order.

Educational Implications

WONDER AND OTHER EMOTIONS IN THE CLASSROOM

A first step in nurturing students' capacity to "see" might be by looking for opportunities to work with their feelings of wonder, curiosity, and amazement. Good teachers have always sought and used teachable moments for such experiences; wonder cannot be forced, but teachers can offer opportunities in which wonder has a chance of rising into the regular curriculum.

I start with wonder because of its unique role in spiritual and moral sensitivity, but other emotional antecedents of the complex emotions inherent in traditional Jewish concepts present opportunities for engaging students' emotional and cognitive attentions within the context of the study of traditional texts. A few concepts that immediately suggest themselves, together with their related antecedent emotions, are fear and *yirat shamayim* (awe of heaven); caring and *chesed* (compassion); excitement and *hitlahavut* (spiritual enthusiasm); disgust and *treif* (not kosher); respect and *k'dushah* (holiness). We need to be careful not to "dumb down" the traditional concepts by conflating them with these simpler emotions, but rather by exploring and honoring the feelings that relate to these concepts. This is especially true when they arise in the context of text study, which can be a powerful preparatory element of children's growing cognitive-spiritual Jewish development.

While inner emotional life is *not* inherently spiritual, it is hard to understand how we can expect children to develop rich spiritual lives if they come to believe that emotions are unimportant, secondary, or embarrassing, a common phenomenon Peter Stearns has termed "American cool."[53] If students are to experience wonder and other emotions antecedent to full religious and moral feelings, they need to have a level of comfort in experiencing and expressing their own emotional lives.

STUDENTS' INNER LIFE AND LANGUAGE

Language is our entrée into developing that sense of ease. In both the general and Judaic studies curricula, teachers can find almost daily opportunities to work with emotional language in literature discussions (trying to understand and describe the frustrations, joys, annoyances, and pleasures of characters in reading material) and in the writing that students are asked to do. Teachers can promote students' development of a language for emotions by focusing on the emotional experience of characters in literature, including Jewish texts, and the students' own emotional responses to reading about them. By exploring emotions with the serious intent (but playful manner) with which subject matter is explored in the classroom, teachers can transmit the message that the inner life matters. In this way, they can develop in students the sensitivity that emotional "seeing" permits in both the moral and spiritual domains, as I have described above.

The observation that literature broadens our emotional experience by providing us with language to express it is as relevant for children as it is for adults. This implies selecting literature, Jewish and general, that dwells on characters' emotional experience and that employs rich emotional language and themes, even in the elementary grades; guiding students to attend to the specific nouns, verbs, and adjectives used to describe protagonists' emotions; asking students when writing to describe emotional experience (their own and the individuals about whom they write); and honing students' understanding by asking for more precise emotional language in their own expression. Doing so opens the eyes to an empathetic way of seeing.

Negative emotions can be as valuable as positive ones in the classroom. First of all, negative emotions are often fun for students to explore. Second, for example, in a cooperative study group of high school students who found a video displaying the dissection of a dead animal disgusting, the discussion could well lead to the realization that their disgust results from their own identification of slimy innards with animalistic aspects of their own bodies; this in turn might lead to a discussion of the human connection with the animal or even of mortality. Disgust could therefore be a step toward sensitivity. Not that this kind of depth needs to be the immediate goal. If students were only to tease out and play with the subtle differences between feeling disgusted, nauseated, and "grossed out," or if they come to realize that contempt for people is often closely related to disgust for objects, they will have deepened their inner awareness.[54] The negative emotion is as much an opportunity for developing sensitivity as are positive ones. Multiple such opportunities, positive and negative, already exist in science, social studies, and language arts curricula, but they need to be planned for and investigated in class with the guidance (but no heavy-handed direction) of a sensitive teacher.

I want to embody these ideas in a concrete example in order to spell out my intentions, and so as not to fall into the trap of asserting what is right—hypothetically—and leaving to others the "petty" detail of translation into reality. As an appendix to this chapter, I therefore include the summary of a lesson sequence that develops, at an age-appropriate level, the notion of reliability in a way that supports cognitive and emotional (and, hopefully, spiritual) learning. Appropriate for fourth- or fifth-graders, it is, at first, a science lesson on the properties of solutions but then moves on to the larger theme of reliability, both physical and emotional. Then it proceeds to analyze the prayer *Maariv Aravim* (from the evening prayer service) from that perspective. With no claim to pedagogical perfection, these lessons do present evidence that with forethought, students' critical and emotional capacities can be developed while engaging in significant content learning, both general and Jewish.

ASKING FOR MORE

In a lovely classroom discussion about *t'shuvah* (repentance), a student describes with gusto a wrong he had committed against his brother. He ends with a heartfelt "I felt really bad about what I did to my brother that time, and I knew I would never do anything like that again." The teacher could have been happy with that much. After all, she had succeeded in eliciting from the student key elements of the concept of repentance, all freely and authentically given and expressed. Instead, she chose gently to prod the student, to see if he could go a little deeper.

"What you said is really touching," the teacher said, "and I'd like to understand it a little better. You said you 'felt really bad.' Could you tell us what feeling bad felt like?" The student seemed lost in trying to find an answer, so the teacher helped by asking him to be more precise in his *language*. "What I mean is," the teacher said, "when you say you felt *bad*, does that mean you felt sad? Or did you feel guilty? Or stupid? Or something else?" The speed and body language with which the student delivered his response vouched for its emotional authenticity: "Well, yeah, I felt sad," he said, "but I kind of realized how much I love my brother—and I didn't want *him* to feel sad!"

What a difference between that answer and the bland "I felt really bad." With the right question, this teacher helped her student go a step deeper emotionally. And, often the right question is one that prods a student to be more precise with his or her language. The teacher then spun out the discussion so that everyone seemed to fully understand the difference between his first answer and his second, with as much emphasis on language as on the emotion itself. If the time and setting had been appropriate, the teacher might have asked other students to describe similar instances or to put themselves in either the student's or his brother's place and to try to articulate how they would have felt, again pushing them for more specific and explicit vocabulary. She might have introduced the term "compassion," or *chesed*, or tried to link the student's statement with something previously studied in which those terms occurred. Would these moves have been a lesson in using more precise language or a lesson in deeper emotional understanding? Both, I think.

But even without that extension of the lesson, this teacher helped her students develop a sense of the importance of emotional experience.

Just as important, she helped them all see inside the thoughts and feelings of the student and his brother. This is precisely the type of sensitivity that might open their eyes to future situations calling for a moral response. As Vetlesen says:

> The art of perceiving and observing the boundaries…between objects that are moral subjects and objects that are not, is something handed down to individuals by their society.…Far from arising de novo, as if within a social vacuum, perceptions are taught to individuals.[55]

This teacher has helped students see a moral boundary and what it encompasses.

BEING SATISFIED WITH LESS

The teacher needs to play the role of elicitor and facilitator, pushing students to refine (and, one hopes, appreciate) their understanding of the nuanced difference, for example, between being angry at a friend and being disappointed with her, or to develop a more complete notion of what it feels like to be truly sorry. But force-feeding in the form of preaching or supplying students with the words we want them to say is counterproductive to the development of sensitivity. Students need to be encouraged to express and compose, not parrot.

Our traditional texts, with their enduring values, powerful concepts, and generations of accretions and memories, are an uneven weight against our children, with their relatively insubstantial Judaic backgrounds, minimal Hebrew, and school-age developmental levels. It is terribly tempting for us as teachers to serve as supplier of ideas and words to students. But telling them too much undercuts the opportunity for students to develop their own spiritual power. Leading the witness is no more legitimate in the classroom than it is in the courtroom. Much depends on the teacher's pedagogical and psychological sensitivity. Guiding, "scaffolding," and priming are legitimate and necessary teaching tools, and knowing when one exceeds the limits is one of the arts of teaching. Artful teachers find the sweet spot, the point at which they have given just enough ideas and words to prime the engine so it can rev up without flooding it. The greatest error made by teachers in handling material of this kind is in subtly, or not so subtly, hinting at an expectation of hearing certain ideas or words.

If we say too much, students will try to please us by giving us what we want to hear. We can insert prodding questions into kids' minds, but not words in their mouths. The words the student chooses may be childish and the thoughts may be simple, but above all they must belong to the student. The teacher's questions can push for more.

Needless to say, such endeavors can take root only in classrooms in which children are free to express themselves, where children know that teachers take their thoughts and daily feelings into account.[56] A teacher may press for greater precision or higher-quality work, but in ways that challenge and stimulate without threatening personally.

SPIRITUALITY RESEARCH NEEDED

There is a rich research base on children's moral functioning. Although research on children's spiritual functioning is growing, there is a lengthy agenda of research needed particularly in a Jewish context. Among the issues that need to be addressed are the validity of relational consciousness as a core concept of children's spirituality across religions; whether there are naturally built-in structures for spirituality and how they develop in people; relating the existing literature on the development of religious concepts as ideas with the growing literature on spirituality; understanding how the precursors to awe, mystery, and wonder are experienced by children; and how neuroscience can in the long term help us to understand spirituality and its relationship to emotions, cognition, and self-image.

On a practical level, we should know more about how parents nurture (or not) both the religious and the spiritual within their children; how to use aesthetic and natural experiences to nurture sensitivity, both moral and spiritual; how to use the teaching of traditional texts to enrich spirituality (and vice versa); and how to expand the formal classroom with a greater use of experiential educational techniques.

Being Emotional, Being Spiritual, Being Jewish

It is worth reiterating that being emotional and being spiritual are *not* the same thing. In this regard it is interesting to note that much of the research claiming to be devoted to children's spirituality is at least as much interested in their psychological and emotional well-being. These are matters of worthy concern, to be sure, but they are not spirituality, which almost by definition entails a relationship with another.

We have all met people who feel passionate about everything—but their passion extends only to how everything affects *them*. By contrast, spiritual and moral emotions reach from deep within oneself to deep outside so that, somehow, we experience the "other" within ourselves. Being spiritual is much *more* than being emotional, but no matter how hard I try to imagine it, I cannot understand how someone could possibly be spiritual *without* being emotional. I have emphasized so much the idea of helping children develop emotional awareness and expression not because these are the *same* as spirituality, but because I am certain that *without* them spirituality is impossible. Developing moral and spiritual sensitivity is only one part of a comprehensive program of moral and religious education, as I have tried to make clear above.

Jewish education is charged with the urgent need of ensuring that our children grow into adulthood committed to participating in Jewish life, supporting Israel and the Diaspora, and with the intent of bringing up their own children with those commitments. It also has the urgent charge of sustaining knowledge of Hebrew and increasing the knowledge of Jewish texts and literature, and doing so in a cultural environment that neither requires nor encourages it. Hebrew and study of traditional texts are prerequisites for anyone engaging in serious Jewish study throughout their lives. If we want our children to contribute to Jewish life and culture as adults, we need to give them authentic Jewish knowledge, and this requires study.

Yet we want children not only to know Judaism. We want their study of Torah to inspire compassion for the downtrodden. We want their knowledge of Jewish history to provoke love of Israel and a lasting desire to work for its success. We want students to be fascinated with Torah and to respect those who are learned in its varied meanings. We want our children to be drawn to prayer, to esteem the proper performance of Jewish rituals, and, not least of all, to experience awe and reverence for God. These are, to borrow Israel Scheffler's wonderful expression, intellectual emotions, the kinds of emotions that help us find meaning in life.[57] By finding meaning in life, discovering their connectedness to others, learning to be guided by compassion, wonder, and awe—and discovering these profoundly important things through

Judaism and their Jewish schooling—our students may become good, sensitive people, and good, committed Jews, too.

Appendix: A Teaching Unit on Reliability, Science, Family, and Maariv Aravim[58]

This lesson sequence for fourth or fifth grades grapples with the concepts of regularity and reliability in science and in the everyday. It starts with scientific principles and moves on to discussion of a relevant prayer, *Maariv Aravim*.

Lesson 1

Students are given cups of water and small amounts of gravel, salt, and powder. Experimenting with mixing them, they learn that some things don't mix at all, like gravel and water; that other things, like powder, mix in water but don't dissolve; and that still others, like salt, both mix and dissolve. They also learn that solutions are special kinds of mixtures.[60]

Lesson 2

After reviewing the previous lesson, the teacher leads a hypothetical discussion along these lines: Suppose these things didn't always happen. Let's say that when your mom tried to bake chocolate chip cookies, sometimes she could mix the ingredients and make dough, but other times all she got was a bowl of flour, water, sugar, and chocolate chips. The teacher explains that scientists talk about "regularities" to describe the reliability of events such as these.

In responding to the teacher's request for other examples, students may bring up examples of *human*, as opposed to scientific reliability. If they don't, the teacher gives a couple of examples: "I know I can count on my gardener to cut the lawn every Wednesday. I know I can count on school to end at 3:15 every day. I know I can count on some students to want to stay and talk to me during lunchtime." Students will now start to offer examples such as the following: "I know I can count on my mom to take care of me when I'm sick"; "I know I can count on my older brother to help me with my Hebrew homework if I run into a problem"; "I know I can count on my friend Sandra to make me laugh if I get upset." The discussion now goes in the direction of the following questions: "Has anyone ever let you down? How did you feel? Have you ever let anyone else down? How did you feel? What can other people count on *you* for? Is this something you like?"

LESSONS 3 AND 4

The teacher reads the students, "An Offspring's Answer,"[61] a story about a mother bird who, while flying her three chicks on her back across the sea, asks them, "When I get old, will you take me on your back?" The first two chicks each answer, "No" (with disastrous results that the teacher may choose to expurgate), but the third chick answers that she can't promise: "I may not be able to fly you across a sea because I may be busy flying my own children on *my* back just as *you* are doing for *me*." Students immediately identify the mother's anger and shock at the first two chicks' answers, but here is precisely the opportunity to expand emotional vocabulary and sensitivity by pushing for more nuanced answers. If the teacher insists that students describe the mother bird's reactions in full sentences, some will move from just "anger" to describing her disappointment that the chicks seem not to care, her sadness at their ingratitude, and so on. When discussing the mother's feelings about the third chick's answer, the teacher needs to push beyond "happiness," which is the inevitable, easy answer: "Is it as simple as that? Do you think she might have other feelings, too?" With guidance—not heavy-handed—the students can identify that the mother was both saddened and happy at the third chick's response, that she must have been deeply moved and gratified that the third chick understood the concept of responsibility (reliability).

The teacher introduces the prayer *Maariv Aravim*,[62] which praises God, "who speaks the evening into being, skillfully opens the gates,...Creator of day and night, rolling light away from darkness and darkness from light."

After directing students to key phrases, such as "opens the gates," and "rolling light away from darkness," the teacher asks how this description is similar to the scientific laws they have been discussing. With choral readings and graphic display of the prayer, she can show

how reliability and regularity are built into the rhythm of the prayer in its repetitions, parallelisms, and use of repeated short phrases.

At some point in these discussions, students will raise the question of disasters, illnesses, and other ways in which the world is unreliable. This important objection can only partly be addressed by the teacher's pointing out the *ultimate* reliability of the laws: for example, scientists are making progress on predicting earthquakes, engineers have learned to build stronger buildings, and doctors are constantly finding cures for diseases such as AIDS, which no one understood enough to treat thirty years ago. The point is not to try to justify evil, and the point is not to intellectualize these issues. The point is to acknowledge that at times the world *is* unreliable and scary, to help students see that beneath the surface there are things we can count on and that their own efforts can make life more reliable for the people around them, and to create a connection between an important Jewish text and these ideas and feelings.

4

Spirituality and
Moral Education[*]

JUDD KRUGER LEVINGSTON

"I just don't see how Oren can believe that the Torah *really* comes from God," Marc said with an air of disbelief.

"But Marc," Rabbi Hartsfield countered, "can you understand that if it's hard for you to believe that the Torah comes from God, it's equally hard for Oren to believe that the Torah does *not* come from God?"

"Maybe," Marc said in a resigned voice, trying to accept the irreconcilable differences between him and his classmate.

The teacher's attempt at mediating their differences led to a silence between Marc and his classmate as they both considered and then held onto their beliefs.

As I stood in the back of the classroom, I was enjoying the privilege of observing pluralism in action. The teacher, Rabbi Hartsfield, took his

[*] I wish to express gratitude to my colleagues and students at Jack M. Barrack Hebrew Academy (Bryn Mawr, PA), where I work. The teachers see themselves as moral educators, and the students hunger for moral education. I am fortunate to work at a place in which this is valued. Note that all student and teacher names and school names (with the exception of Jack M. Barrack Hebrew Academy) that appear in this paper are pseudonyms.

55

role seriously, not advocating for one position or the other. Instead, the teacher was trying to help his students understand one another while they learned to articulate their own beliefs.

The class discussion that day about revelation from God transcended the moment. Even though the ringing bell signaled the end of the classroom conversation, a feeling lingered among the students that they had encountered Marc's and Oren's deeply held moral convictions. In the safety of the pluralistic Jewish day school that they attend,[1] the students were defining the role that they believe God plays in revelation, sharing their convictions out loud with their peers while their teacher guided them.

Moral education in one of its broadest senses encompasses this kind of thought about the nature of God and human relationships with God. What could be more spiritual in a classroom than deep, contemplative thought as part of an intellectual and personal journey?

Spirituality and Moral Education: Ethics and Beyond

The word "spirituality" often calls to mind the faraway look of an individual in rapture, eyes closed, neck tilted back, body released from tension. Someone help up as a role model for Jewish spirituality might have a tallit draped like a hood over the head, the body swaying to the prayers. Can this kind of spirituality be taught? "Jewish educators should not give up on spiritual education even if they aren't in a position to promote spiritual experiences such as prayer or meditation. Spiritual experiences in many forms are vitally important in Jewish classrooms."

For the purpose of this chapter, I understand "spirituality" to include emotional and physical states such as yearning, surrender of the ego to an intellectual quest, surrender of the ego to a being or life force, and feeling connected to other people and beings. Spirituality can be part of open-ended intellectual activities in research, and spirituality can emerge in the arts and nature, and even play.

If spirituality is this broad in scope, then we could label almost any adolescent experience as a spiritual experience, from pitching a great softball or baseball game to dancing in the front row of a rock concert; from delving into new research to writing poetry; from having a deep conversation with friends that goes late into the night (or early into the morning) to plumbing feelings that rarely get expressed.

Rabbi Abraham Joshua Heschel provides a useful point of departure in his essay "On Children and Youth," based on a talk he gave in Washington in 1960 at a White House conference:

> The problem of our youth is not youth. The problem is the spirit of our age: denial of transcendence, the vapidity of values, emptiness in the heart, the decreased sensitivity to the imponderable quality of the spirit, the collapse of communication between the realm of tradition and the inner world of the individual. The central problem is that we do not know how to think, how to pray, how to cry, how to resist the deceptions of too many persuaders. There is no community of those who worry about integrity.[2]

For Heschel, we cannot teach goodness and ethical practice without paying attention to the soul and without focusing on the integrity of each individual. Later in the same essay, Heschel argues that while we try to fill the minds of young people with knowledge, we cannot afford to ignore values and emotions.[3] We should not live mechanized lives; we should not allow ourselves to become "spiritually stunted."[4] Instead, we need to enlarge our sense of mystery and awe, cultivating an appreciation for "the beauty and grandeur of the universe."[5]

While moments of spirituality may lift a student out of the confines of any particular day or classroom, moral education, which encompasses several different areas of inquiry, may be a more frequent part of the rough and tumble that is part of school life. Moral issues may be introduced as part of the curriculum and in informal, unplanned ways as well.

The study of ethics may be the most familiar and the preeminent arena for moral education, but it is just one of four areas that I have observed in public and private school classes. The four areas of inquiry include the following:

- Questions about ethical practice: How am I expected to behave toward others, and what are my ethical responsibilities as a citizen?
- Questions about character: What does it mean for me to develop a strong moral character with values such as courage and patience? What values should guide and fortify me as I go out into the world?

- Questions about dignity, civil rights, and abstract principles of justice: Why do human beings justify going to war and killing one another? How do people justify enslaving one another? What should be the role of a government?
- Questions of meaning and questions about existential issues: Is there a God? What, if anything, is my role in the world? How do I define my own identity? What is the nature of beauty, truth, love?[6]

The first area of moral education, concerning ethical practice, includes discussions about topics such as honesty, speech, property, and right and wrong. Parents and caregivers begin to coach their children in ethical behavior from the time that they are young and told to share their toys and to put away their things. Once in school, a young person may be coached by teachers and other adults in ethical behavior countless times during the day, from mediation offered at recess to encouragement that directs students to take responsibility for honest behavior, the ethical treatment of one another's property, and fair play.

The second arena of moral education, concerning character, also begins at home, when parents start to shape the moral character of their children. Character education is not limited to instruction in behavior (Say thank you! Don't fight with your sister! Make sure everyone is invited to the party! Go out there and play with courage—you can do it.). Character education involves shaping the qualities that become part of one's outlook or personality. The ancient Greek philosopher Aristotle identifies several character traits that are part of a virtuous life, including patience, courage, modesty, friendliness, magnanimity, proper ambition, and righteous indignation. He also describes a series of corresponding vices: patience gone awry, for example, becomes anger, irascibility, or a lack of spirit; friendliness mismanaged can become obsequiousness or insincerity.[7] In the modern era, there may be other character traits that we believe need to be included, such as integrity and an appreciation for the aesthetic.

The Character Education Partnership (CEP), based in Washington, DC, offers several tools to help educators define a core set of values to guide their school communities, setting expectations for students, teachers, and administrators. The CEP materials suggest different approaches for schools to create a culture of academic excellence while teaching students to assume responsibility in their own school buildings.

In "schools of character" that follow the principles of the CEP, values such as respect and citizenship will become part of a young person's repertoire of behavior. Students are encouraged to question, discuss, and develop their behavior in advisory programs, citizenship classes, assemblies, community service programs, and regular classes. Schools of character can and should become places where people trust one another and where students see the importance of serving one another and the community.

The CEP has identified eleven standards for schools to meet to become a school of character. Standards that are relevant for this chapter about moral education and spirituality include such categories as the following:

> Principle 1: Effective character education promotes core ethical values as the basis of good character.
>
> Principle 4: Effective character education creates a caring school community.
>
> Principle 5: Effective character education provides students with opportunities for moral action.
>
> Principle 8: Effective character education engages the school staff as a learning and moral community that shares responsibility for character education and attempts to adhere to the same core values that guide the education of students.
>
> Principle 11: Effective character education assesses the character of the school, the school staff's functioning as character educators, and the extent to which students manifest good character.[8]

This set of principles can function like a statement of mission for schools to create caring communities that nurture character and spirit while providing for the safety of every student. The tools for principle 11, for example, include space for an evaluator to note the extent to which school staff members "regularly assess the character of the school as a moral community," and also for the evaluator to note the degree to which student progress and student behavior are linked to the student's expression of core values. Students at schools who sign onto these principles receive evaluations in their regular report cards or progress reports based on their character development, community service, performance in student-led parent-teacher conferences, and their own self-assessments.[9] While it would be a stretch to ascribe a level of spirituality to anti-bullying programs, strong student-teacher relationships and high self-esteem in classrooms point to a culture that nurtures mentoring, positive role models, and a positive school spirit.

The current climate requires attention to character development, especially as it relates to ethnic differences, sexual and gender orientation, and bullying. In Philadelphia, public schools were forced to confront simmering tensions between African Americans and Asians in early December 2009, when several Asian students at a South Philadelphia high school were attacked by African American students. The legacy of the attacks continues to affect public perceptions of school safety and protection from bullying. In New Jersey, an anti-bullying law was passed in November 2010 to protect gay and lesbian students who have been bullied and attacked.[10] Newspaper stories are exploring the impact of bullying on individual lives into adulthood in the news sections and ideas sections as well.[11] A school culture that fails to pay attention to moral and spiritual development risks becoming a place in which violence will prevail.

A strong program of character education that also includes bystander education could teach young people how to intervene when bullying begins, stopping destructive violence and cruelty among students. At the "Jerusalem Jewish Day School" in the Philadelphia area, one of the schools in which I did field research, students take part in one such program both in the lower school and middle school. The program, called Second Step,[12] helps students to develop the kinds of skills necessary for self-advocacy, to learn to intervene in bullying situations, and to help with conflict resolution. Through role-playing and intensive classroom discussion, led by teachers trained to use the materials, students play out different scenarios and rehearse moral dilemmas in the hope that they will be prepared to take a stand and intervene, if necessary, should these dilemmas become real in their lives.

While Second Step is designed for implementation in large public schools and also in smaller schools, there are materials intended for a smaller, mostly independent school audience that have been published by the Council for Spiritual and Ethical Education, based in Portland, Oregon. Their materials tend to be oriented toward a student's spiritual development as nurtured in a school with advisors and teachers who know the students well. A teacher who can sense changes in both the moral *macro*-climate of a school and in the *micro*-climate of an advisory group or classroom will be in a good position to stop harmful behavior if it occurs. The CSEE handbook for advisors and a booklet on character education are tools that offer recommendations and handouts that teachers can use for communicating with their advisees and for activities that promote group building, a sense of shared purpose, and friendship instead of bullying and tension.[13]

While the first two areas of moral education identified above (ethical practice and character development) are closely related, the third area, concerning human dignity and civil rights, is more abstract and sometimes more difficult to tackle, especially within the limited time frame allotted to any given class on any given day in a school's daily schedule. Nevertheless, these kinds of questions about human dignity and civil rights may arise in discussions about slavery in the Americas, in discussions about war and peace in the modern era, and in contemporary conversations in the principal's office about discipline. In a New York City public high school that I visited, I observed a history class in which the teacher challenged the students to consider the role of the Constitution of the United States. The teacher had an open-ended question on the board to prompt discussion, asking the students which groups in American society were neglected, oppressed, or deprived of rights. Students readily named a wide variety of groups from Hispanics and blacks to gays and lesbians. One student even identified teenagers as an oppressed group because they lack a public voice. Having observed that class in session within just a few weeks of the high school shooting in Columbine High School in Littleton, Colorado, I was not surprised by the moral empathy for teenagers that I was observing were prepared to offer for teens who lived elsewhere.[14]

The time doesn't always exist for moral questions that touch upon such deeply felt societal issues, and teachers might not necessarily be prepared to take them on, even if they were allowed to be asked. Katherine Simon describes a classroom situation in which a question about civil rights and dignity had the potential to throw a class off track and even undermine a teacher's efforts. In one class that she observed as part of her research, a student asked what to make of the lives of slaves in the antebellum South who may have been treated better as soldiers fighting for the Confederacy in the South than as soldiers fighting for freedom under the Union flag. An exasperated teacher told the student,

"We could argue about that all day," in an effort to put off the subject while the students moved forward in the curriculum. Nevertheless, it was clear that the topic was compelling and needed further exploration. Such topics related to dignity and civil rights do not necessarily arise in every class, so teachers have to remain attuned to the possibility of teaching moments that might lead to rich moral inquiry.[15]

The fourth area of moral inquiry, regarding questions of meaning and existential issues, may be the most challenging for any school to cultivate and promote, even in a Jewish educational setting. Jewish studies teachers may feel comfortable providing instruction in reciting prayers and performing ritual acts, but the same teachers may feel cautious and even uncomfortable about asking students to describe what they believe about God while they recite a blessing. It may feel intrusive. One could imagine a discussion about the meaning behind the blessing over Chanukah candles or over the bread that they eat. In making blessings, do Jews thank God or praise God? Is the Jewish God abstract and beyond expressions of praise? Or is the Jewish God one who appreciates the praise and who sends blessings, rain, and joyful days to people who offer words of praise and worship?

Existential issues naturally arise in classes when students read the Bible, discussing the different motivations of biblical characters from Abraham, who dares to argue with God about destroying the depraved cities of Sodom and Gomorrah and who complies with God's wish to bring up his son as a sacrifice, to the beloved and storied King David, who could be judged in some respects as a failure. To raise questions about Truth (note the capital letter *T*) requires a leap in a teacher's planning to allow unstructured time for these kinds of far-ranging and probing discussions, and it also requires a welcoming atmosphere that is conducive for students to share their convictions so openly. In the opening vignette with Rabbi Hartsfield, I observed how he succeeded in creating the kind of atmosphere that allowed Marc and Oren to share their deep beliefs about the nature of divine revelation. Wars have been and continue to be fought about conflicting beliefs about revelation and the human condition, making it all the more important that educational settings allow for diverse expressions of thought.

A moral discussion about existential issues may be confusing for students because such discussions tend to be inconclusive and oriented not around a set of answers but around a thinking process, so it may not be clear how to take notes. The teacher has to give up some attention to pacing and the clock. If Rabbi Hartsfield had been trying to prepare the students for a test, a factual discussion would have been methodical and thorough, not exploratory and open-ended. A class discussion about what students believe God might expect of them requires time for both believers and skeptics to air their thoughts, to write, to think, to listen, and to probe deeply. In a fundamental way, discussions about existential issues and questions of meaning are not only important to an academic experience; they are part of one's spiritual growth, too. Education in ethics, character building, and citizenship may help to prevent violence, promote understanding among students, and create a more positive school climate. Spiritual development comes most readily in the fourth area of moral inquiry.

Outcomes of Spiritual Education in Faith-Based and Nonsectarian Schools

While conducting field research for my book *Sowing the Seeds of Character: The Moral Education of Adolescents in Public and Private Schools*,[16] I visited several faith-based schools, including a Quaker school, a Muslim school, a Roman Catholic school, and a Jewish school. In each school, teachers feel a sense of investment in the students' spiritual development, seeking to instill a sense of ethical practice and a strong sense of religious faith, and each school takes a different approach to moral and spiritual education.

For many schools, formal religious services provide opportunities both for acculturation and for spiritual education. At the "Fairhill Friends School," where I observed a Quaker meeting for worship, the entire upper school student body and their teachers sat in silence that was broken only a couple of times by prayerful comments from teachers about growth that can come through change.

At an Episcopalian school in New York, where I observed regular upper school "chapel" meetings, the school chaplain led the students in worship services that were meant to be educational and celebratory, marking the winter holidays of Chanukah, Christmas, and Kwanzaa or the spring festivals of spiritual liberation such as Passover and Easter. Sometimes chapel time was a time for the community to gather to consider subjects such as art and music in a purely secular manner, referencing the religious dimensions for historical purposes, not for devotional purposes. Today, under the new leadership of a different school chaplain, students meet with the chaplain to discuss ways to engage the student body in contemplation to raise awareness of great spiritual matters of the day.

Jewish schools have two significant challenges in promoting spiritual education through prayer: skill development and issues of relevancy. At the "Jerusalem School," as at many Jewish day schools, middle school morning services are set up to fulfill both goals. Students learn skills of leading prayer and reading from the Torah scroll, and they also break up into small groups known as minyanim (small prayer groups meeting the minimum of ten individuals necessary for the required quorum) in which they engage in discussions about theology, poetry and prayer, and even contemporary issues drawn from newspapers that raise moral questions about identity, spirituality, and ethics.

At Barrack Hebrew Academy, where I currently serve as director of Jewish studies, the school's secular Jewish founders did not include time in the regular school day for religious services, so middle and upper school students and teachers attend *Shacharit* services on a voluntary basis before the school day begins on Tuesdays, Wednesdays, and Fridays. In response to student and parent interest in spiritual education and in promoting the spiritual life of the students, the school has launched a *Minchah* program that includes the afternoon religious services for those who prefer and feel obligated to recite the formal liturgy. The *Minchah* program also has numerous options for students who prefer other forms of spiritual reflection such as a nature walk, meditation, yoga, writing in a journal, and silent reading. These students can answer the need for relevancy by choosing a setting that is the best fit for their interests. In a faculty meeting prior to launching this *Minchah* program, the teachers reached a consensus, concluding that they have a moral obligation as educators to attend to the spiritual lives of both the observant and the less observant students by giving them opportunities to feel a connection to God, to their own inner yearnings, and to the community. As much as many of the teachers would like to see the students find meaning and develop skills in the traditional Jewish liturgy, they also believe that a rich spiritual life may be the most important outcome, even more important than any specific skills or practice. Building on the success of the *Minchah* program, Barrack teachers now lead the students in a regular *Shaharit* that includes a similar range of options.

Rabbi Elliot Dorff, a professor of philosophy at the American Jewish University in Los Angeles, confirms the important link between moral education and spiritual education when he writes that the practice of prayer "can help us clarify our values by reminding us of the big picture, confess our sins so that we can move on with our lives, and remind us daily of the kind of people we should strive to be and the kind of world we should try to create."[17] For him, spiritual development belongs in a school and should be part of a curriculum.

Many faith-based schools use religious studies classes for spiritual education. On one of my visits to the "Fairhill Friends School," in a class on Quaker philosophy, the teacher gave each student a Girl Scout Thin Mint cookie to eat "mindfully" as part of a lesson on "mindfulness." Eating the cookie became a spiritual exercise under the teacher's guidance, in which students were asked to awaken the senses while feeling deep gratitude for plenty and for the sense of taste.

When I visited the Muslim school, "Al-Aqsa Islamic Academy," the middle school students enjoyed a spirited flow of discussion, probing the degree to which they should share their food in a case when neither they nor their friends were in a position of plenty. The teacher shared her moral perspective, speaking with piety and hope. She explained to the students that giving to one another is not merely an ethical practice of kindness; it is a spiritual practice that establishes a connection with God. She told the young people, "Students, when you do something for *Allahu subhanahu wa ta'ala* [Allah, Glorious and Exalted be He], you will get the same reward." In the same class, she sought to instill a sense of goodwill in her students, saying, "A simple act of *salaam* [greeting] is *sadaqah* [justice]. A thank-you or a paycheck is not necessary."

In Rabbi Hartsfield's class, which I described at the beginning of this chapter, the students had the spiritual experience of connecting their personal theologies to the text; they also had the spiritual experience of defining their religious identity through questions that probe the extent to which they believe that the Torah came from God in a moment of revelation. If they disagree with their peers about such basic theological concepts as revelation, the students have to consider whether what they say will affect their relationships in the future. Teachers in Rabbi Hartsfield's position can help students to understand that even if they and their friends may have some incompatible beliefs and practices, they can learn to live with differences.

Some might argue that a mix of spirituality and religious education does not belong in the classroom because it is too personal. For Marc and Oren to share their deepest religious convictions requires intensive teacher involvement; once the bell rings, who will offer support for anybody's positions or beliefs, whether the beliefs are mainstream, radical, or orthodox? Teachers need to be aware of what they are opening up when they begin to navigate these complicated spiritual waters with students.

While faith-based schools are the most likely settings for spiritual education, it has a place in public schools as well. The Character Education Partnership concludes in a blue-ribbon report that schools have much to contribute to a student's spiritual development. The report, titled *Smart and Good High Schools: Integrating Excellence and Ethics for Success in School, Work and Beyond*, identifies eight "strengths of character" for all students to aspire to reach under the guidance of their school leaders. The eight strengths represent a progression from the first level and a more narrow focus on character traits well suited for learning and thinking to the latter strengths that involve acquiring a broad, global perspective that extends beyond the individual's immediate world toward a life nourished by a sense of spirituality. The eight strengths are as follows:

1. Lifelong learner and critical thinker
2. Diligent and capable performer
3. Socially and emotionally skilled person
4. Ethical thinker
5. Respectful and responsible moral agent
6. Self-disciplined person who pursues a healthy lifestyle
7. Contributing community member and democratic citizen
8. Spiritual person engaged in crafting a life of noble purpose

These eight levels or strengths might move a student from concrete action and concrete thinking into areas of greater responsibility that require abstract thinking and an interest in solving one's own problems, the problems of others, and problems in society.

It is easy to imagine cultivating these character strengths both in full-time schools, where educators have daily opportunities to work with young people, and in after-school programs, where skills for life-long Jewish learning may be taught as well. The authors of the report, Thomas Lickona and Matthew Davidson, conclude that schools can de-velop a young person's character not only through ethics education, and not only through giving each student a sense of place as a citizen in the school and in the larger community, but also by inspiring each student to reach beyond community service and honest practices toward a spiri-tual practice.

For independent schools, the Center for Spiritual and Ethical Education (CSEE), noted above in a connection with advisory pro-grams, serves as an important resource in these same areas of commu-nity service, spiritual education, and education in ethics. In the words of its mission, the CSEE aspires to provide "an active forum for ethi-cal growth and spiritual development in schools" through printed re-sources, newsletters, and workshops that help schools to develop and strengthen advisory programs, service learning programs, and char-acter education programs. The CSEE tries to work at the institutional level to have an impact on curricular choices, counseling, worship or other kinds of gathering times, school rituals, and the total school environment. The CSEE seeks to nurture moral growth without regard to the specifics of any one particular curriculum.[18]

In schools that permit a full range of spiritual expression, teachers are in a position to use the arts, personal prayer, meaningful common times, and academic work to touch on soulful questions and to stimu-late spiritual growth. In the realm of informal education, two particu-larly innovative programs fuel a young adolescent's spiritual education through activities and discussion that promote community building. The programs, sponsored by Moving Traditions, use gender as a frame-work: *Rosh Hodesh: It's a Girl Thing!* has been implemented in numer-ous communities for girls since it was launched in 2002. A parallel, though differently structured program for adolescent boys, is called *The Brotherhood*. Both programs structure discussions around issues of friendship, inclusion and exclusion, and an appreciation for different models of femininity or masculinity, with examples from contemporary life, Jewish texts, and Jewish life. Following the guiding principle in the group leader's handbook, "seamlessly infuse Judaism,"[19] one session prepared for *The Brotherhood* has the young men first create a "Manliness Barometer"[20] in which they stand in a line based on their own response to statements, such as the following, beginning with the phrase "It's a *guy* thing to..."

...know how to sew on a button
...tell someone else how you feel about them
...be obsessed with video games
...make the first move
...be the family provider
...suffer silently[21]

In the same session, the young men turn to a Jewish text, looking at the ideal qualities of a Jewish male as described in the Bible in Psalm 34:

Who is a man? Someone who appreciates life,
who loves each day,
who sees the good,
who holds his tongue from evil and his lips from lies,
who turns away from bad,
who does good,
who seeks and pursues peace.[22]

As the young men discuss what it means to be a man, comparing ancient and contemporary expectations and standards with the guidance of a trained facilitator, they cannot help but grow spiritually as they consider how to bring ancient wisdom into their own lives.

Programs like *Rosh Hodesh: It's a Girl Thing!* and *The Brotherhood* succeed in part because they allow time for the young people to play with ideas and with one another in game-like activities. A young person today is unlikely to accept the moral obligations of a man as described in Psalm 34 just by reading and discussing the text, but after playing with ideas in the Manliness Barometer, he might be more likely to see the wisdom in the biblical vision. Under the guidance of the right adult leader, he might be able to transcend the day-to-day concerns of the average teenage boy and consider great existential questions, complicated moral issues, and new spiritual practices that might even seem uncomfortable at first.

One might argue that experiences of play are essential to a child's moral and spiritual development. Play captivates children in day-care settings and in kindergarten classrooms, at playdates and family get-togethers, and out in the park where they can quickly become immersed in their own worlds. Whether they are playing dress-up, house, school, or store, and in the case of older children, whether they are doing artwork or playing a pickup game of basketball, the satisfying experiences of play enable them to try out different identities and test the extent of their physical and intellectual stamina. Play can be a form of spiritual exploration through the arts in which young people paint an idea, translate experiences of nature into music, or write a poem or story that they hope will last for all time. In a favorite scene of religious and social play from Hollywood, the popular film *Keeping the Faith* shows Brian Finn, the boy who grows up to become a priest played by Edward Norton, and Jake Schram, the boy who grows up to become a rabbi played by Ben Stiller, sharing a mock communion and other mock ceremonies together. In doing so, they reenact religious dramas that they had seen in adult settings.

Not all play is so spiritual. When school-age children at play develop rules, negotiate with their peers, show an appreciation for the meaning of a team, and develop a set of goals, they are echoing and re-creating for themselves the structures of adult society. Research on the connection between recess time and academic achievement shows that children who have opportunities to play in unstructured recess time are likely to improve their grades.[23] It is in the interest of educators to promote play by giving it a priority in the schedule.

Johan Huizinga makes the connection between moral development, spiritual development, and play in his seminal book *Homo Ludens: A Study of the Play-Element in Culture.* One can promote moral development by teaching about justice and by providing opportunities for ethical discussion; he argues that play transcends those more academic experiences. He writes, "Play cannot be denied. You can deny, if you like, nearly all abstractions: justice, beauty, truth, goodness, mind, God. You can deny seriousness, but not play."[24]

We can conclude that as much as teachers can and should encourage moral development in classrooms and chapels, whether through ethics education or spiritual education, through text study or ritual, whether on the playground or in Rabbi Hartsfield's classroom, students need opportunities for spirited play in which they can identify what is meaningful for themselves. Educators cannot force spiritual development or moral development, but they can create a setting conducive to the moral and spiritual development of every student.

5

Where Ethics Meets History:
A Synthesis of Values, Sacred Texts, and the Humanities

JAN DARSA
AND MARTIN E. SLEEPER

Introduction

E DUCATION IS HOLY WORK, and teachers can play a significant
role as spiritual guides in the lessons they impart to their students. It is an awesome task because the journey educators take
with those they teach can profoundly impact the way their students
view and live in the world. Facing History and Ourselves explores the
lessons from the history of the Holocaust and other cases of collective
violence that have threatened or destroyed democracy and examines the

choices and decisions people make as citizens in their societies. As students examine historical content, combining an intellectual endeavor with ethical reflection allows them to engage both head and heart in their educational journey. When this study is interdisciplinary, it creates the opportunity to have the Facing History ethos of good citizenship, social justice, responsibility to each other, *derech eretz* (respect), and *tikkun olam* (repairing the world) seep into the whole school culture.

Facing History and Ourselves

For nearly four decades, Facing History and Ourselves has been working in classrooms and communities that are characterized by increasing religious, ethnic, cultural, and national diversity. Facing History provides a model of educational intervention and professional development that helps teachers and their students make the essential connections between history and the moral choices they confront in their lives. Through in-depth study of historical cases of mass atrocity and genocide, Facing History engages teachers and students of diverse backgrounds in an examination of racism, prejudice, and anti-Semitism, as well as courage and compassion, to promote development of student capacities for active, responsible participation in a pluralistic democratic society.

In Facing History and Ourselves classrooms, students learn to think about individual and group decision making and to exercise the faculty of making moral judgments. Drawing on the seminal work of developmental theorists, including Dewey, Piaget, Erikson, and Kohlberg, the pedagogy of Facing History and Ourselves speaks to the adolescent's newly discovered ideas of subjectivity, competing truths, and differing perspectives, along with the growing capacity to think hypothetically and the inclination to find personal meaning in newly introduced phenomena. Facing History recognizes that adolescents are budding moral philosophers who come to their schooling already struggling with matters of obedience, loyalty, fairness, difference, and acceptance, rooted in their own identities and experience. They need to build the habits, skills, and knowledge to help them find the connections to the past that will inspire their moral imaginations about their role in the future. By exploring a question in a historical case study, such as why some people willingly conform to the norms of a group even when those norms encourage wrongdoing, while others speak out and resist, Facing History offers students a framework and a vocabulary for thinking about how they can make a difference in the world they inhabit.

Facing History's intellectual and pedagogical framework is built on a synthesis of history and ethics for effective history education.[1] Its core learning principles embrace intellectual rigor, ethical reflection, emotional engagement, and civic agency. Its teaching parameters engage the methods of the humanities: inquiry, critical analysis, interpretation, empathic connections, and judgment. Facing History and Ourselves teachers employ a carefully structured methodology to provoke thinking about complex questions of citizenship and human behavior. Teachers stretch the historical imagination of their students by urging delineation of what might have been done, choices that could have been made, and alternative scenarios that could have happened.

The focal case study of Facing History and Ourselves—the failure of democracy in Germany and the steps leading to the Holocaust—is the most documented case of twentieth-century indifference, dehumanization, hatred, racism, anti-Semitism, and mass murder. Embedded in the study are difficult and complex questions of judgment, memory, and legacy and the necessity for responsible civic participation to prevent injustice and protect democracy in the present and future. The language and vocabulary that are taught throughout are tools for entry into the history—words like *perpetrator*, *victim*, *defender*, *bystander*, *opportunist*, *rescuer*, and *upstander*. Students learn that terms like *identity*, *membership*, *legacy*, *denial*, *responsibility*, and *judgment* can help them understand complicated history, as well as connect the lessons of that history to the questions they face in their own worlds.

Facing History materials draw on content from history, literature, art, and science. They include such resources as propaganda posters that demonstrate the power of labeling and the use of words to turn neighbor against neighbor. Students make connections to other situations of collective violence based upon hatred and discrimination, such as South Africa and the American South. Throughout the unit, they learn and practice the skills of in-depth historical thinking and understanding, including knowledge of chronology, analyzing historical context, evaluating evidence, determining causality, and confronting multiple perspectives.

Students learn that violence and injustice begin with small steps of indifference, conformity, and not thinking about what is happening. They discuss what words like *perpetrator,* *bystander,* and *upstander* can mean in the context of both everyday and extreme situations. First-person narratives, as expressed in writings, in video testimonies, and by guest speakers, constitute a compelling element of the program. Holocaust survivors, as well as victims of more recent genocides in Cambodia and Rwanda, tell of their experiences and talk about the need to confront and to bear witness to history. Students also hear about individuals whose actions reflect courage and resilience and whose determination to stand up for human rights have influenced subsequent public policy.

Case studies of other examples of dehumanization, hatred, discrimination, mass violence, and destruction, such as the history of the eugenics movement and the civil rights struggle in America, broaden and deepen these themes. Each component of these histories is linked to issues and decisions in the present and the constellation of individual and group choices, decisions, and behaviors that compose "ourselves." Teachers provoke the intellectual, ethical, and emotional impulses of their students to draw the connections between past, present, and future. Students learn to distinguish between false parallels and simplistic comparisons, while discerning the universals in human behavior, choice, and decision making. Often, it is the distance provided by studying such themes in a historical case study that facilitates discussion of how they are played out in their own lives.

The Teachers

For many educators, the experience of learning and teaching Facing History and Ourselves resonates with the deepest aims and goals that brought them to the profession. Teachers are usually introduced to the program through workshops that are offered in school and community settings or online. Professional development seminars, all of which include face-to-face interaction and online components, provide intensive sessions about the latest scholarship and methodology of teaching sensitive issues in the classroom. Content is interwoven with pedagogy to engage participants in fundamental issues of teaching:

- How to come to grips with the prejudices and preconceptions teachers and students bring to difficult and controversial subject matter
- How to address moral decisions with students without preaching or evasion
- How to build a classroom environment of trust and respect for diverse opinions
- How to orchestrate discussion in which students truly talk and listen to one another
- How to use journals and personal writing and reflection
- How to ask the additional question that complicates the simplistic answer and provokes critical thinking
- How to assess learning about citizenship, judgment, and participation

Through their own confrontation with the issues of history and human behavior, teachers think together about the meaning and the challenge of bringing those issues to their classes. They also contemplate the necessity of evoking and honoring student voices to build together a reflective learning community in which a climate of respect, multiple perspective taking, and acceptance and understanding of difference predominate. Once they become part of the Facing History and Ourselves educator network, teachers continue to receive follow-up support through interactive portals on the website that offer new resources and modules for in-depth examination of particular topics and themes in the program.

Teachers of Facing History and Ourselves have consistently reported that its professional development reinvigorates them, increases their commitment to teach, and reaffirms their aspirations and their sense of efficacy as teachers. Their students display several characteristics: greater engagement in learning, increased skills for understanding and analyzing history, greater empathy and ethical awareness, increased civic knowledge, and an improved ability to recognize racism, anti-Semitism, and other forms of bigotry in themselves and in others.

Evaluation

In the most comprehensive evaluation of the program, a two-year study using an experimental design confirms that Facing History and Ourselves helps to create effective teachers who improve their students' academic performance and civic learning.[2] The study involved seventy-six schools from across the country, where Facing History and Ourselves had not been taught before. Half of the schools and teachers were selected at random to participate in Facing History and Ourselves professional development in the first year of the study; the other half received the program in the second year. The study was designed to assess the impact of Facing History and Ourselves' professional development on these teachers and on the academic performance (e.g., skills for analyzing history), social and ethical awareness, and civic learning and engagement of their students. The report found that the professional development services of Facing History and Ourselves engage teachers and increase their efficacy in promoting their students' academic and civic learning. Those teachers who received Facing History and Ourselves services, relative to those who did not, demonstrated a statistically significant increase in efficacy in promoting community and learner-centered classrooms, deliberative skills, historical understanding, and civic learning. These findings for teachers corresponded with the study's findings for students: Facing History students reported more positive classroom climates, demonstrated greater historical understanding, and exhibited better civic skills and dispositions, including tolerance, awareness of the power and danger of prejudice and discrimination, and a belief in their power to make a difference.

While much of the work of Facing History and Ourselves has been in public and independent schools, the program has also been implemented in many Jewish settings. Its longtime presence there, however, has recently taken on increased emphasis. Recognizing a profound need in Jewish day and congregational schools for both the content and pedagogy that Facing History could provide, additional materials were developed that addressed the specific concerns of educators in those settings. In particular, it became clear that to study the Holocaust and the destruction of two-thirds of the European Jews without first examining the rich and vibrant culture that existed in pre-war Europe would be a missed opportunity. For Jewish students, it is especially important to understand that Jews were a people who contributed to the societies in which they lived and had communities that flourished across Europe. Only with that knowledge can students appreciate the magnitude and irreversibility of what was lost. With the publication of *Facing History and Ourselves: The Jews of Poland*, a resource that provides teachers and students with materials on Jewish life in Eastern Europe before the war, as well as on Jewish identity and the legacy of the Holocaust for Jews today, many congregational and day schools joined the Facing History network.[3] The program was increasingly integrated into Jewish middle and high schools across disciplines, spiraling throughout grade levels and across the entire curriculum.

The Jewish Text Project

Resources from Facing History's Jewish Education Program have been incorporated into the general studies programs of middle and high school grades in such subjects as history, social studies, language arts, art, psychology, and science. Yet many of the themes of Facing History's sequence of study embody ethics and values that are seen throughout Jewish sacred texts and provide a moral compass for how Jews live in the world. *Sacred Texts, Modern Questions: Connecting Ethics and History Through A Jewish Lens*, is Facing History's newest work and involves five units that align Jewish texts with the themes of Facing History. Further, the new study guide, along with other resources, encourages the part-nering of Judaic studies teachers with general studies teachers to teach Facing History with a spiritual and theological lens. These affiliations have increased Facing History's impact in schools, built teams across departments, and reinforced student awareness of the holistic nature of their Jewish learning. What they learn in history, science, literature, and the arts cannot be separated from their Jewish lives.

These new resources are a component of Facing History's larger Jewish Education Program and can be used in conjunction with the reg-ular Facing History sequence of study (anywhere from a six- to eight-week unit or a semester- or year-long program) or as a separate program that can be used as an elective, embedded in Judaic studies, or in advisories. Its content demonstrates the centrality of the complex and difficult moral issues within Jewish tradition. The resources of the Jewish Text

Project, many of which are in the new study guide, draw upon biblical, Rabbinic, and contemporary Jewish texts, so that students can reflect on a culture that embraces textual questioning and analysis to form a basis of how one lives an ethical life today. Its integration of the framework and materials of Facing History and Ourselves with Jewish texts, both Rabbinic and modern, highlights how Jewish tradition and ethics relate to the events in the real world. It does this both in history and in our students' lives today.

The lessons included in the Jewish Text Project exemplify the continual interweaving of choices and decision-making in the past and present that underlies the core *Facing History and Ourselves: Holocaust and Human Behavior* case study.[4]

The relationship between the individual and society, for example, is an underpinning of the Jewish Education Program, as is the connection between history and ourselves.

IDENTITY

The initial set of lessons examines the forces that shape who we are, how the labels that we are given impact how we think about ourselves, and how the multiple identities we assume influence who we think we are and how we see others. Through a range of activities, students consider the many factors that influence their identities as individuals and as members of a community. For educators in a Jewish setting, these first lessons guide students in connecting the concept of identity to their particular situation as Jews living in the Diaspora. They read excerpts from interviews in which Jews of different backgrounds reflect upon their identities.[5] They see that Judaism is more than a religion; it encompasses a broad culture in which a significant component of their individual identities is rooted.

Students are also encouraged to think about their connection to their Jewish communities at large. What are the threads that bind us to each other? What traditions and practices contribute to our collective identity and sustain us throughout time? One story that is used to illuminate the components of ritual that make us who we are as a people is attributed to the Ba'al Shem Tov:

On his deathbed, a rabbi told his students, "I've always served as a messenger for you to God. When I die, you must face God yourselves. You know the secret place in the forest where I pray, you've seen me light a fire, and you've heard me recite a blessing. Do all of this and God's Presence will surely come." After the rabbi died, the first generation of students did as they were taught, and God's Presence came. By the second generation, the people had forgotten the blessing. Still, they stood in the secret place in the forest and lit a fire, and God's Presence rested with them. By the third generation, the people had forgotten how to recite the blessing and how to light the fire. Still, they stood in the secret place in the forest, and...it was enough: God's Presence rested with them. By the fourth generation, everyone had forgotten everything: how to recite the blessing, how to light the fire, and even where to go in the forest. One person still remembered the story about it all and told the story. And...it was enough: God's Presence rested with them![6]

This story raises the question of what is needed to maintain a dispersed community. Is telling the story (learning the history) enough to sustain a people bound by tradition and ritual? Can the one who tells the story help restore the missing and forgotten pieces? What happens to our identity without the stories, rituals, and traditions?

MEMBERSHIP

Another set of lessons introduces the concept of membership: how groups—whether they be peer, ethnic, religious, or national—define themselves and their constituents and the relationship between individual and group identity. The theme of membership includes identity and belonging, inclusion and exclusion. After addressing a Facing History and Ourselves theme called "universe of obligation"—Helen Fein's term for the circle of individuals and groups toward whom a government "has obligations, to whom its rules apply, and whose injuries call for [amends]"— students consider the concept of *areyvut* (responsibility) in Judaism.[7] It is a term central to the Jewish tradition and refers to an individual's obligation toward others. Judaism advocates a continuously expanding sense of *areyvut*, as individuals are encouraged to take responsibility for the world in which they live.

The related Jewish Text Project lesson uses the biblical story of Joseph to show how groups or individuals can become "the other." The Joseph story can also be read as an account of the development of *areyvut*, particularly if the focus is not only on Joseph, but also on Judah, his older brother, who becomes an example of an individual who learns to reach beyond himself and take responsibility for others. Although all the characters in the story of Joseph belong to one family, the text tells us that there are competing groups within that family and shows how even members of the same family can be removed from the "universe of obligation" of the rest of the family.

The theme of membership is explored in history as well. As students in the Facing History and Ourselves program confront the failure of democracy in Germany and the steps leading to the Holocaust, a central theme is that of who is within and who is outside the "universe of obligation." Students consider the issue of obedience to authority, especially when such obedience involves ethical choices and moral decision making. Again the Facing History and Ourselves conceptual framework is brought to bear on biblical text. The history includes examples of "upstanders"—individuals whose actions embodied courage and compassion in the face of extraordinary evil. Biblical stories like those in the Book of Exodus also illuminate such situations and the responses of individuals who act on the basis of their internal moral compass. "Upstander" can be a lens through which to view the figures of Moses, as well as Shiphrah, Puah, the midwives, Moses's mother and sister, and Pharoah's daughter, in their actions in violation of dictatorial authority. Each of these figures takes a moral stand that is in direct conflict with the edicts and psychological factors that shaped their decisions to resist authority and take action. By analyzing the context in which these figures from the Exodus story operate, students are prompted to reflect upon history and their own personal decision making. When juxtaposed with some of the individuals in the history of the Holocaust who took huge risks to defy the Nazi system, save people's lives, and act on their conscience and not on the "law of the land," students see that such dilemmas and examples of moral courage are universal issues. The discussions that emerge are as important and engaging in the history class as they are in the Judaic studies class.

SOCIAL RESPONSIBILITY

In another section of Facing History's sequence of study, *Choosing to Participate*, students are asked to think about how their own choices, however small, can have a positive impact on their society and the world at large. In the Jewish Education Program, they examine how social responsibility is illuminated in Jewish sources as well as examples of civic participation in Jewish tradition. One resource used in these lessons is a brief film entitled *Pigeon*.[8] Based on a true story, the film opens with a Jewish man waiting nervously for the train to Grenoble, in France's unoccupied zone. As he checks his forged papers, we sense that this may be his only chance for escape. The man watches as two young boys taunt a small bird on the station platform. He intervenes for the bird's sake and confiscates the boys' slingshot. But in the melee, his passport is stolen. Only after he has boarded the train does he realize his predicament. It's then that something amazing happens. Echoing his earlier kindness, a stranger intervenes on his behalf, risking her own life to save his.

After viewing the film and reflecting in class discussion or in journal entries about what may have motivated the stranger, students consider several selections (some examples below) from biblical and Rabbinic texts, contemplating the meaning of each, its connection to the film, and implications for choices in their own worlds:

Do not stand idly by while your neighbor's life is in danger. (Leviticus 19:16)

When there is no man, you must try to be a man. (*Pirkei Avot* 2:5)

If I am not [concerned] for me, who will be concerned for me? But, if I am concerned only for me, what am I? If not now, when? (Hillel the Elder, *Pirkei Avot* 1:14)

Every moment one delays his efforts to redeem captives when he could have helped them is considered as if he had shed blood. (*Shulchan Aruch, Yoreh Dei-ah* 252:3)

Rabbi Shimon ben Eliezer said, "Act while you can: while you have the time, the means, the strength." (Babylonian Talmud, *Shabbat* 151b)

After using this lesson, one teacher commented:

The students watched the film, and then chose from a bank of textual quotes they thought were relevant to it. They presented the interpreted the quotes and then connected them to the story, and by doing that they learned how our sources serve as a moral guide in their own lives, the Facing History course, and in their conversations about Jewish values/ethics. What I loved the most is how the students made a connection between something rabbis wrote so long ago to take action nowadays.

Memory and Repair

In the final section of the study guide, students have the opportunity to explore concepts of how we remember events from our collective past and what are the avenues we can take to mend the world. For Jews who believe in a supreme and compassionate being, the notion of evil raises complicated questions. Theology after the near total annihilation of European Jewry provokes particularly troublesome and complex issues. How can we reconcile this profound evil known as the Holocaust with our faith? The question "Where was God?" is one that has evoked diverse responses among Jewish theologians since the end of World War II and continues to this day. It is also one that often troubles young people. As Facing History engages the moral thinking of students in Jewish settings, the question of God and God's role in history often arises. Texts that address theological responses to the Holocaust are used to provoke deeper conversation and reflection as students struggle with their own questions and doubts. A lesson here might begin with a presentation of works by Samuel Bak, an artist and Holocaust survivor whose work is an integral part of Facing History resources.9 The Bak painting *Creation of Wartime II* is a painting based on the Michelangelo painting from the Sistine Chapel, *The Creation of Man*, which depicts Adam and God reaching out to each other. Bak's painting depicts the Adam figure in complete disarray, with a shaved head and clothing resembling that of a concentration camp inmate. The space in which God was depicted in the original painting is vacant, with only the outline observed in the clouds and a wooden hand visible. The painting is often analyzed and interpreted twice: first, as a catalyst for students' thinking about the question of where God was during the Holocaust; and second, as a point of discussion about how different perspectives in post-Holocaust theology might lead to different interpretations of the painting. Students are asked to describe the painting and then to think about its meaning. What do they see, and what is the artist saying about God's presence or absence in the world? They are also asked to reflect on how the various theologians might interpret the painting. This lesson gives students a chance to struggle with their own doubts and uncertainties in a space that encourages them to question without judgment or thinking there is a right or wrong answer to some of their deepest questions.

Facing History's Jewish Education Program and the materials that have been developed specifically for this program, like *Sacred Texts, Modern Questions* and *The Jews of Poland*, offer educators in Jewish day and congregational schools an opportunity to integrate general learning with Jewish values. It is important that in their hearts and minds, students can understand that the whole of life, like the whole of learning, can combine their spiritual self with their academic self. We are never far from the ethics and values that we have learned as we move through our lives. Sometimes, though, the academic world can seem very separate from the spiritual world that is also part of our being, whether consciously or unconsciously. Even the division in many schools between "general" studies and "Judaic" studies, Jewish history and general history, sanctions the notion of two different worlds. Many of our materials and our teaching strategies foster a synthesis of these two worlds and allow students the benefit of a learning environment that encourages the merging of the intellect and the spirit.

6

Fine-Tuning the Listening Heart:
Weaving Together the Teaching of Jewish Ethics and Socio-emotional Learning through the Open Circle Program[*]

SHOSHANA SIMONS AND RUTH GAFNI

WHEN SOLOMON was a young king, God told him that he could have anything that he wished for. Solomon wished for a listening heart (I Kings 3:9). What is a listening heart? Why do you think a wise young man like Solomon wanted a listening heart?

[*] Special thanks to Dr. Marsha Mirkin, who was instrumental in the development of the Judaic links to the Open Circle curriculum.

This quote is taken from a Judaic adaptation of a core lesson from the *Open Circle Curriculum* called "Being a Good Listener." In 2004 Open Circle curriculum consultants and Jewish educators from Jewish day schools spanning the spectrum of denominations partnered to develop a set of links with the *Open Circle Curriculum* to make more explicit the connections between Jewish ethics and values and social and emotional learning (SEL) core competencies. With the generous aid of a CAJE (Center for Advancement of Jewish Education) grant, the group created in-depth curriculum links for nine Open Circle lessons, including a sample lesson for each, to assist educators in finding creative ways to bring the content to life. This chapter explores how the Open Circle Program has been adapted to meet the needs of Jewish day schools by deeply integrating key Jewish social and ethical values into the implementation of the Open Circle in practice.

We begin this chapter by reviewing the foundational principles and practices of the Open Circle Program, addressing the congruence between the program's structures and processes and key Jewish concepts and principles. We go on to offer three examples of core SEL competencies addressed by the *Open Circle Curriculum* that have been adapted to incorporate Jewish values and ethics, central to the development of *menschlichkeit* in our children. We use these to frame an exploration of how one school, the Solomon Schechter Day School of Bergen County NJ (SSDSBC), has used the principles and practices of Open Circle to weave Jewish spiritual traditions, ethics, and values deeply into the life of the school community. This chapter itself reflects the close nature of the collaboration between the Open Circle Program and its school partners. Shoshana Simons is the former training director and director of special programs for Open Circle and was consultant to SSDSBC from 2002 to 2006. Ruth Gafni is the head of school of SSDSBC and is also a trained Open Circle teacher and consultant.

What Is Open Circle?

The Open Circle Program, based at the Stone Center, Wellesley College, Wellesley, Massachusetts, was founded in 1987 by school psychologist Pamela Seigle in partnership with a small number of teachers in the greater Boston area. Its mission is to work with school communities to help children become ethical people, contributing citizens, and successful learners and to foster the development of relationships that support safe, caring, and respectful learning communities of children and adults. It has since expanded to become a nationally recognized SEL program, serving 272 schools in 98 communities in the Northeast, including a number of Jewish day schools in Massachusetts, Rhode Island, Connecticut, New York, and New Jersey. Open Circle is listed in the U.S. Department of Education Expert Panel guidebook *Exemplary and Promising Safe, Disciplined, and Drug-Free Schools Programs* and has been designated as a "select" program by the Collaborative for Academic, Social and Emotional Learning.

THE OPEN CIRCLE CURRICULUM

The program's core vehicle for teaching SEL skills is the *Open Circle Curriculum*, a grade-differentiated multiyear curriculum that serves grades K–5. The curriculum focuses on teaching foundational social skills, including being a good listener, speaking up, recognizing and managing emotions, problem solving, recognizing discrimination, and how to recognize and actively respond to teasing and bullying. The table of contents remains consistent throughout the six grades of the curriculum, with the concepts and practices associated with each topic revisited in each grade at greater levels of complexity. For example, the lesson titled "Speaking Up" in the kindergarten curriculum includes an activity in which each child is asked to say his or her name out loud into a mock microphone, created out of a cardboard tube. By the third grade, children witness a role-play where the teacher tells a story demonstrating how *not* to speak up; she mumbles, covers her mouth, speaks too quietly, and fidgets. She follows this by asking the students to identify how she could have done a better job of speaking up, leading to an opportunity for the students to practice speaking up using their own suggestions for improvement. By the fifth grade, students have built upon their growing foundation of skills as speakers and discuss the concept of speaking up against injustice, making links with social issues. An example of a Judaic adaptation of the fourth grade "Speaking Up" lesson appears later in this chapter.

There is also consistency within the *Open Circle Curriculum's* activities. Each lesson begins with an evaluation of how quickly, quietly, and cooperatively students got into the Open Circle meeting space. Next is a review of the homework from the prior Open Circle meeting, followed by either a continuation of the prior lesson or the initiation of the new lesson in the intentionally sequenced curriculum. Each lesson is accompanied by visuals of key vocabulary words and their meanings. Teachers are encouraged to display these visuals in the classroom and use them as prompts for students to practice social skills throughout the day. The curriculum also includes supplementary lessons and resources to assist teachers in helping students "carry over," that is, generalize concepts addressed in Open Circle into the rest of the school community throughout the school day. Additionally, the curriculum features a unique set of vocabulary words that all members of the community draw upon to encourage smoother communication and to facilitate the development of a "meta-culture" across what can be large cultural and linguistic differences in a given school. Some examples of the Open Circle vocabulary that carries over into the whole school are the "School Listening Look," which signals to students to be quiet, sit still, and look at the speaker; "Double D's," which indicates a behavior that is dangerous and destructive that must be reported to an adult; and "non-negotiable rules," which are rules set by the teacher or other adults in the community that cannot be challenged by the students, distinct from "classroom norms," which are collaboratively developed by students and teachers at the beginning of each new school year. In addition, individual classrooms as well as the larger school community develop their own nonverbal signs to ease communication among large numbers of people. An example of this is when the teacher raises her hand, and as the students notice it, they also raise their hands and move toward becoming silent. Many Jewish day schools have adapted the latter nonverbal sign by raising their three middle fingers to signal the Hebrew letter *shin* as a symbol for *sheket*—silence.

OPEN CIRCLE'S APPROACH TO TRAINING

The Open Circle teacher training model draws from multiple theoretical roots, including the Stone Center's relational-cultural theory,[1] emotional intelligence theory,[2] group development theory,[3] and the "heart-centered pedagogy" associated with the work of Parker Palmer.[4] Through a highly experiential yearlong program, teachers are trained to create classroom and school communities that embody the core principles of caring, respect, and cooperation within which both adults and students can not only thrive socially and emotionally, but can also experience and cultivate the *relational trust* that is a prerequisite for academic achievement.[5] Teachers are supported in their personal learning and development by an Open Circle consultant who visits their classroom three times throughout the school year, modeling lessons in individual classrooms as well as observing individual teachers as they implement lessons. Open Circle consultants and trainers aim to model in their interactions with teachers the respectful, open, and nonjudgmental behaviors that they, in turn, hope to see teachers model for their students.

A WHOLE SYSTEMS APPROACH

The program is rooted in a whole systems approach. In addition to training teachers, it offers a peer consulting and coaching program, a districtwide train-the-trainer program, programs for school leaders and other administrative personnel, a whole school sustainability program, and a program for psychologists, social workers, and school counselors to enable them to train parents in Open Circle concepts and practices. The whole systems approach has been instrumental in facilitating proactive support for school communities in times of stress. For example, after the tragic events of September 11, 2001, several schools held sessions based on the Open Circle model to help parents and caregivers manage and express their own emotions and to learn how they could best respond to their children's needs. School leaders are encouraged to use Open Circle skills to facilitate faculty meetings, with the goals of reinforcing primary social skills at the adult level, building positive adult community, and more effectively managing the ongoing issues arising in the everyday life of a school. Open Circle peer-consultants regularly host breakfast teacher meetings and other events to support the deep integration of the Open Circle program in the school.

OPEN CIRCLE IN PRACTICE

The developmentally sequenced yearlong curriculum is implemented two times per week for fifteen to twenty minutes in the structure of an "open circle," symbolized by the addition of an empty chair, indicating that there's always a space for a guest or another opinion. Open Circle is a space that stands outside of "normal" linear classroom time. Children transition out of their usual classroom layout by bringing their chairs "safely, quietly, and cooperatively" into a circle in a pre-assigned space in the room, signaling a shift in mood and tempo from the rest of the school day. Everyone is seated at the same level and is visible to everyone else. The teacher's keen attention to pacing, body language, tone of voice, facial expressions, calling patterns, and nonjudgmental responses help each child to feel that their presence and contribution are valued and welcomed. As founder Pamela Seigle once described it, "Open Circle may only be fifteen minutes long, but it should feel timeless."

The Open Tent:
Open Circle, Jewish Spirituality, and Ritual

Though the *Open Circle Curriculum* and its related practices are secular in origin, they bear a striking resemblance to Jewish ethical principles as well as elements of Jewish ritual practice. The authors' realization of the congruence between the theories and practices of Open Circle and Jewish principles and practices led to the convening of a group of Jewish educators from schools using the Open Circle Program and Jewish SEL practitioners who spanned the spectrum of Jewish denominations. The group worked together to enhance the embedding of the Open Circle Program in Jewish day schools by more consciously creating links between Jewish ethical teachings and the *Open Circle Curriculum*. A key benefit of implementing the *Open Circle Curriculum* in a Jewish day school context is that the spiritual life of children (and adults) can be directly named and addressed, and the connections Jewish educators using *Open Circle* were already making could be explicitly articulated and built upon.

OPEN CIRCLE AS RITUAL

Open Circle can be seen as a ritual practice, happening twice weekly at specific times within a specific space in the classroom and containing a specific order of predictable events. All members of the classroom community constitute the *kahal* (community) of Open Circle. The accent is on building relationships, enhancing the capacity to experience empathy, and practicing compassion for self and others through being in respectful relationship rooted in the practice of deep listening. Open Circle becomes the holding environment within which students can share what is on their minds and troubling their hearts. A successful Open Circle becomes a sanctuary that is marked by a different rhythm and tenor than any regular "class" in the rest of the school day. As one kindergartner in a Jewish day school in Massachusetts wisely noted, "Open Circle is like Abraham and Sarah's tent! It's welcoming, open, and there's always room for guests." Reflecting this, several classrooms in Jewish day schools have created "chuppah-like" structures by hanging a large piece of fabric across part of the ceiling, conducting Open Circle meetings in the sanctuary of this space. Further, many Judaic studies classroom teachers schedule Open Circle meetings prior to or right after *t'filah* (prayer), extending the sense of sacred space and time out into Open Circle and cultivating a sense of calm and centeredness that promotes open-heartedness and listening.

T'SHUVAH, TIKKUN, AND CHESHBON NEFESH: OPEN CIRCLE AND PROBLEM SOLVING

From the earliest teachings in the Torah we are reminded that we have free will and that our decisions can have disastrous consequences. The concept of *t'shuvah*, "repentance," so central to Jewish philosophy and ethics, helps us to understand the importance of how we *respond* to the mistakes we make and the ruptures we create in our relationships. Open Circle provides a consistent space within which students can fine-tune their listening hearts, practice forgiveness to self and others, learn how to manage problems proactively, and gain skills in generating positive solutions. Over the years, students in Jewish day schools can therefore actively construct meaning by linking personal experience with complex foundational concepts and practices such as mitzvot (commandments), *t'shuvah*, *tikkun* (repair), and *cheshbon nefesh* (accounting of the soul, self-reflection) using Open Circle's six-step problem-solving process and by connecting lived experience with the archetypical stories within the Jewish tradition.

Integrating Ma'agal Midot *into the Open Circle:* *The Circle of Ethics at Solomon Schechter Day School of Bergen County*

At Solomon Schechter Day School of Bergen County (SSDSBC), New Jersey, a pre-K–8 suburban Jewish day school of four hundred students, there is calm in the air; the environment is open; there are no locks on lockers; students welcome each other with a smile and love their school. This supportive school environment is the outcome of a systematic effort on the part of faculty staff, parents, and students to co-create a strong, vibrant, supportive, and respectful community of learners and educators. In addition to developing a curriculum dedicated to academic excellence with a focus on advanced technology for success in a twenty-first-century global world, the SSDSBC community sought to develop a parallel curriculum that would nurture students' inner strengths, cultivate their emotional and spiritual development, and develop their capacity for healthy relationships. The program was named *Ma'agal Midot*, "Circle of Values," aligning Jewish values and text with core Open Circle lessons to create an authentic integration of Jewish "soul traits"[6] into daily Jewish life for SSDSBC students. The school's goals were to create a caring community, joined by a common SEL vocabulary unifying the community of learners. The school sought to build students' self-esteem and confidence in their interactions with one another in a thoughtful, supportive, and collaborative manner, teaching students conflict resolution and problem-solving techniques in a way that would be acceptable to all parties involved.

Ma'agal Midot is the name given to the Judaic adaptation of Open Circle that SSDSBC has been implementing at the school since 2003. The Hebrew name echoes the practice of the "spiritual curriculum" associated with the ancient *musar* tradition that is currently experiencing a renaissance within contemporary Jewish life in the United States whereby a particular *midah* (value) is studied and consciously practiced in one's everyday life for a specific period of time.[7] Chanting, meditation, and visualization practices are woven into *musar*. Likewise, in *Ma'agal Midot*, *t'filah* and ethical teachings, calm breathing, and guided imagery are woven into the teaching of primary social skills as children learn how to manage their emotions, develop communication and relationships, and negotiate their social environment more successfully.

In this sense, *Ma'agal Midot* could be viewed as a contemporary child-centered approach to *musar*.

CREATING *K'HILAH* THROUGH *MA'AGAL MIDOT*

All classroom teachers at SSDSBC are trained in the Open Circle method and curriculum. The training allows for both Judaic and general studies teachers to develop a powerful, common language. It fosters the development of relationships that support safe, caring and respectful learning communities for students and adults. Aligning spirituality and religion has positively influenced the teachers' work as educators. Faculty members, both Jewish and non-Jewish, often begin their day or their lessons with calm breathing, reflection, ethical discussion, and a short meditation. That practice transforms the learning environment into a meaningful, authentic, and joyful one that is a vehicle for personal growth for all.

As classroom teachers began to implement the Open Circle / *Ma'agal Midot* program at SSDSBC, a clear need to train the broader school community became evident. The school continued with the training of special-subject teachers, which facilitated a deeper understanding of core Open Circle concepts and vocabulary, enhancing their work and connection with grade-level teachers. One of the most visible rewards was the Jewish literature connections developed by the school librarian and teachers. This further enhanced thematic ties between Judaic studies and the *Open Circle Curriculum*. Support staff and school bus drivers were offered training sessions, adding another layer of support to the unified language and culture change at the school. The school involved the parent body by offering introductory evening workshops about the program highlighting the Hebrew and English SEL vocabulary connections associated with Open Circle/*Ma'agal Midot* that they could reinforce at home, together with information about the Jewish ethical and textual foundations of the program. The school also implemented the Open Circle multi-session parent-training program. Rooted in Jewish values and text, SSDSBC has focused on teaching children a purposeful approach to SEL at school, at home, and in the greater community, providing students with the tools for deepening self-awareness and the ability to be in relationships with others that foster compassion, insight, and commitment to *tikkun olam*—making the world a better place.

A CLIMATE OF MIDOT

Jewish values and text permeate the SEL focus at the school. For example, *hakarat hatov*, "gratitude," helps students to recognize what is good and hopeful in their lives; *midat hachodesh*, "the value of the month," involves the whole school in performing the same act of *chesed* (kindness, compassion). *Parashat hashavua*—the weekly Torah portion—presents ethical and moral dilemmas associated with the weekly Torah portion through Hebrew language vocabulary, which are explored at each grade level through developmentally appropriate discussions, looking at the big ideas and essential questions arising from the *parashah* through the lenses of biblical heroes, their problems, struggles, actions, outcomes, and ways of solving a conflict. Connections to Torah, Rabbinics, prayer, and history have been integrated into the *Ma'agal Midot* lessons, aligning Judaic and general studies. Through authentic Jewish life and practices at the school, students' understanding, ownership, and development of *midot* are reinforced by acts of *chesed* that begin in the early years. From kindergarten on, SSDSBC students visit the sick, draw pictures to liven up public areas in the community, visit the elderly, send *b'rachot* (prayers or greetings) to families with new babies, dance in *Sheva B'rachot* celebrations following weddings, visit houses where mourning families sit shivah, and open the school's daily student-led *minyan* to community members who are in mourning.

MA'AGAL MIDOT IN ACTION

The following are excerpts from lessons adapted from the *Open Circle Curriculum* that provide examples of *Ma'agal Midot* in practice. We highlight lessons in kindergarten, first-, and fourth-grade classrooms, each with eighteen to twenty-two students. We begin by situating where each lesson appears in the curriculum. It should also be noted that a specific lesson might extend over multiple meetings, depending on the needs of the specific class.

Getting In and Out of the Open Circle
(Lesson 1; Week 2 of the School Year)

The objectives of this lesson are to familiarize the students with the Open Circle Program, to make a plan as to how to get into and out of Open Circle "safely, quietly, and cooperatively," and to experience working together as a class to execute the plan. This lesson is, in effect, the first cooperative "problem-solving" lesson in the curriculum, requiring students to work together toward a common goal. The secular Open Circle lesson is greatly enhanced in the Jewish day school context by weaving the *midah* of *hachnasat orchim* (welcoming guests) into the lesson. At SSDSBC, the Jewish value of building a *k'hilah*, a close, supportive Jewish community, is reinforced through this lesson, as seen in the following example:

> The children of the *Gan D'vorim* kindergarten class were sitting on the rug in a large group singing with their teacher a verse of *v'ahavta l'rei-acha kamocha* (and you should love your friend as much as you love yourself [Leviticus 19:18]). *Morah* Martha ended the song softly. Reviewing the words of the song, she stated, "It is important to learn how to talk to each other, get to know and understand each other, and to solve problems in a way that is fair. We want our classroom to be a safe, happy, and welcoming place like *ohel Avraham v'Sarah* [Abraham and Sarah's tent]."

Morah Martha told the children that they will meet together weekly in a *ma'agal midot*, "a circle of values," an open circle. There will be an open space in the circle to welcome guests who may join the class. She asked them where in the room they thought the *ma'agal* should take place. The children chose their preferred open space. *Morah* Martha then asked them to go there safely, quietly, and cooperatively. She used the three Open Circle vocabulary words in Hebrew: *sheket* (quiet), *yachad* (together), and *batuach* (secure).

On arrival at the circle, *Morah* Martha asked the children to stand in front of their chairs like individual trees and to spread their arms like branches, allowing the palms of their hands to touch one another's. *Morah* Martha said, "In our kindergarten class, we are like a forest—together, strong and united." *Morah* Martha then prepared a sign in the shape of a tablet and asked the children what they saw. "A Torah," said

Talia. "We will place the sign on the empty chair to remind us of the mitzvah of hospitality—*hachnasat orchim*." After reviewing the steps in and out of the *ma'agal midot*, the children went back to their tables. *Morah* Martha complimented them on the way they worked together and asked them to remember the plan they had created to get in and out of the circle. To foster generalization, *Morah* Martha's usual note to the parents included the emphasis on the Jewish values of the program and the Hebrew language vocabulary.

Calm Breathing (Lesson 17)

The objectives of this lesson are to understand what it feels like to be calm and to learn and practice calm breathing techniques. The lesson begins with a short story about a cat. The students are asked to use their imagination and to "feel" the cat stretching, slowly, deeply, and calmly. They are taught to breath in deeply and to describe their feeling after they are relaxed and calm.

At SSDSBC, the Jewish value of *hakarat hatov*, realizing the goodness in our world (with specific connection in Open Circle with recognizing the beauty of Shabbat), is directly linked with the concepts of feeling calm in this lesson. The children are introduced to the practice of visualization, imagining themselves viewing the glowing lights of the Shabbat candles and the beauty of the Shabbat table as a vivid image that they can visit again and again in their memory as a source of peace and calm. This lesson reinforces the idea that when we are calm, we are more likely to make good decisions, allowing us to be better friends and to be positive community members.

> In a first-grade *Ma'agal Midot* meeting, *Morah* Liora was holding a snow globe in her hand. She passed it around and asked the children to shake it and observe what happened. She asked Max to stand up, shake the globe hard, and to tell everyone what he saw. "Nothing," said Max, "only snowflakes." "A busy mind cannot see clearly," said *Morah* Liora. "What do you see when the globe is still?" "A small house," answered Max. "Can you see it clearly?" *Morah* Liora asked. Max answered affirmatively. "When we are calm, we can see everything clearly," added *Morah* Liora.

On Shabbat, *Morah* Liora explains, God wants us to rest, stay calm, and fill ourselves with the goodness of a peaceful day. She asked the children to imagine that they are sitting at *Kabbalat Shabbat* (the welcoming of Shabbat) looking at the candles, drinking sweet grape juice, singing, and tasting freshly baked challah. She asked them how they might be breathing and asked Sarah to demonstrate. She explained that in these situations, at school or at home, they breathe slowly and calmly. She asked the children to sit in a relaxed and comfortable position and taught the children ways to do calm breathing. "Breathe in slowly and deeply, filling your belly with air like a balloon; breathe out slowly. Think about the beautiful flowers on your Shabbat table," prompted *Morah* Liora. "Close your eyes and breathe in, imagine that you are smelling the flower...breathe out with an 'ahhh' sound. Knowing and practicing calm breathing is important. We are able to be good learners, good friends, and good problem solvers when we feel calm," explained *Morah* Liora. "I practice calm breathing before *t'filah* each morning, and especially before I say the *Sh'ma*. When do you think it will be a good idea for you to practice calm breathing?" "Before I go to lunch," Sam replies. "When it's noisy," said Eva. "When I go to dance class," said Dana. "When I am scared," added Josh. "When I am talking to God," said Jake. "I want God to listen." *Morah* Liora prepared flowers to send home with the children for Shabbat, reinforcing the concept of calm breathing—flower breathing—and making the connection to *t'filah*, *Sh'ma*, and Shabbat. She asked the parents to practice calm breathing with their children.

Speaking Up (Lesson 14)

The objective of this Open Circle lesson is to understand how to speak confidently in front of a group. Components of "Speaking Up" include looking at the person or people to whom one is talking, speaking slowly enough, and speaking loudly enough. At SSDSBC, the Jewish adaptation of this lesson in the fourth grade draws from the examples of Moses and Aaron speaking up to help students face their fears and discomforts as they learn to use their voices and leadership skills. Drawing from Torah stories helps students deepen their knowledge of Torah by inviting them to imagine themselves in the shoes of their ancestors, strengthening the sense of continuity between past and present, as demonstrated in the following example:

As the fourth-grade students gathered for their *Ma'agal Midot* lesson, *Morah* Tami sat down holding a short wooden stick. "I am holding

Moshe's *mateh*, the magical stick he held when he spoke to Pharaoh, asking him to free the Israelites. Moshe was our *shaliach*, our leader; he had to be able to speak up. What might it have been like for him? "He must have been scared," said Tamar. "He had his helpers with him," said Adam. "He knew God would help him," said Josh, "so he was not scared."

"Moshe and Aaron held *matot* in their hands when speaking," *Morah* Tami continued. "It was a reminder to them that they could not mumble and that they had to speak up. I will pass our classroom *mateh* around as you will take turns practicing speaking up." She explained to the students that speaking up has several steps, infusing the Hebrew key vocabulary words the students have learned—*lirot, l'dabeir l'at, l'dabeir barur, l'dabeir chazak*:

- Look at the person to whom you are talking
- Speak slowly
- Speak clearly
- Say it loud enough so that everyone can hear

Morah Tami asked her students to practice effective speaking by stating their Hebrew names slowly, clearly, and loudly. Passing on Moshe's *mateh*, she asked the *sh'lichei tzibur* (prayer leaders) of the week to share what they did that morning to prepare for *t'filah*—what was done first, what was done next, and so on. Then, she passed Moshe's *mateh* again and asked the students who were the leaders for reciting *Birkat HaMazon* (Blessing after Meals) to tell the others about their responsibilities. She gave several other students a chance to speak up, handing them Moshe's *mateh*. After each student had finished, she asked the group if the person looked at the group, spoke slowly and clearly, and could be heard by every one while speaking.

"Was it helpful to you to hold onto Moshe's *mateh* as you spoke?" asked *Morah* Tami. "It reminded me that I have to speak loud," said Dina. "It did not help much," said Elliot, "but it reminded me of Moshe and how strong he must have been. I felt strong." *Morah* Tami congratulated her students, "*Yashar kochachem, kol hakavod.*"[8]

Morah Tami shared with the parents that twenty-first-century learning is about communication, collaboration, problem solving, and globalization. She made the connection that SEL emphasizes leadership and the specific values about leadership that have been part of the Jewish people past, present, and future. She asked the parents to practice speaking up at home with their children.

Summary and Moving Forward

This chapter has explored the core principles and practices of the Open Circle program and how these were adapted to develop a specific Jewish approach to SEL called *Ma'agal Midot*. We highlighted the congruence between Jewish principles and values and those of SEL, detailing how these overlap through the lens of three lessons adapted from the *Open Circle Curriculum* as implemented at SSDSBC in New Jersey. Furthermore, we provided some examples that demonstrate how these values can be brought to life both within individual classrooms as well as across the whole school community, strengthening the sense of *k'hilah* through the living practice of *Ma'agal Midot*.

Ma'agal Midot as a Jewish SEL approach is a structure well suited for deeply embedding Jewish ethics, spiritual values, and practices into the life cycle of the school. The *Open Circle Curriculum*, with its secular roots, is geared to a more general school population, with the invitation for teachers to "make it their own." In that sense, it covers foundational SEL areas while opening space for various ethnic and cultural communities to develop specific supplementary lessons that address specific cultural values and norms. *Ma'agal Midot* provides a vehicle through which a fuller range of Jewish ethical teachings can be addressed in the SEL curriculum. The rich array of texts in the Jewish tradition offers almost limitless possibilities for more deeply linking contemporary challenges shaping our children's lives in the twenty-first century with those of our ancestors through a curriculum rooted in the best of evidence-based SEL principles and practices. Moreover, the development of *Ma'agal Midot* provides an example of how the secular *Open Circle Curriculum* can be adapted to the ethics and values of specific ethnic groups. This can serve as an example for other ethnic and religious groups who may wish to tailor the *Open Circle Curriculum* more closely to the needs of their specific cultural and spiritual traditions.

We strongly support the building of the adult community in Jewish day schools that draws from our rich spiritual and ethical traditions. A suggestion for enhancing a sense of "oneness" among the adults is to create moments for shared calm breathing and meditation together. For example, taking five minutes at the start of a meeting to practice the ancient tradition of meditating on the letters of the unpronounceable name of God—*Yod-Hei-Vav-Hei*, exhaling on the *yod*, inhaling on the *hei*, exhaling on the *vav*, inhaling on the *hei*, gently whispering the letters to oneself—can transform a hectic, distracted atmosphere into one that is calm and filled with a sense of the Divine. Furthermore, there is a need for continuing Jewish-informed SEL work at the middle and high school levels, when the practice and the generalization of the *midot* can be even more challenging for students than in the early grades. We invite Jewish educators to build upon the foundation of *Ma'agal Midot* to develop curriculum for older grades, drawing deeply from the source of meaningful texts in our tradition.

7

Nourishing the Souls of Students in Jewish Education

LAURA WEAVER,
RANDI HIRSCHBERG,
AND BATYA GREENWALD

JUST IMAGINE

IMAGINE A CLASSROOM where each child's inner brilliance is nurtured like a precious diamond—where their thoughts, feelings and wisdom are valued, developed and heard. Imagine a classroom where students connect, authentically and personally, to Jewish values—a classroom that allows students to naturally engage with these Jewish values in the classroom and in their lives. Imagine a classroom where students gain the tools they need to cope with the confusing barrage of information and media messages they experience each day, so they don't have to numb themselves with drugs, alcohol, food, or sexual experiences. Imagine a classroom where students are given ways to focus and bring themselves fully to their academic lives and where social-emotional learning is given the stature that the "learning and the brain" research suggests is necessary to provide an optimal learning environment. Imagine a classroom where the teacher is not preoccupied with her own problems or school politics, but instead is fully present in each learning moment with her students. Imagine a classroom where students feel deeply connected to themselves, to others, to their teacher, to their heritage, and to the world. This is what PassageWorks offers to Jewish education.

    —Bev Buncher, former Jewish day school principal[1]

    After a cohort of Jewish educators came to a PassageWorks course in 2006, PassageWorks founder Rachel Kessler attended a conference on Jewish education to explore how the PassageWorks approach could be more intentionally integrated with Jewish education. Conference leader Rabbi Nancy Flam[2] then invited Kessler to attend a retreat and offer her perspective on how Jewish educators could address the inner life[3] of students and support them to experience a personal connection to their Jewish heritage and education. Flam remarked, "The meeting was *bashert* [meant to be]—Judaism has a tradition of instruction in values, but not a clear methodology for how to address the inner life of students." After the retreat, Kessler and colleagues collaborated with Jewish educators to create a customized course integrating the PassageWorks approach with Jewish education and to support the implementation of this work in Jewish day schools and synagogue- and community-based bar and bat mitzvah programs.

The PassageWorks Approach

Founded in 2001 by Rachael Kessler and colleagues, the PassageWorks Institute[4] is an educational nonprofit offering a unique approach to the integration of social, emotional, and academic learning. The PassageWorks approach offers educators and school leaders practices and principles to transform school culture; foster student engagement, motivation, and resilience; and help students navigate the vulnerable developmental transition years throughout the K–12 schooling cycle. The PassageWorks approach also supports educators to bring "who we are to how we teach" and to cultivate our own "teaching presence." "Teaching presence" refers to that essential aspect of teaching that goes beyond technique, strategy, and curriculum. The four dimensions of teaching presence are teaching with an open heart, practicing respectful discipline, cultivating our capacity to be present, and expanding our emotional range.

The child of Holocaust survivors who immigrated to the United States, PassageWorks founder Rachael Kessler knew firsthand the experience of isolation, disconnection, and alienation that so many young people feel. While on an exchange program to the Philippines in her adolescence, Kessler began to discover the power and potency of authentic relationships and a sense of deep connection to a community of people very different from herself. Through her early work with pregnant teen mothers and later work in schools, she saw that the experience of alienation and lack of connection was at the core of many students' "risky behaviors," and she committed herself to creating a secular approach for addressing the "spiritual void" in young people. Her groundbreaking book *The Soul of Education*,[5] published in 2000 and distributed to over 110,000 educators, includes stories of her experiences with students and colleagues and articulates many of the key concepts of the PassageWorks approach.

Over the last few years, exciting new research has proved the efficacy of social and emotional learning. A recent meta-study found that "students who took part in social and emotional learning, or SEL, programs improved in grades and standardized-test scores by 11 percentile points compared with nonparticipating students."[6] The study goes on to say:

> Compared with their peers, participating students also significantly improved on five key nonacademic measures: They demonstrated greater social skills, less emotional distress and better attitudes, fewer conduct problems such as bullying and suspensions, and more-frequent positive behaviors, such as cooperation and help for other students.[7]

PassageWorks partners with educators to create relationship-centered classrooms where students' academic and human development is supported.

A STUDENT-CENTERED APPROACH TO SPIRITUALITY

For years, Kessler engaged students in a practice called council,[8] in which she gave students the opportunity to respond to the question "What nourishes your soul?" Out of her students' stories and responses emerged a kind of map of the inner life, which she called the Seven Gateways to the Souls of Students. The gateways did not come from any particular philosophy, religion, or belief system, but rather from the students themselves. These gateways offer a unique framework for understanding what questions and experiences are stirring in our young people as they move through their school days and lives. The Seven Gateways are as follows:

1. The yearning for *deep connection* describes a quality of relationship that is profoundly caring, is resonant with meaning, and involves feelings of belonging or of being truly seen and known. Students may experience deep connection to themselves, others, nature, or a higher power.
2. The longing for *silence* and solitude, often an ambivalent domain, is fraught with both fear and urgent need. As a respite from the tyranny of "busyness" and noise, silence may be a realm of reflection, of calm or fertile chaos, an avenue of stillness and rest for some, prayer or contemplation for others.
3. The search for *meaning* and purpose concerns the exploration of big questions, such as "Why am I here?" "Does my life have a purpose? How do I find out what it is?" "What is life for?" "What is my destiny?" "What does my future hold?" and "Is there a God?"
4. The hunger for *joy* and delight can be satisfied through experiences of great simplicity, such as play, celebration, or gratitude. It also describes the exaltation students feel when encountering beauty, power, grace, brilliance, love, or the sheer joy of being alive.
5. The *creative* drive, perhaps the most familiar domain for nourishing the spirit in school, is part of all the gateways. Whether developing a new idea, a work of art, a scientific discovery, or an entirely new lens on life, students feel the awe and mystery of creating.

6. The urge for *transcendence* describes the desire for young people to go beyond their perceived limits. It includes not only the mystical realm, but experiences of the extraordinary in the arts, athletics, academics, or human relations. By naming and honoring this universal human need, educators can help students constructively channel this powerful urge.

7. The need for *initiation* refers to the longing in youth to be consciously supported through the transition from childhood to adulthood. Adults can give young people tools for dealing with all of life's transitions and farewells. Meeting this need for initiation often involves ceremonies with parents and faculty that welcome them into the community of adults.

As Kessler and colleagues worked with students, they introduced practices that addressed and evoked these gateways. They actively invited students' questions, passions, hopes, dreams, and visions into the classroom. Through this process, they began to see that nourishing the inner life of young people directly impacted students' focus, motivation, academic performance, and resilience—an observation that has been confirmed by brain research and learning theory. As Robert Sylwester, author of *A Celebration of Neurons* says, "Emotion drives attention, attention drives memory, memory drives learning and just about everything else."[9] Referring to Sylwester, Kessler said, "Even if all we cared about were test scores, it would be essential for our schools to support the emotional lives of young people." When content and teaching practice are "emotionally rich and resonant," students are eager and available to learn.

PASSAGEWORKS CORE PRACTICES

PassageWorks offers a variety of practices that can be used in any classroom. The approach fosters the growth of authentic relationships and supports students to develop focus, learning readiness, communication skills, and a sense of meaning, purpose, and relevance.

PassageWorks core practices include the following:

- **Active and reflective focusing activities:** This practice involves beginning and ending a class with a brief activity that helps students come into presence and "learning readiness," or to acknowledge a learning or connection they have had that day. Focusing activities also provide a necessary transition between classes. Examples are journaling on a relevant theme, taking a moment of silence, engaging in a playful, kinesthetic team-building activity, or writing a notecard to the teacher on a prompt.

- **Systematic building of classroom community:** This practice involves the scaffolding and sequencing of activities and lessons that build trust among classmates, develop communication skills, and support intrapersonal and interpersonal awareness. One essential component of this process is creating student-based classroom agreements.

- **Deep listening and authentic speaking (council, sharing circles, and dyads):** In this practice, students take turns deeply listening to one another as their peers speak for a prescribed time on a theme introduced by the teacher. Council is one particular form of deep listening that supports the cultivation of the inner life. Since ancient times, diverse cultures have used various forms of council for communication and community building. In council, students and facilitator(s) sit in a circle and pass a talking piece. The person with the talking piece then has the opportunity to speak on a particular theme for a prescribed period of time while the others in the circle listen without interrupting the speaker. The four intentions of council are to listen with an open heart, speak from the heart, speak leanly, and speak spontaneously. Council provides students the opportunity to feel seen, heard, and known.

- **Creative and symbolic expression:** These practices foster self-awareness and critical and creative thinking. Examples include students creating a personal symbol for their hopes and dreams or using symbolic objects to discuss what is important in their lives.

- **Inclusion of developmentally appropriate social and emotional themes:** This practice asks educators to link content to their students' personal lives, to include lessons that helps students develop awareness about the transitions they are undergoing, and to offer tools for stress, change, and anger management.

- **Mystery questions:** This practice, offered halfway through the year after a community of trust has been established, involves asking students to anonymously write down what they wonder about regarding their own self, peers and other people, and life and the universe. These questions are not to be answered but are later shared anonymously in an environment of reverence and respect.

PassageWorks and Jewish Values and Concepts

Jewish middle school educator Arlene Fishbein talks about her experience with PassageWorks and Jewish education: "Although my school is a place where Torah values are strong, and indeed addressed daily in our curriculum, I often wished that students' hearts and minds could be moved at a deeper level."[10] Randi Hirschberg[11] had a similar experience at the Jewish day school where she taught:

> One of the most important challenges of Jewish schools is avoiding fragmentation of Jewish values and teachings. Students typically learn Torah teachings and Jewish values in specific classes but leave those teachings behind as they move through the rest of their busy days. There are also students who feel that the Torah teachings have been "shoved down their throats," leading them to disavow much of what they have learned as they move into adulthood.

Hirschberg goes on to share this story about this fragmentation:

> When I was teaching at a Jewish day school, I had a profound experience of this disconnection between the idea and practice of Jewish values. In this setting, high school students participating in a *Chesed* Club generously engaged in community outreach to the developmentally disabled, while simultaneously cyberbullying a student with a learning disability from their own class. This brought to light the students' difficulty applying the Jewish values they were learning into practice in their everyday relationships. I wanted to find a methodology that would help students put values into practice in their classroom communities and beyond.

Batya Greenwald[12] told this story of being a parent visiting a Jewish day school:

Once, a number of years ago, I was helping a friend find an elementary school for her daughter. There was a Jewish day school in her area, so we went to check it out. One of their selling points was that their students were testing two grade levels above the national average in standardized tests and were getting excellent academic attention. The day we visited, we were talking to the teacher on duty when two children in conflict came over to us. One student was blaming the other, the other was screaming back, and the teacher told them both to sit down on the bench and work it out. In an exasperated tone, she said this was a common argument for these students and that they just had to figure it out themselves. I left that day feeling sad for those students. Although they might have been receiving excellent academic instruction, they were not being taught the most basic skills to help them mediate conflict or be kind. It left me wondering about the priorities we were focusing on in Jewish education. Were academic achievement and high statistics trumping attention to the social and emotional lives of our children? Weren't we also in the business of building *menschen*? In the end, my friend chose a school where the social and inner lives of children were as important as teaching students to be creative thinkers and excited learners.

These stories are not unique to Jewish education—they exist in every school across the nation. Thankfully, they can help us reexamine our priorities and ask ourselves how we can effectively help students to understand, grapple with, and embody the values we deem essential to their learning and well-being.

Because of its emphasis on community building, social and emotional learning skills, and the inner life, the core practices of PassageWorks invite students to engage with values and express and enact them "from the inside out." Fishbein speaks about her experience working with the PassageWorks program:

> As the weeks progress, so do the activities in the curriculum. We move into dyads and circles and the topics become deeper. They reflect the children's greatest hopes and fears. As we debrief, students frequently note that we all share the same things. Students talk to people they may not usually talk to and a level of trust has been established.[13]

In a PassageWorks course for Jewish educators, faculty member Batya Greenwald reflected:

> As I worked with this cohort of teachers, we began to see that Jewish values are embedded in the PassageWorks approach. The Jewish educators felt like PassageWorks gave them a *vehicle* to support students to make a very personal connection with Jewish values. By utilizing PassageWorks activities to teach Jewish values, students could then understand how to internalize and practice these values in their daily lives.

The Jewish values and concepts listed below are meant to be illustrative of the kinds of connections that naturally exist between Jewish education and the PassageWorks approach. This commentary is intended to illuminate this relationship and inspire educators to engage PassageWorks practices in the teaching of Jewish values to enrich the experience for both teachers and students. This list is by no means exhaustive.

MISHKAN: SANCTUARY, A SACRED VESSEL OR CONTAINER

In the PassageWorks approach, "creating a container" or vessel for the work we do with students is essential for learning and emotional and intellectual risk taking. Learning does not happen in a vacuum—it happens in a very particular context and environment that directly influences what is possible for our students. In an "unsafe" or leaky container, learning is compromised, as students do not feel safe and discipline may be arbitrary, dictatorial, or nonexistent. When we create a strong, healthy container, students feel connected to themselves and one another. They trust that their classroom is a place where they can learn, grow, and take risks. We create this container by intentionally building community through a series of lessons that take students deeper into self-knowledge, giving them opportunities to share their stories, passions, and hearts in a variety of ways. We create group agreements that support students to take responsibility for participating in maintaining the container—knowing we, as teachers, are ultimately responsible for the well-being of the *mishkan*. We offer students opportunities to know each other in new ways by asking them vital questions that relate to their inner lives. A healthy container can be likened to a beautiful spiderweb. In this web, students understand that they hold a unique and essential place. They can see how their own behavior and presence impact others. When this kind of container is created, the souls of students can emerge in surprising, creative, and delightful ways.

A tenth-grade student, Sarah, shares the following story about her engagement in the Mystery Questions activity. In her story, we can witness her increased sense of belonging once she felt there was a container that allowed her to risk sharing authentically:

> I remember our council on the "Mystery Questions." We were asked to anonymously write down questions that we wondered about in relation to others, the universe, and ourselves. Our teacher typed the questions up so that we wouldn't recognize each other's handwriting and passed them around the council to read aloud. We each read a question from the list one at a time, going around the full circle. Hearing all of those questions in our own voices was powerful. After the reading, we were given time to make connections to some of the questions. Someone had submitted the question "Am I beautiful?" While I was sure everyone could connect to this question, no one mentioned it in their "connections." All the way around the circle I was nervous, knowing that I was the one who would connect to it directly. Somehow, I found the courage to speak that question out loud. When people were commenting afterwards, my friend said, "Yes Sarah, you are beautiful," and several others in the council agreed and nodded their heads. Passageworks taught me that it's okay to be open in front of groups, even if I'm scared to share.

HINEINI: "HERE I AM"

Hineini, meaning "here I am," refers back to two stories from the Torah.[14] The first reminds us of the moment after Adam had eaten from the Tree of Knowledge and was hiding in the Garden of Eden. God sees Adam and calls him out of hiding, "Where are you?" Adam answers, "Here I am." In the story of Moses, God calls to Moses to lead his people by saying, "Moses! Moses!" from the Burning Bush, and Moses answers, "Here I am" (Exodus 3:4). In both of these situations, when Adam and Moses announce, "Here I am," they reveal themselves fully, take responsibility for their actions, and assume their divine charge.

Imagine a classroom where this call of "here I am" has new meaning for students—where they feel safe enough to reveal themselves in this way, to authentically express themselves, and to begin to understand their own purpose and divine charge? Each of the PassageWorks practices invites students into this inquiry, sharing, and exploration of what is deeply meaningful to them. For example, in a "Senior Passage" class, we hold a council in which students have the opportunity to speak to the following question: "What do you know now about your purpose in this life, even though you know it may change? What gifts are you here to offer?" This kind of classroom is about seeing and being seen in a way that creates a different kind of belonging and engagement with life.

KAVANAH: INTENTION, PRESENCE, DIRECTION OF THE HEART

In PassageWorks we engage in activities that assist students to focus, direct their attention, and come into full presence in the moment. These focusing activities bring our bodies and minds into alignment so that learning and concentration are possible. When students come in from recess wild and rowdy, we might put on some quiet music and engage in a "golden moment" of silence to calm and settle the students. If high school students are sluggish and sleepy after lunch, we might invite them to come into a standing circle and play "Ah-So-Ku"—a game that invites students to repeat a series of gestures in order. This activity requires tremendous focus and generally provokes quite a bit of laughter. These activities support students individually and collectively to come into "learning readiness" and also bring students into the experience of community. As Arlene Fishbein says, "While the games progress, there is an obvious change. There is concentration on the part of all of the children. Instead of working as separate units, we are working as one unit."

YETZER HATOV: INCLINATION TO DO GOOD

An old story tells the tale of a woman who had spread cruel gossip about another woman in her village. Feeling guilty for what she had done, she went to her rabbi and asked, "What can I do now to make up for my act?" He said, "Take a goose down pillow, tear it open, and scatter the goose feathers on the wind." She did as he instructed and then returned to him for further guidance. He said, "Now, go and gather all the feathers again."

What if our students understood that their words and actions can have this kind of impact on their peers? With Facebook, texting, and e-mail at their fingertips, students are more apt than ever to thoughtlessly say or do harmful things and to commit acts they later regret. When students are practicing social-emotional skills that give them the opportunity to know the person behind the social mask, they are less likely to harm themselves and others. As one PassageWorks student said, "When I really know my classmates, I don't want to hurt them."

In the sometimes insular communities of Jewish schools, students often feel they know each other very well (too well, in fact). However, the way in which they know each other is often based on labels, roles, and assumptions. When students go to school with the same group of peers for years, they form opinions of each other early on and remain stuck in these patterns of perception over time. Sometimes students even begin to see themselves in the limited way their peers have come to see them. PassageWorks practices, such as personal storytelling in council and the Mystery Question process, are designed to break this habituated way of seeing and relating to one another. Through these activities, students see that they share common dreams, visions, questions, and hurts with those they judged to be different from themselves. When teachers and students create collaborative classroom agreements in a PassageWorks class, students identify what behavior breaks trust and safety and what behavior sustains and builds a healthy learning community. Then, as a group, the students commit to developing greater awareness of these "needs for safety" and apply themselves to upholding the agreements. All of these practices naturally grow the *yetzer hatov* within us.

KAVOD: RESPECT, HONOR, DIGNITY

Each student in our classroom is a precious gift. At times we may not feel this way about our students, and certainly there are times when students do not feel this about each other. Students sometimes avoid those who seem different, strange, or threatening to them. In PassageWorks we bring in intentional practices to erode these perceived boundaries between students, so that each student's *n'shamah* (soul) is more visible to all. From this place, not only do students "tolerate" each other, they respect, honor, and listen to one another. An international baccalaureate student from a PassageWorks advisory class in a large public high school shared how he never had the opportunity to get to know any of the students who were native Spanish speakers. After being in a class where students regularly shared their stories, hopes, and dreams and engaged in deep-listening activities, this student forged friendships with students who had previously been virtually invisible to him.

Batya Greenwald shares a story from her kindergarten classroom about one student who always felt "different":

> Ben, who has severe speech apraxia, was hardly speaking in class for fear of being misunderstood. When the talking piece came to him in our sharing circles, he would "pass" the talking piece on to the next person without speaking. After a few weeks, I invited the students to think about what "superpower" they would most like to have. There were many wishes for the power to fly or to be invisible. When we got to Ben, he hesitated a moment and then said he would like the power to speak clearly. I repeated it back to the class to make sure everyone understood, and Ben smiled with relief. Since then, he has taken many risks sharing his ideas in the classroom. If we don't understand the first time, he is now confident enough to act it out, clap out the syllables, or try other strategies to help us understand. I see the PassageWorks principles in action as I watch the patience and compassion of the students when they work with Ben to understand and include him. A core component in the PassageWorks curriculum is equipping students with the capacity to develop *chesed* (loving-kindness) and dignity for themselves and all people. When students first engage in deep-listening dyads, they are often partnered with students they do not know well. At first they are typically uncomfortable or bored or want to interrupt with their own responses. However, over time the students develop the capacity to quiet their own thoughts and to listen—over time, they *want* to listen to other students. From this process of listening, a different quality of community is created—one in which every student voice is welcomed and appreciated. This community can then become a microcosm for students' interaction with the outside world.

CHEVRUTA: PARTNER STUDY

Deep-listening dyad practice can be a wonderful addition to *chevruta*, because it teaches students a different kind of listening and speaking. Instead of interrupting and debating, students are invited simply to take on the role of speaker or listener and to focus wholly on their particular role in the moment. Different insights arise when we are not interrupting or interrupted by others. We access aspects of our thinking that might have been cut off or rerouted in a typical dialogue or classroom discussion. And, it is often in the pauses between our thoughts that new insights emerge. In this way, deep-listening practices provide a reflective complement to our rich and vibrant traditions of debate and dialogue.

LIMUD: STUDY

Central to Jewish identity is the value of study and interpretation. Students learn stories of their ancestors to provide a deeper understanding of Jewish holidays and traditions. Students are encouraged to actively engage with Torah teachings through inquiry. This facilitates personal meaning making and intellectual curiosity and supports students to develop an authentic relationship with Jewish spiritual life.

A lesson from early on in the tenth grade PassageWorks curriculum illuminates one way of actively developing creativity and critical thinking skills in relation to texts. The lesson is titled "Building Community." Creativity is fostered in the warm-up activity, "The Wild Wind Blows," which asks students to identify something that is true for them and to move about the circle accordingly. The main lesson engages students in a process called "Text-Rendering." Students read a handout on emotional intelligence and underline sentences, words, or phrases that feel relevant to them. After the "text rendering," students gather in a circle and share the words and phrases they have underlined—allowing every student's voice to come into the room. Finally, the group discusses emotional intelligence and how it relates to their lives and experiences. This mode of reading and analyzing assists students to make a personal connection to the concepts of the text.

Tikkun Olam: Repairing the World / Personal Responsibility

Part of Jewish identity involves accepting responsibility for the care and repair of our world. In order for students to participate in this work of repair and renewal, they need to both understand themselves deeply and experience their connection to others and the world around them. One lesson plan that addresses *tikkun olam* is titled "Serving Others, Being Served." This lesson begins with a reflective writing task where students journal on the following quote from Nobel Peace Prize winner Elie Weisel:

> But where was I to start? The world is so vast; I shall start with the country I know best, my own. But my country is so very large. I had better start with my town. But my town, too, is too large. I had best start with my street. No, my home. No, my family. Never mind, I shall start with myself.

Then, through reflection and dialogue, students are asked to identify all the ways they are supported and "served" by others. This realization most often evokes a profound sense of gratitude and experience of interconnectedness. From this place, the spirit of generosity and the authentic desire to give to others well up. So often, in the face of local and global issues, young people feel disempowered, overwhelmed, or apathetic. Giving them the opportunity to discover how they long to participate in the "repair of the world," first through personal inquiry and later through service or action, can move them to a true place of passion, empowerment, and engagement.

L'cha Dumiyah T'hilah: "For You, Silence Is Praise"

The PassageWorks approach regularly integrates silence into the classroom as a way of offering students the much-needed time to pause, digest the learning from other classes, and listen to what is present in themselves. Hirschberg shares a story about using silence with a *b'nei mitzvah* Sunday school class to help students quiet their minds and appreciate the sensory experience of a menorah:

My students, who had been practicing silence in our PassageWorks classes, provided feedback that it was one of their favorite parts of our class. They commented that they were surprised both by how much they enjoyed the silence and by the realization that silence was absent from their regular lives. At the beginning of this particular class, we lit the Chanukah menorah together. After saying the blessing, the students and I sat in silence and just noticed our breath. Following this minute, I quietly instructed the students to rest their eyes in silence on the menorah. We sat in silence together for several minutes, admiring the beauty of the flickering lights. After concluding the silence, my students had so much to say. Many agreed they had never fully realized the visual magnificence of the menorah. Others reflected a feeling of deep connection to their ancestors and the ancient rituals of the Jewish people.

Providing periods of silence is also a way to invite students to sense their inner connection to God in a very personal way. Jewish educator Abra Greenspan[15] talks about the power of silence in the Jewish classroom:

> When students slow down, it develops their awareness and sensitivities. Silence provides a time when they can let God in. Students then realize that Judaism isn't just about arguing key points and social action, it is also about paying attention to the still small voice within.

Greenspan also notes how essential it is for students to realize that contemplation and meditative silence are an ancient and essential part of the Jewish tradition. "Often students associate these kinds of practices with Buddhism, or other religious or spiritual paths, but Judaism has always had a deep contemplative strand."

"TEACHING PRESENCE": WALKING OUR TALK AS TEACHERS

Imagine a classroom where teachers' hearts are open and they can naturally express their care and compassion for their students. Imagine a classroom where teachers are neither permissive nor authoritarian but have found an authentic approach to teaching that balances *chesed* (loving-kindness) and *g'vurah* (used in the sense of firm boundaries). Imagine a classroom where teachers understand how they can share personal stories in appropriate ways and clearly see the difference between being a mentor and being a friend. Imagine a classroom where the teacher's own social and emotional skills and capacities are sufficiently developed so that they can truly hold the full range of emotion in young people.

Arlene Fishbein remarks:

> Within each and every class is the need for presence. This means that as a teacher I have to be conscious of my own feelings and thoughts and present an openness that my students can model. Hopefully I will set an example and the environment of my room will change as the children become more open as well.[16]

Fishbein speaks of what we refer to as "teaching presence"—that aspect of teaching that goes beyond curriculum and technique and relates directly to our embodiment of the principles we teach. Teaching presence refers to

1. Teaching with an *open heart* and knowing what tends to close our heart in the classroom
2. *Being present* in the classroom—bringing our attention fully to the present moment and leaving other distractions behind
3. *Respectful discipline*—being willing to establish clear, firm, and loving boundaries for our students
4. Expanding our *emotional range*—making friends with the full range of emotions in ourselves and others

Fishbein goes on to say:

> This year as I sit in the councils with each of my classes, I too have to be present. I am able to see my children in a different light. They reveal themselves to me and give me glimpses into their souls, and I allow them to look back into mine. I become more human in their eyes and therefore am building stronger bonds with a larger percentage of my students.

When teachers actively engage with developing their own teaching presence, they more easily motivate their students and create emotionally rich and academically rigorous classrooms.

In our work, we ask teachers to consider adopting the disposition of the "self-scientist," in which they deepen their relationship with their "observer self" who sees when we are able to be present and when we are distracted; when our heart is opened and when it is closed; when we are reacting to a student because we are emotionally "triggered" and when we are offering an appropriate clear boundary; and when we are unable to witness or support certain emotions in our students because we have cordoned off that part of ourselves. One of the most simple and profound self-scientist practices is to ask ourselves when our hearts are opened and when they are closed and how our hearts open again when they have closed. Engaging in this inquiry over a number of days, weeks, or months can offer us profound realizations about how we live our life inside and outside the classroom.

Why is this important? How does our teaching presence relate to academic achievement for our students? Brain research and learning theory confirm that relationships are central to creating a positive classroom environment conducive to learning. When we have little awareness of where our own behaviors and biases come from, we develop relationships unconsciously, and our own perceptions and reactions can interfere with our students' learning. Perhaps we have a radically different worldview from a student, and whenever that student speaks, we don't want to listen. Or perhaps a student continually sabotages our class, and we develop feelings of resentment and cut off the possibility of a positive relationship with that student. Perhaps a highly "successful" colleague brings up our own insecurities, and we avoid contact with that colleague. Or perhaps we get angry whenever a colleague speaks in a faculty meeting because that colleague reminds us of someone else in our lives we have conflict with. These are highly instructive observations that can give us essential information about how we impact our classroom, our students' capacity to learn, and the culture of our school.

Developing awareness about ourselves as teachers can also increase our own "resilience." As we feel more empowered to bring our whole selves to the classroom, create the kind of teaching environment we long for, observe ourselves compassionately, and learn from our successes and challenges, we find that our passion for the art and science of teaching grows.

Rites of Passage Model:
B'nei Mitzvah and the Transition Years

> Transition does not require that you reject or deny the importance of
> your old life, just that you let go of it. Far from rejecting it, you are likely
> to do better with the ending if you honor the old life for all that it did
> for you. It got you this far. It brought you everything you have. But now,
> although it may be some time before you are comfortable actually doing
> so—it is time for you to let go of it. (William Bridges)

Underlying the PassageWorks approach is a deep understanding of
the potency and vulnerability of the developmental transition years in
young people. Across the nation, we see that risk behaviors increase any
time there is a developmental or school-initiated transition. When students are offered a structured rite of passage, guided by trusted adults
who acknowledge these new challenges and emerging capacities, this
time of risk can be transformed into one of rich opportunity for growth.

To support students who are navigating major periods of change,
PassageWorks developed curricula for the transition years into and out
of elementary, middle, and high school. These social and emotional
learning programs are based in part on an anthropological model for
rites of passage. After studying the practices of diverse indigenous cultures around the globe, anthropologist Arnold van Gennep coined the
term "rite of passage" in 1909. He found that throughout the world,
there were commonly three phases associated with adolescent initiation:
severance, threshold, and reincorporation. *Severance* describes the time
when we let go of or separate from an old identity; *threshold* describes
the in-between or liminal place where the old identity is no longer and
the new identity has not been formed; and *reincorporation* describes the
phase of bringing the knowledge and understanding that emerge during the severance and threshold experiences back into daily life and the
community for the benefit of all. The new understanding and awareness
gained through an individual's rite of passage then nourish and sustain
the community and connect the generations to one another.

Though transitions are present throughout a human life, beginning
in birth and ending with death, our culture has a tendency to avoid
the emotions and experiences that naturally emerge during these times.
Transitions may be fraught with anticipation, exhilaration, uncertainty,

and fear and often give rise to important questions about meaning and purpose, love and its shadows, and beginnings and endings. When we do not take time to acknowledge and honor the tremendous importance of transition, our students can easily fall into regression, cynicism, anxiety, and confusion and miss this potent opportunity to develop and express new capacities and awareness within themselves.

The Jewish life cycle has its own powerful rite of passage—the bar or bat mitzvah, which marks a young person's coming of age. The year preceding b'nei mitzvah is often stressful for both parents and children. Both are grappling with saying goodbye to the student's childhood self and welcoming the unknown that this new phase and identity will bring. The "severance" aspect of the Gennep rites of passage model is embedded in the b'nei mitzvah process—at thirteen, young people become more directly responsible for themselves and their relationship to Jewish values, laws, and religious practice—leaving behind the identity of the "child" who does not have such responsibility or opportunity. At this time, it can be helpful to offer youth practices that assist them with the "sifting and sorting" process that naturally happens during the threshold phase of transitions. We can ask students to consider a variety of questions:

- What qualities, habits, or tendencies in myself do I want to let go of now that I am moving into a new phase of life?
- What aspects of my old self are important to carry with me (for example, creativity, wonder, imagination)?
- What are the new capacities that I want to grow into?

These kinds of explorations can encourage deep reflection and more conscious choices about the new identity that students are stepping into.

The thirteenth-year transition also coincides with physical changes that accompany puberty. These serve as reminders that old, familiar roles will shift and the unknown lies ahead. When conscientious attention is not paid to this period of time, anxiety in both parents and students can snowball. This can surface in a range of adult behaviors—such as parental pressure on their child to deliver a flawless Torah reading, the tendency to pay attention solely to the details of a fancy party, or the denial of the fears the child is dealing with. Family relationships often become tense as parents are challenged to let go of familiar ways of parenting and to discover new tools and tactics to guide their child who is now ready for more responsibility and freedom.

The PassageWorks approach to transitions offers a forum to support *b'nei mitzvah* students and parents to meaningfully navigate this passage. The core practices and lessons can be interwoven into an already existing *b'nei mitzvah* class or to extend the *b'nei mitzvah* process. Students are offered a safe container to express their fears and anxieties, while developing a capacity for resilience. They can learn tools for managing stress and uncertainty and discover how to engage this new phase with a sense of wonder and delight.

Abra Greenspan is quite familiar with the tensions of the *b'nei mitzvah* process. She utilizes PassageWorks practices to connect with parents of students at the beginning of the *b'nei mitzvah* year:

> We have an entire logistical evening about the upcoming year. However, before we move on to the logistics, we do a deep-listening practice called "wheel within a wheel." I put students on the inside and adults on the outside of the circle. The students turn toward an outside adult who isn't their parent. They are given timed prompts to speak with each other and then switch pairs when the prompt is over. Some of the prompts I use are "Describe a neighborhood you grew up in," "Describe your after-school activities," and "Talk about your connection to Judaism." For the parents, I have them respond to each prompt by sharing their answers to these questions from the perspective of where they were in their lives when they were twelve years old (i.e., "Describe the neighborhood you lived in when you were twelve years old"). After we complete the activity, we debrief with the question "Why did we just do that activity?" The connection becomes clear to everyone in the room: it takes a village to support students through this time of transition. Parents and students gain the insight that they are not alone in this process. Students begin to make connections across time and see that their parents were dealing with similar issues and thinking about the same things when they were their age. The culmination of the PassageWorks Transitions program is an "honoring ceremony" that is designed to celebrate each student's gifts. In one version of this ceremony, parents and students participate in a witness council. In the first part of the council, the students speak openly about how they are navigating the transition they are in. The parents

simply witness and listen. In the second part of the council, the parents are asked one at a time to turn to their child and, witnessed by the community, to speak to the growth they have seen in their child over the years. Students are hungry for this kind of acknowledgment, and parents are longing for just this opportunity to authentically acknowledge their children. In these ceremonies, there is often not a dry eye in the room.

The PassageWorks approach can also be used to augment and extend the *b'nei mitzvah* journey beyond the initial year. Often students go through the powerful *b'nei mitzvah* passage but don't understand how to "reincorporate" the learnings and experiences back into their lives. Many educators wonder, after *b'nei mitzvah*, how do we keep our students engaged in Jewish life and learning and the deeper meaning of *b'nei mitzvah*? How do we support them to continue to mine the jewels that Jewish life has to offer them? Creating an intentional time and safe space where students can continue to reengage with these profound teachings assists young people to integrate this *b'nei mitzvah* experience into their lives and to recognize the places in life when those same themes may emerge again.

Rachael Kessler's Return to Judaism: Bat Mitzvah and Cancer Journey

Founder of PassageWorks Rachael Kessler was raised in a secular Jewish family in Detroit. As a deeply spiritual individual, throughout her life Rachael explored her connection to God in nonreligious ways. It was not until late in her life that she began to fully explore her ancestral roots. Just after her sixtieth birthday, she embarked on a two-year course to prepare for an adult bat mitzvah. She found great joy and solace in this path and in the deepening connection to her Jewish community. Unexpectedly, one year into her bat mitzvah training, Rachael received a diagnosis of uterine cancer. A year later and a day before her own bat mitzvah, she learned that her cancer had metastasized. In her typical character of "welcoming the unwelcome" and meeting "obstacles as allies," Rachael participated fully in her rite of passage the following day.

The following is an excerpt from her Torah portion speech on the parting of the Red Sea:

B'shalach, which means "the sending," is the story of the Hebrew slaves being wrenched out of Egypt and, with great resistance and complaint, being led and protected by an angel to the shore of the Sea of Reeds. It is about the terror of going forward, the impossibility of going back, and the faith of one man, whose courageous act of diving in head deep catalyzes the parting of the waters. It tells of the strong east wind—the force of nature that God sends to rage all night long to part the waters—and of the joyful song that arises spontaneously when the former slaves arrive safely on the other side.

Rachael remarked on those powerful moments of life when great uncertainty arises and tests our faith. She invited us to consider the richness of these times where we are asked to go into unfamiliar and sometimes terrifying territory with intention and courage:

Where in *your* life do you have to go... "all the way," before you can discover the miracles of personal growth and the loving support that surround us when we enter the swirling sea or the endless, dry wilderness of Change?

Rachael passed through her final transition one year after she shared this bat mitzvah speech with friends and family. Throughout her final year of life, she continued to embody the principles that were deeply embedded in the PassageWorks approach and met her cancer journey with grace, honesty, courage, and wisdom. Rachael was present with the difficult feelings in her dying process and also experienced times of profound joy and transcendence. Commenting to a colleague in an interview completed during the last months of her life, she remarked, "It's so easy for me to focus on the cup half full, because I've let go... it's so *joyful*." Rachael showed that death, too, can be a gateway to transformation.

Conclusion

Imagine a classroom where students experience deep meaning, purpose, and connection, where educators join "soul with role"[17] to bring their whole selves to their work. Jewish educators who have intentionally engaged with the power of the transition years and offered their students principles and practices that support the inner life have found that this kind of classroom is possible—with rich rewards for all.

As Batya Greenwald noted:

> The Jewish day school I had experienced a year earlier entered into a profound process of reassessing the values they were consciously modeling and teaching their students. They took time to build their student, parent, and faculty community and committed to bringing social and emotional learning into their classrooms. They found new approaches to address the bullying that they were seeing and taught conflict resolution skills, and teachers felt a renewed sense of passion for their work. The results were remarkable.

A semester into her PassageWorks class with seventh graders, Arlene Fishbein commented:

> As for myself, I am changing as well. Though my classroom environment has always nurtured a comfort for students, I am now in that process of making that final leap from teacher to human or person. I am still the adult in charge, yet I find myself connecting with more of my students than ever before.[18]

The "connection" Fishbein speaks about is at the very heart of our students' learning. It allows educators to create an environment where students can take the emotional and intellectual risks necessary to truly excel academically and to grow, transform, and express all of who they are in their community and world.

Postscript

When the idea for this book was first conceived, Rachael Kessler was the intended lead author of this chapter. After Rachael died in 2010, editor Jeffrey Kress approached our writing team to see if we would be willing to continue on with the original plan for the chapter. We have been most grateful for the opportunity to share this profound body of work that Rachael tended and stewarded for over two decades. This chapter builds on many discussions with Rachael and includes the wisdom of

many colleagues. Many thanks in particular to Bev Buncher for her contributions and insights. We dedicate this chapter to Rachael and give
thanks for her unique and beautiful spirit that lives on in the minds and
hearts of educators and young people around the world.

8

Evidence-Based Bully Prevention in Jewish Schools:
The BRAVE Experience Addressing Problematic Social Behaviors and Building Social Leadership

RONA MILCH NOVICK

J EWISH SCHOOLS are places of learning, but they are also places of community and connection. Parents choose Jewish schools hoping to connect their children to an ancient heritage and to build friendships with modern-day peers.[1] Recognizing a mandate larger than simply conveying knowledge, the mission statements of Jewish schools emphasize not only the promotion of Jewish identity, but the building of

127

care for others, citizenship, and social responsibility.[2] Like all schools, Jewish settings must meet these goals in the context of significant challenges. One pervasive challenge confronting today's educational institutions is bullying. The popular and research literatures are replete with examples of the devastating impact of bullying on students[3] and schools.[4] Public and private schools may address bullying in order to appropriately protect their students. Jewish schools also want their students to be safe, but beyond safety, they hope to create an environment for personal and spiritual growth. For Jewish schools, bully prevention programming, which entails educating students in peer refusal, leadership, and social responsibility, is an attractive vehicle for fostering individual students' development and a school climate consistent with their multifaceted missions.

This chapter will describe the implementation of the BRAVE Bully Prevention and Social Leadership Development Initiative in modern Orthodox Jewish middle schools in the United States. A brief review of the phenomenology of bullying, including common characteristics of bullies, victims, and bystanders and the implications for Jewish schools will be provided. A similarly brief review of the critical components of effective school-wide bully prevention will be offered. It was from the years of careful research in bullying and social relationships that the BRAVE initiative from as it began work with Jewish day schools. The process of implementation in over a dozen Jewish middle schools will be described, with particular attention to the unique role bully prevention can play in Jewish curricula, lessons learned, and implications for future research and practice.

Defining Bullying

The subject of hundreds of headlines and thousands of academic articles, bullying must certainly be clearly and consistently defined and measured. Educators, students, and researchers, however, employ a variety of definitions that make comparison across settings and populations challenging. Researchers generally agree that bullying is a subtype of aggression, and three characteristics—intentionality, repetition, and imbalance of power[5]—are alternately included or questioned as essential to the definition. Olweus, a seminal figure in both research on and prevention of bullying, defines it in the instructions to students on his questionnaire as including these three elements:

We say a student is being bullied when another student or several other students

- Say mean and hurtful things or make fun of him or her or call him/her mean and hurtful names
- Completely ignore or exclude him or her from their group of friends or leave him or her out of things on purpose
- Hit, kick, push, shove around, or lock him or her inside a room
- Tell lies or spread false rumors about him or her or send mean notes and try to make other students dislike him or her
- And other hurtful things like that

When we talk about bullying, these things happen again and again, and it is difficult for the student being bullied to defend himself or herself. We also call it bullying when a student is teased over and over in a mean and hurtful way. But we don't call it bullying when the teasing is done in a friendly and playful way. Also it is not bullying when two students of about equal strength and power argue or fight.[6]

Vernberg, Jacobs, and Hershberger eliminate the element of power imbalance from the definition of victimization, defining it simply as "actions taken by one or more youths with the intention of inflicting physical or psychological injury or pain on another youth."[7] Others have argued that single incidents may be categorized as bullying, given their damaging and long-lasting effects on victims.[8] Distinctions in definitions across cultures have been noted,[9] such as the Italian translation of bullying conveying more physical and violent acts, and the Japanese term *ijima* placing more emphasis on bullying in social manipulative and relational contexts.[10]

Research definitions aside, what do teachers and students consider bullying? Teachers consistently demonstrate a narrow conceptualization of bullying as physical, with some recognition of verbal and emotional bullying and a very limited recognition of social exclusion as bullying.[11] Boulton, Trueman, and Flemington demonstrated how similarly narrow secondary students are in their understanding and definition of bullying.[12] They found that when asked to determine which behaviors constituted bullying, the vast majority (80 percent) of students agreed that physical aggression, threatening others, and forcing people to do something against their will was bullying. A somewhat smaller percentage (54 percent) viewed name calling, telling nasty stories, and taking the belongings of others as bullying. Less than half (40 percent) of the students viewed laughing at others, and only 20 percent categorized social exclusion as bullying.

How bullying is defined impacts how frequently it will be said to occur and how it will be addressed.[13] In countries with broader definitions, incidence rates are typically higher.[14] The largest study of bullying in American schools found almost 30 percent of middle school students to be moderately or frequently involved in bullying, with 13 percent identifying themselves as bullies, 10.6 percent as victims, and 6.3 percent as bully-victims.[15] Bullying in American Jewish settings is only beginning to be explored. Research on bullying definition, incidence, and intervention in Jewish Israeli schools,[16] while substantial, may have limited relevance for American Jewish schools.

Ancient and modern Jewish history provide numerous examples of intentional, repetitive, and power-imbalanced aggression, often resulting in dire consequences for the Jewish people. Moses is appalled at the chronic and escalating aggressive Egyptian management of their Hebrew slaves. Sodom is destroyed because its citizens fail to protect visitors from the repeated aggression of the inhabitants. Inquisitions, expulsions, and the Holocaust are all part of the Jewish historical experience of the abuse of power to cause harm. How has this historical experience shaped Jewish understandings of bullying and, in particular, the definition and recognition of bullying in Jewish schools? The author's work with dozens of Jewish schools suggests no uniform answer. Consider a Jewish high school that experiences a hazing incident during a school-wide retreat. Younger students were coerced by seniors to engage in midnight calisthenics and muddy walks, wearing limited clothing and in a humiliating manner. The school requested assistance but required that the words "hazing" and "bullying" not be used, since the actions of the seniors were felt to be an example of well-meaning, albeit misplaced desire to help younger students integrate. Another Jewish school felt extremely uncomfortable with the notion of using the word "bully" to describe a Jewish child, choosing to describe specific aggressive behaviors.

Other Jewish schools have prominently included language identifying bullying and defining its consequences in their handbooks and policy guidelines. Such differences in approach to definition are not immaterial, as whether one views bullying as an accepted rite of passage or as an unacceptable social ill will determine what resources are afforded to address it.[17]

Characteristics of Bullies, Victims, Provocative-Victims, and Bystanders

Significant efforts have been invested in understanding the major players in bullying, assuming that identifying characteristics of bullies, victims, and provocative-victims would foster the development of effective intervention strategies.[18] Research on bullies suggests that while they are not a uniform group,[19] common characteristics include a strong need for dominance and limited empathy for the suffering of others.[20] Bullying has been associated with moral disengagement, poor emotional understanding, diminished guilt over aggression,[21] and a lack of faith in human nature.[22] Recent MRI research has provided biological evidence of limited empathy in adolescents with conduct disorder, which often includes bullying.[23] Examining collegiates who currently engage in bullying, Pontzer found that college-age bullies had also been bullies during childhood, were impulsive, had a tendency to displace shame, were more likely male, and had been exposed to parental stigmatization.[24] Peeters, Cillessen, and Scholte, however, suggest significant complexity and heterogeneity of bullies.[25] Their research confirms the seemingly divergent views of Sutton, Smith, and Swettenham in finding some bullies to be socially intelligent[26] and the assumptions of Crick and Dodge that bullying behavior is the result of incompetencies or deficiencies, including poor social information processing.[27] For both boys and girls, it seems likely there are high social status, socially intelligent bullies, as well as socially unintelligent and unpopular bullies.

Concerns with the significant psychological and social sequelae of peer victimization[28] have resulted in considerable research on victim characteristics. Victimization appears quite stable, with approximately 10 percent of public school children experiencing chronic victimization by middle childhood.[29] Of the two types of victims, passive victims are the most common.[30] These inhibited, submissive, and socially with-drawn youngsters are easy targets, often not retaliating and providing attackers with the additional "reward" of strong negative emotional re-actions.[31] Less common is the provocative or aggressive victim, who exhibits poorly controlled anger and responds aggressively to attack. These youngsters may be irritable and restless[32] and are the most vul-nerable to psychological symptoms and distress, including depression.[33] Anxiety in victims has been explored as both a precursor and response to ongoing victimization.[34] Both types of victims demonstrate deficits in social skills,[35] struggling with receptive processing of social cues and lacking expressive social competencies such as skill in entering social groups, cooperativeness, and humor.[36]

Bullies and victims comprise a relatively small percentage of students at any school. The majority of students are, however, aware of bullying, with estimates ranging from 60 percent[37] to over 80 percent.[38] These bystanders can both have an impact on bullying and be impacted by its presence in the school culture.[39] Unfortunately, the actions of bystand-ers typically support bullying rather than stop it,[40] with many serving as "reinforcers" who actively encourage bullies, acting as "assistants" or followers, or remaining as passive "outsiders."[41]

Research provides a fairly comprehensive picture of bullies, victims, and bystanders in public and secular settings. Research in private or religious settings may offer a closer approximation of the social dynam-ics in Jewish schools. Delfabbro and colleagues explored bullying in Australian school settings, allowing comparison of single-gender and coeducational schools, an issue relevant to Jewish day schools, which may be single gender or separate boys and girls for all or part of the school day. Interesting interactions were uncovered, with boys more likely to be bullied at single-gender schools and girls experiencing greater victimization at coeducational schools.[42] Coleman and Byrd ex-plored victimization in a "small private, religiously affiliated school in the south-eastern United States"[43] and found overall levels of victimiza-tion comparable to public schools (i.e., 10 percent). Compared with public settings, however, there was a significantly lower level of direct aggression. The researchers suggest that covert forms of social aggres-sion may be more likely in private religious settings, which provide clear guidelines for and narrower expectations regarding acceptable behavior.

Bullying in Ecological Context

When Espelage and Swearer published their book *Bullying in American Schools*, they bemoaned the lag in bullying research in the United States and the need to rely on the decades of research in Europe, Australia, and Canada.[44] Jewish educators are in an equally difficult position, having to extrapolate from research in settings quite unlike their own. Astor, in his insightful consideration of Jewish involvement in school violence research, suggests that initially the American Jewish community operated as if school violence was "a problem for other groups in the United States," with the Jewish "presence" in violence prevention research evident in settings such as inner city schools, but not in American Jewish schools.[45]

Researchers and practitioners have argued that bullying is highly contextual and must be studied and addressed within the ecological culture in which it occurs.[46] Bullying, they suggest, is discouraged or nurtured based on individual, family, peer, school, community, and cultural influences. For example, Rodkin argues that the American view of bullying as a normative element of childhood and adolescence, in contrast with the Scandinavian view of bullying as a threat to basic human rights, requires that US educators not assume all adults are committed to bully prevention.[47] Within the United States, research exploring ethnic/ cultural distinctions in attitudes toward bullying has documented a differential between African American students' and their white peers' reporting of having been victimized.[48]

How might the culture of a faith-based, mission-driven school impact bullying? In their qualitative exploration of spiritual and moral development in religious (including Jewish) and public Chicago schools, Blain and Revell document an implicit belief in character education as a central task in faith-based schools.[49] Formal character education programming, however, was seen as unnecessary by such schools, since both administration and faculty felt it was "connected" to everything they taught or did. The power of a school culture that embodies spiritual and moral values was also documented in a study of Israeli schools that were unusually safe and nonviolent, compared to surrounding norms and context.[50] Schools that were "atypically nonviolent" came from both the secular and faith-based sectors and were unique for missions that "not only aimed at creating a safe school environment but had an outward orientation geared toward changing society as well."[51] The faculty at such schools saw it as critical to empower students to make a difference and contribute to a just, democratic society. These schools were led by inspired principals who embodied and demonstrated the school mission, and signs of warmth, caring, humor, and emotional and social support were evident to the researchers embedded for months in the school.

The above studies hint at the potential for American Jewish schools, but the impact of mission and culture on bullying cannot be assumed. Fried expresses serious concern that Jewish schools are not necessarily kinder, gentler places[52] and may suffer from a "disconnect between Torah learning and Torah living."[53] Fried's chilling anecdotes include parents being advised by Jewish educators to make their bullied son "normal" so others "won't hit him"[54] and the subtle and outward ways Jewish educators communicate that *mitzvot bein adam lachaveiro*, commandments regarding behavior between individuals, are of minimal concern. If Jewish schools are to create an ecological environment of caring, they will need a commitment to teaching, modeling, and celebrating, in practical and consistent ways, Torah principles for human relationships.

Research on bullying in American Jewish schools is extremely limited,[55] with only one published study exploring teacher responses in Jewish schools.[56] Through the BRAVE initiative, described below, the author has amassed a significant data set including over three thousand student and five hundred teacher responses to surveys regarding school climate. Initial analysis suggests rates and patterns of bullying are quite similar to those in public settings.[57] Hopefully, these preliminary reports will spark much needed additional research and intervention efforts to address bullying in Jewish schools

Effective Bully Prevention

Numerous bully prevention programs and curricula have been employed in US schools. The pioneering work of Olweus in Norway[58] served as a template for most later programs.[59] A program component that appears necessary but not sufficient is awareness raising.[60] To be effective, programs also must change the norms and climate of the school, empower all members of the school community (teachers and students) to respond in a pro-social way when bullying occurs, and include systems for recording, reporting, and disciplining bullying. All this must be paired with a commitment to ongoing efforts. Limber's review of the Olweus Bullying Prevention Program, which includes all these components, summarizes its substantial success in European implementation.[61] Although less substantial, promising US results have earned it designation as a Blueprint program by the Center for the Study and Prevention of Violence at the University of Colorado.[62] *Bully-Proofing Your School*, which incorporates the same elements as the Olweus program, has had similar positive outcomes, including decreases in self-reported bullying and improvements in overall school culture.[63]

There is by no means universal agreement about the positive outcome of school-based bully prevention. Merrell, Isava, Gueldner, and Ross argue that the literature has been largely limited to descriptive studies.[64] Only recently is the effectiveness research sufficient to allow synthesis or critique. Their meta-analysis, including sixteen studies, found a small but meaningful decrease in student self-reported bullying and other positive changes following bully prevention programs. Given relatively small effect sizes and variability of outcomes, the authors "tentatively" conclude that there is "some evidence" supporting the effectiveness of school bullying intervention. Considerable research deficiencies (lack of control group, non-experimental designs, threats to internal validity, and reliance on indirect measures) were cited in a call for continued and increasingly controlled research. An earlier review by Smith, Schneider, Smith, and Ananiadou (2004) concluded that the majority of school-wide anti-bullying programs failed to demonstrate significant changes, although some had positive results.[65]

Jewish schools, often with limited resources for addressing bullying and other social-emotional issues, face considerable challenges in selecting and implementing effective programming. This makes the "translation" of secular research and programs for bully prevention in Jewish schools particularly compelling.

The BRAVE Initiative:
A Secular Start and Empirical Tradition

In 1999, the Alliance for School Mental Health (ASMH), a school consultation program housed at a major teaching hospital in the New York metropolitan area, began receiving requests from schools for professional development and prevention/intervention programs to address bullying. Some requests were prompted by the integration of special needs students into general education settings, and others by schools' growing concern, in the aftermath of Columbine, about school violence and bullying. Committed to evidence-based practice, the Alliance faculty reviewed the extensive international research and began work with local schools to develop programming that would incorporate the components of effective prevention first documented by Olweus in Norway[66] and echoed in much of the literature.

Increasing knowledge about bullying throughout the school community and fostering a sense of shared responsibility among all constituents (i.e., students, teachers, support staff, families) to address bullying when it happens were critical to include. Although not present in existing programs, Alliance faculty and school professionals felt that direct skill building of socially responsible bystander skills was equally essential. Student, faculty, and family materials were developed, piloted, and reworked. Two years after the program was introduced, BRAVE was manualized and delivered through a turnkey training institute for schools throughout the region. Public schools were extremely positive in their response to the program, and requests for involvement resulted in an expanded network of BRAVE schools across the region.

BRAVE Finds a Jewish Home

Shortly after BRAVE was introduced to schools in the public sector, private schools, including secular private schools, parochial schools, and some Jewish day schools expressed interest. Unlike public counterparts, these schools were not responding to governmental school violence prevention mandates and had limited funds to support their efforts, but were committed to creating more positive school environments. As BRAVE began implementation in Jewish day schools, overlap between

Jewish concepts and bully prevention concepts began to emerge. Teachers attending BRAVE workshops provided biblical or halachic references to support the bully prevention paradigms, and students made connections to lessons about Jewish holidays and beliefs. Most powerful, however, was the comfort Jewish schools voiced regarding the core values of bully prevention, spelled out in the BRAVE acronym: a belief in the rights and value of everyone.

The author's affiliation shifting from a secular health system to a university department of Jewish education afforded the opportunity to expand BRAVE to specifically respond to the needs of Jewish schools and students. Supported by a department with both academic and practical emphases, BRAVE began a research protocol to investigate social-emotional issues in Jewish schools, as well as exploring implementation and outcome issues for bully prevention in Jewish settings. BRAVE program content and process are discussed below, with particular exploration of the unique challenges and opportunities in application to Jewish settings.

BRAVE Content

BRAVE targeted bullying but hoped to have wider impact, strengthening the place social-emotional development occupies in Jewish schools. BRAVE allows flexibility for schools to tailor content to meet their needs but always includes the four components of effective school-wide bully prevention documented in research:

1. Increasing awareness about bullying and its consequences across the school community
2. Engendering a sense of shared responsibility to address bullying among all, but particularly among student bystanders
3. Providing ongoing mechanisms for processing and discussion of bully-related issues
4. Creating clear expectations/policies regarding pro-social behaviors and consequences for aggressive behaviors

In addition to these components, BRAVE included focused, skill-based instruction and social problem-solving tools germane to bully prevention. The BRAVE content addressing the first three of these bully prevention elements and its skill-building approach is described below. The creation of expectations and policies are discussed in the section on BRAVE process.

Increasing Awareness and Shared Responsibility

In the original Olweus initiative, education about bullying and its various forms is accomplished through administration of an anonymous questionnaire[67] and dissemination of the results to students and faculty through an assembly or other activity. BRAVE uses surveys for research and to provide feedback to schools, but developed a mock trial of comic-strip bullies as the initial activity to engage students in the exploration of bullying and shared responsibility. While serving as attorneys for alleged bullies and their accused *accessories*, the *judge* (workshop leader) provides a definition of bullying and elucidates its subtypes. Student legal teams defend or prosecute those who directly bullied, as well as bystanders who failed to aid the victim. The "trial" concludes with students serving as jurors and a discussion of comic characters' behaviors and responsibilities. Finally, students are invited to consider who in their school environment has the opportunity and responsibility to address bullying situations.

Recognizing that students are only one part of the school community, BRAVE includes family and faculty presentations. These workshops provide information on bullying and bully prevention, including characteristics of bullies and victims, the critical role of bystanders, and particularly, the role of adults in supporting pro-social behavior. Faculty attendance is often mandated by school administration, or workshops are incorporated into existing professional development. Guaranteeing parent attendance is significantly more challenging. Although this phenomenon is not unique to Jewish schools, some yeshivot and day schools draw students from a wide geographic area, making it less likely that parents will attend evening programs. Within the past few years, several of the Jewish day schools in the BRAVE research project have held joint parent-student programs, some even inviting parents to "Night Court" to view their children's legal prowess in the BRAVE mock trial.

Building Bystander Skills
and Focused Social Problem Solving

Student, teacher, and parent feedback after initial BRAVE workshops is positive but tentative. That bullying should be addressed and that all members of the school community can and should play a role in addressing it is largely accepted. The tentativeness most often results from the limited behavioral options both students and adults consider regarding bullying situations. In fact, research on teacher responsiveness to bullying suggests that as much as 82 percent of the time, teachers do nothing when witnessing bullying.[68] Many teachers admit they feel unprepared to address such situations.[69] Students generally see as possible responses standing up to the bully or telling an adult, but are leery of doing either, fearing negative consequences .[70]

To enhance these limited response sets, the second BRAVE student workshop introduces concrete strategies that allow students to proactively and reactively impact bullying. These LEADERS (an acronym for the strategies) tools are carefully explained and discussed to avoid misuse. For example, the strategy labeled "Amuse with humor, make light of dark situations" involves using novelty and humor to diffuse bullying, but never to make others feel bad. Students serve as screenwriters, using LEADERS strategies to complete and perform scene prompts that include bullying. Audience participation during the workshop includes fellow students labeling the various strategies employed in scenes.

In addition to expanding the behavioral repertoire of student bystanders, this second workshop offers adults in the school community a shared language and set of tools for encouraging pro-social behavior and problem solving. The notion of building leadership skills is attractive to families and educators, and many BRAVE schools have created LEADERS posters or bulletin boards and connected the strategies to literature or other assignments. Jewish schools have related the notion of leadership and pro-social bystander behavior to holidays (the Maccabees BRAVE-ness on Chanukah), Bible lessons (Moses's defense of the Hebrew slave preceding the Exodus from Egypt), and critical events in Jewish history (Holocaust education).[71]

Ongoing Processing, Discussion, and Skill-Building Vehicles

Addressing a problem as socially complex as bullying and building students' pro-social skills cannot be accomplished with two workshops. Research on bully prevention, social-emotional learning, and teaching social skills and social problem solving all underscore the need for ongoing opportunities for students to apply and expand their skills.[72]

Olweus's program borrowed a tool from the world of manufacturing to facilitate ongoing social processing. Quality circles, when used by organizations, aim to shift attitudes toward shared responsibility, cultivate individuals' skills and potential, build team spirit and collaboration, and improve organizational culture.[73] Production crew quality circles meet together to evaluate their combined performance in creating a quality product, discussing as a group what each individual can and should do to improve the collective outcome. Transplanting quality circles to schools, the "product" of concern is the school's social environment, and the most convenient "production unit" is the individual class. In quality circles aimed at bully prevention, students engage in practical discussions about social relationships, bystander responses, and shared responsibility.

BRAVE incorporates monthly quality circles after the initial workshops. These circles are generally conducted with the naturally occurring classroom group, although a unique feature of some Jewish schools involves the fluctuation between mixed- and single-gender arrangements. BRAVE quality circles have been employed in varied settings (boys and girls in the same school, but with all separate classes; distinct boys' and girls' schools, totally coeducational schools, schools with coeducational general studies classes and single-gender religious studies classes). Considering who is included in each quality-circle discussion requires understanding of the social culture of the school as well as sensitivity to religious issues.

BRAVE quality circles are unlike typical classroom discussions and have a specified format and content, focusing almost exclusively on the response of bystanders. Students may initially expect to be asked to serve as "informers," providing evidence that adults will utilize to lay blame and assign consequences. When students share an incident in a quality circle, however, questions such as "Who else was there?"

or "Who else was aware it happened?" keep the focus on bystanders. Using Socratic dialogue, encouraging perspective taking and forecasting, and providing opportunity for logical problem solving, quality circles expand the discussion beyond the bully-victim dyad. Bystanders are challenged to consider what message their actions sent to the bully or victim and how they might use the LEADERS strategies to intervene in a pro-social way. Students are encouraged to question assumptions that are antithetical to positive social environments such as that being uninvolved is safe or that one only needs to aid one's friends. In Jewish schools, previously taught prohibitions and mitzvot, such as the ban on rumors (*lashon hara*) and the requirement to love one's neighbor as oneself (*v'ahavta l'rei-acha kamocha* [Leviticus 19:18]), can be applied to real situations and the challenges they bring.

The BRAVE Process

BRAVE was originally delivered by a corps of trained clinicians, who visited schools using the program. While this guaranteed high-quality workshops, it quickly became clear that the expense was prohibitive for many schools (Jewish schools in particular) and that no resident expertise was developed. To foster sustainability, BRAVE radically shifted its delivery method, offering an annual BRAVE Instructor Training Institute (BITI). Schools sent members of their staff to what was initially a four-day training program that prepared BRAVE instructors to turnkey train faculty at their schools and to provide BRAVE content to students, faculty, and families. It also offered guidance on strategic planning and systems change.

The BITI has evolved in several ways. Schools that sent one person to the training did not seem to do as well as those who sent a team who were able to share responsibility for catalyzing the efforts in their schools. Since personnel changes are common, multiple trainees decreased the risk of a school losing all resident BRAVE expertise. For Jewish schools, of particular relevance was the inclusion on the team of both religious and secular studies staff, providing shared ownership of bully prevention and social leadership programming. Another adaptation was decreasing the number of days of the training. This allowed BRAVE to move from a program for local schools to one that was accessible to schools across the United States, also critical for application to Jewish day schools.

With support from a university-based Jewish education research/service initiative, further changes in the process of bringing BRAVE to schools were possible. Currently, schools are asked to commit to three-year participation, including collecting data from middle school students and faculty, sending a team to training, and implementing BRAVE with at least one middle school grade annually. Schools are provided with up to four days of on-site consultation in their first year, decreasing to one day in their third year. On-site consultations allow extension of BRAVE training and partnering between BRAVE faculty and resident school staff in planning and implementing existing program elements, as well as innovative programming for students, faculty, and families. Novel approaches have included parent-child evening programs, teacher mock trials, lessons on the traditional *Vidui* prayer of Yom Kippur and social responsibility, and girls-only retreats.

Equally essential to successful implementation is review and adjustment of existing school policies and procedures to support BRAVE efforts. Meetings with school administrators are critical components of BRAVE consultation visits. Unlike in the public system, however, where administrative structures and governmental mandates are standard, Jewish schools have no uniform hierarchical structure and vary greatly in their approach to the content and even existence of formal disciplinary policies. In some instances, schools included administrative staff in the team they sent to BITI, virtually guaranteeing administrative buy-in. Others delegated teaching and support staff to be trained and spearhead BRAVE programming, requiring additional effort to create the administrative access and support needed to address policy and discipline codes.

Prior to their BRAVE experience, many of the participating schools had a discipline code, and many of these codes included general statements about the conduct of students as *b'nei* and *b'not Torah*. Some specifically mentioned bullying, but few had specified procedures or consequences for addressing bullying incidents. Several schools were grappling with issues regarding behavior beyond school hours or off-site, such as cyberbullying, and welcomed guidance from BRAVE consultants.

Lessons Learned: Challenges and Opportunities in Bully Prevention and Social Responsibility in Jewish Schools

From a research pilot with five Jewish coeducational middle schools, BRAVE has expanded to include fifteen schools in North America. Engaging a diverse group of Jewish schools from large and small communities has elucidated several unifying factors. In many cases, what appeared as challenges also provided unique opportunities.

Scheduling student workshops and monthly quality circles is challenging for all middle schools. Jewish middle schools have additional dual-curriculum requirements, with educators highly protective of teaching time. Whereas in public schools, BRAVE was often "located" in English or social studies classes, the schedule tightness forced BRAVE in some Jewish schools to engage more teachers across the curriculum. This requires deeper front-end training of more faculty but can result in broader buy-in and a shared vocabulary and vision for developing prosocial student behavior. Given the evidence for limited teacher awareness of and response to bullying,[74] increasing teachers' involvement with bully prevention is clearly a valuable investment.

Public schools have a full complement of support professionals, including counselors, psychologists, social workers, and others. Such support staff frequently served hundreds of students in large, public middle schools and were selected by their administration to shepherd the BRAVE program in their settings. Jewish schools have a more limited array of support staff, many of whom have multiple portfolios (e.g., administrative duties, teaching assignments). As a result, many Jewish schools sent a combination of administrators, support staff, and teachers to BITI, allowing for a variety of perspectives and facilitating creative teaming and planning. BRAVE consultants were often impressed by support staffs' knowledge of students, families, and community, which was extremely useful in adapting BRAVE programming and materials to meet schools' needs.

BRAVE consultants have been equally impressed by schools' contradictory responses of regularly relating BRAVE to Jewish studies content and failing to capitalize on "Jewish teachable moments."[75] When activities to build community in a socially divided sixth-grade class in a coeducational community school were suggested to the rebbe, he asked if such programming should be allowed to supplant time for teaching Torah. Many Jewish educators and Torah scholars would agree that engaging Jewish students in learning and living *mitzvot bein adam lachaveiro* is among the most critical components of teaching Torah.[76] In stark contrast, a school struggling with social dissension in a girls' class devoted significant time and effort to a two-day retreat focused on building community.

As the number of Jewish schools utilizing BRAVE increases, it has become clear that implementation fidelity varies considerably. Some BRAVE schools scrupulously provide all program elements on time, with well-trained staff facilitating student, family, and faculty workshops. Others struggle, due to scheduling, staffing, or other infrastructure issues, and may skimp on or totally skip vital program elements. In bringing evidence-based obesity prevention programming to Jewish schools, Benjamins and Whitman noted the repeated, professed needs of schools to take "baby steps" in making policy and procedural changes (e.g., removing high-calorie snack machines).[77] The BRAVE initiative has experienced a similar "tread lightly" stance among some Jewish schools in addressing bullying.

How programmatic fidelity affects outcome is a crucial question. In a preliminary and informal review of fidelity across schools, neither school size, financial stability, academic excellence, nor programmatic experience seems critical. The factors that seem most salient are administrative support and BRAVE leadership in the school. When there is a strong BRAVE coordinator, with strong ties to administration, the program seems to have greater fidelity and greater likelihood of continuity both within and beyond the three years of the BRAVE initiative. These initial findings are impacting recruitment, with administrative connection to the program now explored early in the process. BRAVE has also initiated conversations with schools prior to BITI to help identify strong candidates for training who will serve as coordinators of the project in the school.

In over a decade of bringing BRAVE to secular and Jewish schools, I have become accustomed to inconsistent application of bullying policies and schools' struggles to increase their awareness of and appropriate responding to those incidents that occur outside adult view. More recently, while I have been working exclusively in Jewish schools, particular challenges to the BRAVE notion of belief in the rights and value of everyone have become apparent. Whether justified or not, many Jewish educators express the belief that consequences for bullying and other social misconduct are delivered inconsistently not because of sloppy administration, but because of differences in social and financial power and prestige among students' families. These educators sense that Jewish schools, reliant on private funding, treat donors' children differently from other students. Clearly, a major challenge for Jewish schools is the creation of truly just and equitable schools in the context of long-standing and current fiscal paradigms. Can major school donors be educated to appreciate that the lofty goals of Jewish education are significantly undermined when donations are paired with expectations of special treatment? Are Jewish schools sufficiently steadfast in their mission and secure in their finances to clarify donors' roles and desires? Schools will rightly add that the issues of equitable social treatment and social responsibility extend beyond donor issues and are larger than schools alone can tackle. Recently, a Jewish school was unable to arrange a small meeting to discuss social issues in a family's home because some parents were unwilling to attend in other parents' homes. It is not surprising that the grade is beset with exclusionary cliques and social nastiness, given that among parents, not one universally accepted home could be found! Synagogue rabbis and community leaders need to embrace their "bully" pulpit and encourage the development of communities of care and acceptance. If in our communities individuals are shunned on Shabbat and *Yom Tov* because they have less social clout or are treated cruelly for whatever reason, we cannot expect to raise a generation of Jewish children who, in their schools or in their lives, live spiritually enriched Torah lives, imbued with the value of *tikkun olam* (improving the world) and *kol Yisrael areivim zeh lazeh* (all Jews are responsible one for another).

Conclusion

Educating Jewish students to be socially responsible and creating Jewish educational environments where bullying and other social cruelty are minimized are not new goals. Considerable attention to bully prevention and social-emotional learning in the secular world can, in some measure, inform research and intervention in Jewish settings. Research and intervention specific to the unique needs and realities of Jewish schools are sorely needed. Such tailored approaches allow for a synergy between Torah learning and Jewish precepts and character and social development that both seems natural and may offer great promise.

Martin Buber's remarks at a 1939 meeting of educators in Palestine championed social-emotional learning:

> Education worthy of the name is essentially education of character. For the genuine educator does not merely consider individual functions of his pupil, as one intending to teach him only to know or be capable of certain definite things; but his concern is always the person as a whole, both in the actuality in which he lives before you now and in his possibilities, what he can become).[78]

Today's Jewish educators can be worthy of the name when, through bully prevention or other vehicles, they see the potential of their students as social leaders. It is easy to be overwhelmed by the enormity of the task and the high stakes of failure. Virtually every week another news story brings to the fore the potential deadly consequences of unaddressed bullying. Buber's words, over half a century ago, are still relevant:

> Nothing remains but what rises above the abyss of to-day's monstrous problems, as above every abyss of every time: the wing-beat of the spirit and the creative work).[79]

With a dedication of spirit, and creative use of time, resources, knowledge, and their own personal humanity, Jewish educators can make a substantial contribution to their students' potential social growth, and therefore to the vibrancy and social justice of the Jewish community of the future.

9

Educational Jewish Moments:
A Methodology for Educators to Self-Audit

SHIRA D. EPSTEIN

A GUIDING MISSION of many graduate education programs is
to support novice teachers in developing a methodology for
ongoing "reflective practice," continuous inquiry about one's
teaching.[1] Participants in the William Davidson Graduate School of
Jewish Education's day school track become "junior faculty" for a full
year in a mentor teacher's day school classroom. In addition to gaining
experience in lesson planning and teaching core content knowledge,
they engage in ongoing dialogue with their mentor teachers about their
own pedagogy and practice, as well as participate in a weekly practicum course at the Jewish Theological Seminary. While junior faculty
occasionally discuss struggles in fostering positive relationships with
students, the primary case studies and incidents that they share within
the practicum indicate an uncertainty with how to attain proficiency in

pedagogical content knowledge, what Shulman refers to as the amalgam between having knowledge of a particular subject area and knowing how to convey their expertise through the most appropriate pedagogy.[2] The dominant concern of the junior faculty with whom I have worked is that of establishing "expert power,"[3] an authority that stems from firm command of material.

In radical contrast to the preoccupations of pre-service teachers, the requests for support that I receive from graduates in the field reflect a concern with developing "referent power,"[4] elevating their influence with students through the cultivation of interpersonal bonds. Newly minted full-time teachers often reach out to brainstorm how they can "be there" for students who are in need of social-emotional support and share that they are most caught off-balance by the unanticipated, unscripted moments that arise during the day. Furthermore, while they want to develop a strong rapport with students, they are often unsure of whether their students will welcome them as allies or view them as role models. New teachers desire perfection in their pedagogical choices and will abdicate their role of "being there" if they think this connection will be ineffective or that students will view teachers as inappropriately interfering with their lives. This desire to "get it right" can become paralyzing and often results in avoiding classroom conversations that might touch on sensitive, personal issues.

This desire for day school teachers to learn how to successfully "be there" for students deserves attention. With the recent increased spotlight on bullying and "relational aggression,"[5] the discourse on the responsibilities of the day school educator has included conversation on maintaining schools as safe spaces and how teachers can be proactive agents of fostering a communal environment. However, teachers report that while intent or declaration of schools to be safe spaces is a necessary first step, they require further support in exploring the range of their roles. They seek professional development that moves beyond the how-tos of implementing school policies and procedures, to consider how they can best guide learners in their emotional and spiritual journeys while simultaneously balancing the demands and constraints of daily teaching. Day school teachers need help developing as responsive educators[6] and require methodologies to support them in becoming active listeners and in seizing opportunities for dialogue and for cultivating connections with learners.[7] Koplow describes an "emotionally responsive curriculum" as one that "allows children to focus on issues that preoccupy them or hinder their functioning at school; it also gives teachers tools that facilitate emotional well-being and the evolution of community and cognitive growth."[8] In my own work, I have attended to this need by developing a lens for Jewish educators to address "evaded issues."

What Are Evaded Issues?

The American Association of University Women (AAUW) report *How Schools Shortchange Girls* identified that in addition to taught subjects (the explicit curriculum), schools often have an *evaded curriculum* encompassing gendered issues that learners confront and negotiate in their daily lives and that are typically not addressed in the formal classroom environment: harassment and bullying, sexuality, gender and sexual identity, eating disorders, body image, and substance abuse.[9] As opposed to issues that are often simply overlooked, "evaded" connotes actively sidestepping and avoiding particular subject areas. The AAUW recognized that the exclusion of subjects relating to the emotional lives of learners sends an implicit negative message that the areas of students' daily struggles, which very well might be on their mind as they sit in our classrooms, are irrelevant to their schooling. Are our educators equipped to relate school content to these adolescent realities, as well as create space for content areas that might not readily emerge from a Jewish educational curriculum?[10]

Evaded issues are often circumvented because they are uncomfortable to address. The following scenario encapsulates a set of circumstances in which an educator might experience unease:

Your junior high [students are eating lunch in the cafeteria]. You walk past some of your favorite students (yes, ones who really like you and you've built a trusting teacher/student relationship with). Some of the kids there are not your students, though you recognize them. You hear that they are talking about Jeff, a boy in their grade who is not present at the table. It is clear they have been doing so for a few moments. Some of the boys refer to him as the "fag." Most of the kids are laughing, except one or two. They move onto talking about another subject that involves other people soon after that moment.[11]

One can recognize the many circumstances within the above scenario that would lead the educator to second-guess whether he or she should intervene: the exchange does not occur during regular teaching time, and therefore, the students would not consider it to be the educator's responsibility to step into their private conversation; an educator might wonder what type of response he or she could offer during this down-time that would have any long-term effect or be taken seriously; the educator might worry that interfering will only bring undue attention to a remark that might be best left alone. What educators most often share in our training sessions is that they are not sure how to craft a response that straddles the line between conveying their own values of respect, tolerance, and inclusion while at the same time, not being perceived by students as dogmatic or preachy. They wonder what can be stated that simultaneously holds educational value as well as long-term effectiveness in shifting the students' attitudes or behavior. Furthermore, educators want to explore the implications of addressing scenarios such as the one above that might manifest during actual teaching time, when often they feel that the stakes for intervening might be even higher and costlier to their credibility and referent power.

The Rationale for Crafting Educational Jewish Moments

Although social-emotional learning encompasses so much more than gendered issues, I focus largely on scenarios that relate to gender and sexual identity, harassment, intimate relationships, and body image because they are often named by educators as the top evaded issues in their settings and are recognized as areas that they are least comfortable addressing. The Educational Jewish Moments (EJM) methodology was developed for both formal (i.e., day school and supplementary school classroom) and nonformal, experiential (i.e., camps, youth groups, service learning) settings. In this chapter, I focus specifically on formal teaching, as I have found that a stronger case often needs to be made for attending to social-emotional issues within the confines of day schools. Teachers repeatedly express uncertainty as to whether this type of relational work fits into their job descriptions. What message does it send to a learner if we evade issues that relate to their emotional lives? How can we help equip educators to relate school content to learners' daily realities?

As part of the Evaded Issues in Jewish Education project, which I developed, my colleague Naomi Less and I created the Educational Jewish Moments (EJM) methodology as a two-pronged approach to addressing evaded issues: (1) help Jewish educators reflect upon the evaded gender topics that arise within their teaching settings; and (2) offer a protocol for institutions to target a particular area for change. It is a schema through which educators can consider how to develop spaces in which social-emotional issues can be understood through the lens of Jewish values. Ideally, the three-part training is enacted with a faculty cohort. This cohort model enables a progression from focusing in the first session on professional development and strengthening individual practice to brainstorming and strategizing in the second and third sessions on potential systemic institutional changes.

This methodology for professional development stems from the recognition that while several curricula exist for teaching young people about specific gendered issues such as bullying, body image, healthy and abusive relationships, and sexual identity, there are few forums available to help the educators, themselves, reflect upon their own roles in establishing their schools as domains for safety and support. Naomi Less refers to this element of education as "soul work":

> The *soul work*, the social and emotional pieces of our connection to Judaism and to Jewish life … how we approach our teaching styles … how do we make that work a consistent part of our teaching practice, and what do we need as educators, as institution heads, as administrators, what kind of genetic work do we need in our DNA to enable that soul work to happen? What kind of training do we need? Who are the kinds of professionals that we need? How do we enable this work to be part and parcel, not an add-on … of the total soul character development of our kids?[12]

Often "unsafe" refers solely to the presence or manifestation of physical violence within a school. In contrast, a discussion of evaded issues enables a wide-lens picture of the environment in which students are learning and suggests that a non-safe classroom is also evidenced when students do not feel that they can participate fully or voice their opinions. A methodology such as EJM acknowledges a need to train teachers to view an integral part of their job descriptions as creating emotional safety.[13] In our training materials, we have included the following quote by Elie Wiesel: "Neutrality helps the oppressor, never the victim. Silence encourages the tormenter, never the tormented." A teacher witnessing the above scenario has a choice to ignore what is overheard. However, the question to consider is this: What opportunity is lost by evasion? Conceptualizing the addressing of evaded issues as "soul work" positions teaching beyond the enactment of effective pedagogical content knowledge; it includes a strong emphasis of the teacher's role in cultivating a comfortable learning environment. It connects the day schools' spiritual work of teaching Jewish studies, connection to God, and Jewish practice to the teacher's personal spiritual practice of "building mindfulness,"[14] being present to the moment-to-moment interactions between learners.

In contrast to the formal or planned curricula of our schools, an educational Jewish moment is "off the page" and can arise as Jewish educators proactively respond to these unanticipated student remarks, questions, or conversations related to gender issues (e.g., overhearing a student refer to a girl as a "bitch"; student-generated questions about a Jewish text that suggests condoning of rape; two girls talking during health class about "being really bad" by overeating at lunchtime and "feeling fat"). The methodology offers a schema for educators to engage learners in dialogue and make connections to Jewish values and resources that might extend or expand unforeseen conversation. Through facilitation of EJM trainings, we have heard firsthand from teachers the challenge of having time to pause and craft a response that feels both effective and authentic. For this reason, the trainings offer a framework for helping educators to prepare in advance for how they might react. In this way, we honor the idea that in order to help teachers feel that they are strong stakeholders in developing safe schools, they need opportunities to engage in the praxis cycle of reflection and action on their teaching.[15]

"Critical Incidents" as the Centerpiece of Constructing Educational Jewish Moments

The methodology of EJM builds upon the literature and framework of "critical incidents." While this term may connote a dire and explosive interaction, the terminology is misleading. Tripp notes that critical incidents are not the interactions themselves; as stand-alones, they are simply "happenings." Critical incidents are *created* when an educator decides to reflect back on an interaction with a student or group of students and consider what occurred, why, and what can be learned. He notes that they are "produced by the way we look at a situation . . . we have to ask both what happened and what allowed or caused it to happen."[16] The construction itself of a critical incident enables a launching point for strengthening one's teaching practice. Griffin explains that this strengthening of practice occurs when the educator moves beyond describing the incident itself to identifying the emotions and feelings that arose in that moment, which then allows consideration of why they responded to the students in the way that they did.[17] These second and third steps offer opportunities for shifts in practice, as teachers consider alternatives to how they chose to interact with learners.

It can be quite powerful for an educator to construct a critical incident. The process facilitates a stepping back to consider how split-second actions and responses do or do not align with educational philosophy and how, sometimes, the most immediate response is a dam-release of emotions and not always the response that the educator would choose in hindsight. For example, a teacher witnessing the above scenario of two students referring to another as a "fag" might in the moment yell at the students because that feels like the expected and appropriate response from an authority figure. Novice teachers in particular rely upon the "coercive power"[18] of reprimands and punishment because they do not feel as comfortable with other means of relating to students. However, if that same teacher had the opportunity to step back and reflect with colleagues, she might identify the initial reaction of anger that bubbled up inside as she overheard this conversation, and then move beyond that feeling of anger to pinpoint and describe the response that best aligns with her values and goals for "being there" for learners.

The focus within the construction of a critical incident on the description of teachers' affective states positions this particular approach as a natural support for teachers in better preparing to be present in emotionally charged situations. When introducing the framework of critical incidents to educators in EJM trainings, I describe it as akin to "pressing the pause button" on the DVD/DVR (or whatever form "pause" takes in the current media player technology!). A critical incident helps us to consider that in any given moment of teaching we are flooded with so many thoughts of how we might respond. When we take time with colleagues to reflect on the range of emotions that we experience in our teaching, we are better equipped when difficult moments arise to be present for our learners, to achieve the goal of "being there" that we desire.

EJM Training Session One: Building Mindfulness

The first EJM training session enables participants to define and identify evaded issues that might present within their settings, develop a lens for mindfulness building, and practice the "pressing of the pause button." The pausing enables an educator to respond from core values, rather than simply what might be raw emotions. The session focuses upon helping educators to understand the need to respond; in my work as a trainer I have come not to take this step for granted. Many educators will share that they are not sure even if they *should* respond at all.

In the first part of the session, the facilitator reads a scenario (such as the one above) to the educators. Participants are then asked to identify some of the issues that they think are embedded in the scenario. For example, issues that are often identified as connected to the above scenario include talking behind someone's back, using derogatory or inflammatory language, and using language that suggests homophobic beliefs. Participants then spend a few minutes reflecting upon a time in their settings that they can recall an evaded issue as present during their teaching, and they practice naming what they view as the core issue they would want to address were they to once again confront that issue during school time. This piece, also integral to developing a critical incident, is the first step in learning the slowing down and pressing of "pause."

Constructing the Critical Incident: The Barrage Activity

While many educators can vividly describe the moments in which evaded issues arise and can acknowledge that they want to respond or interject their own values, they are often paralyzed by the many reluctances that race through their minds. The teacher in the above scenario overhears the word "fag," and during the one second when he must make the decision as to whether to let on that he has overheard, he is overwhelmed by a multitude of anxieties. The word that I have integrated into trainings is "barraged"—within the moment of witnessing the evaded issue, teachers are often barraged with the inner-voice messages that run through their mind, such as thoughts about how to proceed or judgments about why one way is better than any other. These messages can serve as inhibitors that prevent educators from responding to students.

The EJM training draws upon the critical incidents framework to help teachers reflect upon potential evaded issues that might crop up during teaching time and consider how they would respond and why. Participants in trainings imagine that they are the educator within the scenario described above. At the moment that they have witnessed this student discussion, they have to make an instant decision. Although there is no clear correct response, whatever decision the educator makes will have implications. When teaching, these moments occur in the blink of an eye. The barrage exercise, the signature exercise of EJM trainings, helps educators practice hitting the pause button and shape the above scenario into a critical incident, a launching point for reflection on the choices one could make for response. It honors that despite the many pressures we experience within these moments, there are techniques that can help us to slow down so that we might respond from a place that feels less authoritarian and more present to hearing what students are sharing and that offers the best possible chance of creating an educational Jewish moment.

The barrage activity asks participants to imagine that the scenario just occurred and the pause button has just been hit: You are the educator, and you are frozen, barraged by reluctances to respond to the laughing students. One participant stands in the middle of the circle and symbolizes this every-educator. The rest stand around her in a circle and are asked to cross the circle one-by-one, pass by the one educator, and give voice to some reason that would derail her from responding, from interjecting, from some sort of interaction. We instruct, "Whatever comes to mind as the person in charge, cross the room and say it to the educator as you pass by. As you cross the circle, you say, 'I am reluctant to respond because...'"

The exercise asks educators to self-audit by literally giving voice to the sources of their potential reluctance to respond. In doing so, they are then able to examine their hesitations from a non-emotional, non-judgmental stance and ultimately to consider how they might engage their learners in discussion. Each time I facilitate or witness the facilitation of the barrage activity, the voiced "reluctances to respond" fall into predictable categories. For example, educators suggest the following concerns:

- The perceived problem isn't really a big deal and any response would be viewed as an overreaction.
- Parents might be unsupportive of the teacher's choice to intervene, and job security could be threatened.
- School administrators will not support their choice to address these topic areas.
- Their limited knowledge of these complex issues stand in the way of offering a worthwhile response.
- They will lose credibility or respect from students who do not agree with or like the way they have intervened.
- Since the teacher has only a few minutes during which to have a serious discussion with students, it is better not to attempt to craft a response.
- Their personal discomfort with the topic area prohibits them from offering an honest or full response.
- They have limited access to resources designed specifically for Jewish educational settings, so it is better not to attempt to offer an educational Jewish moment.

During the activity debrief, the educator is asked how it felt to bear witness to the voiced inner messages, and the barrage participants discuss how it felt to name their hesitations aloud. Many admit that they didn't even realize they held these reluctances until participating in this exercise, and some offer that it was validating to realize that others share what they now recognize might be limiting beliefs. A conversation inevitably arises around how one can address reluctances that might serve as a genuine obstacle—for example, how one might talk about homosexuality within a Jewish school where homosexuality is not considered as halachically acceptable. Under such circumstances, might the educator address the students' use of a slur against another student or the smearing of someone's name behind his back? It is only after this barrage activity that we can ask participants to return to their own developing critical incidents with fresh eyes, with the lens for understanding why they might be afraid to interject and how they can find solutions to their concerns. We tell them that as, with the examination of any critical incident, every choice has implications, and "in the moment, you don't have time to deconstruct—so we're going to do this in slow motion to develop your teaching practice."[19]

Seizing the Moment for Crafting an Educational Jewish Moment

The next step in any critical incident is taking a step back and considering the choices one had at the time for interacting with students. In the EJM methodology, we suggest that there are three choices:

Ignore: Not responding *is* a response choice, even if it is not intentional or one is not aware. Through this training, we want educators to then be aware of the times they do not respond, even if for legitimate reasons such as limited class time or recognizing that a supervisor might disapprove.

Delay: Don't address "in the moment," but make a mental note or tell the class, aloud, that the issue will be addressed in the future.

Engage: This might begin as an immediate attempt to stop the behavior, either for safety reasons or to reinforce school policies, if physical or emotional violence was present. Assuming that there is an opportunity for dialogue, when educators select the choice to engage, they offer an opportunity for learning.

If educators decide that they want to engage in an educational Jewish moment, a four-part schema supports this practice.

1. IDENTIFYing: Identifying key gender issues by asking probing questions such as, "What did you mean when you said . . . ?" It is a method for *slowing down* and focusing on the key issue that you want to address.

2. **CLARIFYing:** Choosing a type of response, such as pausing a formal lesson to talk about what just occurred. In the CLARIFY step, the educator is beginning to determine what type of response is needed: establishing or reinforcing ground rules, such as, "We don't use words like that in this classroom"; deciding that a moral or personal confrontation is needed, such as, "When you use the word 'fag,' I find it personally offensive, and it degrades gay students in our classroom"; or using the incident as a launching point for an educational conversation, by connecting to Jewish resources.
3. **CONNECTing:** Drawing from resources, such as referring to Jewish values or textual sources or to pop-cultural references.
4. **INTERJECTing:** Shaping the response so that it is offered through the educator's own authentic voice. While there are many possible ways to respond, and several textual or media resources might suggest phrasing, the goal is to select one that feels genuine and honest.

In the training, once we have offered the framework, we engage participants in a series of activities through which they practice the "hitting of the pause button" and "slowing down" described above. Through these application activities, they practice asking clarifying questions as part of the process of slowing down and listening to learners, rather than jumping in and immediately responding. They IDENTIFY evaded issues that they view as embedded in particular scenarios, thus gaining practice in identifying the potential entry points within their teaching for creating educational Jewish moments. The practice of asking questions helps them to both receive more information from their learners and gain processes for being present as critical incidents unfold within their teaching.

Beyond Individual Teaching Practice: Building Systemic Change

As noted above, the methodology aims to support individual teachers in expanding their practice while concurrently strengthening schools as communities that feel "safe" to learners. An exploration of the evaded issues within our own institutions requires educators to consider the larger school culture and the teaching practice that sustains this positive and healthy environment for learning. In the second session, cohort participants reconvene to explore research and data around a particular evaded issue that they have identified as immediate and relevant within their setting or institution, such as harassment and bullying, socioeconomic difference, sexuality, eating disorders, body image, gender or sexual identity, or substance abuse. They will be asked to name a critical incident within their institution and share some clarifying questions they have developed to determine what the issue was, as well as the type of response they have selected for engagement. They will then, in teams, develop schema for CONNECTing with their learners—either through institutional resources, existing programs and curricula, or Jewish resources. For example, if they have decided that they wanted to focus on issues of healthy relationship building within their high school, they might examine recent curricula that offer a Jewish perspective on dating, friendships, and relationships.[20]

In session three, participants reconvene and practice INTERJECTing, crafting their responses to learners. They explore a case example from their teaching of a critical incident that involved an evaded issue. This must be something they will feel comfortable examining within the context of the cohort. They consider prompts and questions such as the following:

- Describe the critical incident.
- IDENTIFY the evaded issue. (What, if any, CLARIFYing questions did you ask to determine that?)
- Did you intervene/respond?
- If not, what was your reluctance?
- If yes, describe what you did—what response did you select?
- Describe any resources you CONNECTed?

Ideally, the second and third training sessions model methods and approaches that schools can integrate into recurring in-house professional development sessions. Educators simultaneously examine their own individual practice and appraise the broader landscape of the school's culture. This process can potentially help administrators to consider how the school's explicit curriculum of designed courses, special programs and assemblies, chosen texts, and structured assignments, as well as the tacit, implicit curriculum of policies, selected new hires, and designated materials for hallway and classroom displays, either support the addressing or evasion of particular social-emotional issues.

The Lessons of EJM:
Educators as Partners in Shaping Institutional Culture

Methodologies such as EJM help educators to consider the impact of both the official, explicit curriculum and the hidden, implicit curriculum of their institutions. It is this examination of the hidden curriculum, what Orenstein refers to as "all the things that teachers don't say, but that you learn in class anyway,"[21] that can lead to changes in some of the less overt but similarly problematic practices within schools. Certainly, modifications to course syllabi can influence the scope of classroom dialogue about gender issues. However, in order for systemic change to occur, it is imperative for teachers to have opportunities to consider how institutions, as complex systems, can better sustain a climate for social-emotional learning. An unexplored but significant next step would be to research the outcomes of engaging educators with a methodology such as EJM. For example, a high school that has identified a key evaded issue of "healthy relationship building" might decide to train teachers in a curriculum that they would implement with learners but would in tandem want to track how they have addressed the implicit curriculum. Teachers might advocate for other structural changes, such as expanded advisory group modules during which teachers have opportunities to model methods for positive communication; further informal programming such as weekend *Shabbatonim* that enable students to build relationships with both peers and educators outside prescribed teaching time; or developing with students a parent-student evening programming series that explores the challenges of conversing through the modes of texting, social media, and e-mail.

Adaptability of EJM for Other
Professional Development Trainings

One unanticipated outcome of the EJM trainings has been the adaptation by other professional development initiatives of the barrage activity. Several have integrated this activity into their trainings as a signature methodology for helping educators explore their reluctances to address a range of evaded issues: Keshet Boston has utilized the activity to help educators reflect upon their reluctances in addressing gender and sexual identity issues within Jewish education. Jewish Theological Seminary's Mitzvah Initiative has facilitated this activity to aid rabbis and lay leaders in considering why they might be hesitant to foster with congregants the often challenging conversations regarding personal relationships with and feelings about observing mitzvot. Ma'yan, which currently houses the project Evaded Issues in Jewish Education, has utilized EJM, particularly the barrage activity, to help adults explore the evaded issue of race and class privilege within the Jewish community. The widespread use of the barrage activity suggests that professional development programs that seek to impact a change in practice often desire a process method for engaging participants in self-reflection.

Conclusion

Jewish education and professional development programs require a range of methodologies that place value on helping teachers expand and strengthen their relationship with subject areas and materials that relate to emotions within the classroom.

Enduring changes in the social-emotional climate of schools can occur through intentional modifications to both everyday teachings and the pervading school culture. The inclusion of educators as stakeholders and partners in this endeavor holds the potential for systemic shifts in how gender issues are explored and addressed during formal teaching and less formal interactions. While published curricula that offer lesson plans for teaching can spotlight particular issues for exploration within the classroom, professional development initiatives such as EJM enable educators to deepen their own self-understanding of why they might not feel comfortable addressing particular issues, and to potentially to feel more at ease with incorporating more consistent discussion of feel-ings into teaching).[22]

The emphasis within professional development of aiding educators in "pressing the pause button" can lead to a mindfulness building; this slowing down to self-reflect and assess how we are taking time to con-nect with learners is an indispensable scaffold for learning how to fa-cilitate difficult conversations about sensitive and often emotionally charged topic areas. By giving space for teachers to discuss the wide range of feelings that they experience in teaching, ranging from fear, anxiety, anger, and disappointment to empathy, appreciation, and joy, they are better able to achieve the goal of "being there" that they desire.

10

Facilitating Change in the Culture of Prayer in Day School:
An Intervention Based on a Theory of Practice

SAUL WACHS
AND MICHAEL SCHATZ

I F IT IS GENERALLY DIFFICULT to change the culture of a school, it is particularly challenging to do so with regard to worship and the curriculum of prayer. Prayer is different from other subjects taught in Jewish day schools. One *learns about Tanach*, Mishnah, *sifrut*, and so on,[1] but one *does t'filah* (prayer). The absence of the motive of *chiyuv* (obligation) complicates the study and practice of prayer for many pupils in non-Orthodox day schools. However, the problem is not entirely absent even in Orthodox day schools, where reports indicate that pupils are often unmotivated to pray in the public worship services conducted by the school.[2] For example, Lehmann's research in a modern Orthodox high school revealed a gap in the assumptions of pupils and teachers as to the role of prayer in the school.[3] While teachers saw organized prayer as a daily obligation (*chovah*), pupils saw it as a matter of choice (*r'shut*). Lehmann offered three possible explanations for this gap. The first is developmental: teenagers are naturally rebellious and resent being forced to do something, even when they might choose to do it if allowed. Second, the pupil population of a modern Orthodox day school is varied and includes different levels of commitment to ritual observance. The Judaic studies teachers in these schools, on the other hand, have chosen to live lives of ritual piety. Finally, young people increasingly show a drive toward self-determination and are increasingly unwilling to accept religious ideas uncritically.[4]

The culture of prayer and prayer study in non-Orthodox day schools is also largely determined by the teachers. Many Conservative and community day schools place a great deal of emphasis on the study of the Hebrew language. This connects the school to Israel and its culture and also has the "virtue" of appealing to a wide range of families, since it does not affect religious observance or belief.[5] Because of this great emphasis on Hebrew, it has been common for these day schools to engage teachers who are fluent in Hebrew, many of whom lack a background in prayer and might feel uncomfortable addressing issues that are connected to prayer, God, and belief.[6]

The attitude of the teachers toward prayer is critical in several ways. First, it affects their behavior during services and, therefore, the extent to which they can function as models for the pupils. Second, it affects the degree of comfort they have in teaching prayer. This relates to the priority placed on in-depth study of prayer texts and the extent to which teachers are willing to open this study to areas of unknown perimeters. Teachers who are themselves uncomfortable with prayer will find it more difficult to allow unfettered exploration of theological, halachic, and philosophical questions. Moreover, if teachers are more comfortable with *bei-ur t'filah*, explaining *the* meaning of a prayer, than with *iyun t'filah*, exploring *different* meanings of the text as well as those that represent the personal midrashim (interpretations) that the text evokes, this too will limit the degree to which pupils can experience prayer study in depth. It follows then, that any change in the prayer climate of a school has to begin with the faculty.

Developmental issues are also relevant. *T'filah* in the classrooms of younger children is typically an exercise in skills. Any explanations provided likely take the form of *bei-ur t'filah* (a teacher telling the meaning of a prayer). Because young children enjoy ritual, those observing the services of young children see what on the surface seems to be a successful educational experience. Since fluency in Hebrew is prized above almost all other pedagogical virtues in these settings, many of the teachers who are engaged to teach (particularly in the early grades) possess that strength but might not have any knowledge or pedagogical content knowledge or experience that would prepare them to make prayer experiences meaningful or the study of prayer intellectually stimulating. Moreover, a superficial examination of prayer in the lower classes seems to reveal children who enjoy praying. In effect, prayer becomes little more than an exercise in skills. As the children progress from grade to grade, motivation weakens, and more and more pupils tune out and some begin to become turned off. For many children, skills do not automatically reinforce themselves. Lacking any convincing rationale for prayer and experiencing organized worship that lacks depth, it is not surprising that what was *not* done in the younger grades bears bitter fruit.

Prayer and Gratitude

It is remarkable that, despite the trials and tribulations of some of Jewish history, the overwhelming subjects of most of the formal prayers of the liturgy are appreciation, gratitude, thanksgiving, and praise. This is true of the first three sections of the *Shacharit* (*Birchot HaShachar, P'sukei D'Zimrah*, and *K'riat Sh'ma Uvirchoteha*)[7] and informs most of the *Amidah* of Shabbat and Festivals and part of the *Amidah* of weekdays. In similar fashion, *siyum hat'fillah*, the final portion of *Shacharit*, is predominantly devoted to these subjects. As anyone who has ever experienced tragedy firsthand knows, a human being doesn't need a siddur to get in touch with what one has lost. Many (probably most) people, however, do not wake up and spontaneously get in touch with what they *have*. Typically, one thinks about a limb or a tooth when it hurts; too often, one reflects on a relationship only after it is severed.

But getting in touch with what one *has* is important. It adds a necessary balance to one's view of life and can lead to the kind of reflection that affects attitude and behavior.

There is now an accumulating body of research that attests to the value of appreciation. Professor Robert A. Eammons of the University of California at Davis has devoted years to studying gratitude. He and his colleagues have enriched happiness research in two ways: first, by developing methods to cultivate gratitude in daily life, and second, by developing a measure to assess individual differences in dispositional gratefulness. This research revealed that "those who kept 'gratitude journals' on a weekly basis exercised more regularly, reported fewer physical symptoms, felt better about their lives as a whole, and were more optimistic about the upcoming week, compared to those who recorded hassles or neutral life events."[8] Among other benefits discovered or confirmed by Eammons' research were that "children who practice grateful thinking have more positive attitudes towards school and their families."[9]

In generalizing from this and other research, Eammons points to four areas where appreciation seems to affect people in ways that, both from a Jewish point of view and an educational point of view, can be seen as desirable.

1. Grateful people report higher levels of positive emotions. They derive greater satisfaction from life, greater vitality, optimism, and lower levels of stress and depression. They are aware of problems and negative aspects of life and experience unpleasant emotions, but their positive emotions are enhanced.

2. Grateful people are able to be empathic; their interpersonal intelligence and capacity for generosity and helpful to others are enhanced.[10]

3. Those who regularly attend religious services and engage in religious activities such as prayer (and) reading religious materials are more likely to be grateful. They are more likely to acknowledge a belief in the interconnectedness of life and a commitment to and responsibility to others.[11] Grateful individuals are less materialistic. They are less likely to evaluate success in life in terms of possessions. They are less jealous of others and more likely to share what they have with others than those who are less grateful.

4. Gratitude has been associated with a sense of awe, thankfulness and appreciation of life has been a source of contention for
thousands of life. Cultivated by religions such as Judaism, it has
been seen by others as demeaning and a sign of weakness. If the
bulk of Jewish prayer is about gratitude, a sense of wonder, and
getting in touch with what one *has*, then, ideally, davening can
be analogous to the gratitude journals that Eammons advocates,
or perhaps it can serve a complementary function.

In sum, if our pupils (and we) become accustomed to regularly encountering prayer texts that essentially affirm life, offer hope, and remind us of what we have (individually and as a community), it might
not be too far a leap to transfer that experience to a greater expression
of appreciation to others who enrich our lives.[12]

Intervention Grounded in a Theory of Practice

We now turn to a case example based on our experience as consultant
(Wachs; henceforth "the consultant") and researcher (Schatz; henceforth, "the researcher") in one school to illustrate the challenges of creating a positive prayer culture. In 2002, the Solomon Schechter Day
School of Bergen County, at the urging of then-head of Judaic studies
Ms. Ricky Stamler-Goldberg (henceforth, "the administrator") and supported by then head of school Rabbi Stuart Saposh, decided to initiate an
effort to improve the quality of the study and experience of prayer. They
invited the consultant to study the situation and help begin a program
to improve it. The school clearly exhibited certain strengths. According
to the administrator, "*T'filah* in the lower school is and always has been
an activity performed respectfully by teachers and students alike." This,
together with the teachers' trust and respect of the administrator, who,
for many years, had been a teacher in the school, made the situation at
the focus school somewhat more positive. This respectful stance, however, was limited by a

lack of understanding of both the goals of the school and of the content
area, which often resulted in *t'filot* that were void of spiritual connection and run by faculty with minimal knowledge of or investment in the

subject matter or the experience. Moreover, the service doesn't change very much in a classroom from September to June, and the pupils never get to encounter many parts of the service.

The intervention to be described was grounded in a theory of practice (a theory that is asserted to be valid in situations that share the same characteristics). Since non-Orthodox day schools in general and Solomon Schechter day schools in particular do, in fact, share many characteristics, the intervention is asserted to be of potentially wider utility. The theory reflects reflection upon more than thirty years of observation and practice in day schools. The key components of this theory are as follows:

1. Unresolved issues of theology, theodicy, halachah, etc., can lead teachers to avoid open-ended questions.
2. Some teachers associate professionalism with knowing the answer to questions that are asked by pupils.
3. The questions that "leap out of the pages" of the siddur do not easily lend themselves to a rhetoric of conclusions.
4. Teachers cannot come to terms with something professionally until they have come to terms with it personally.
5. The siddur addresses questions that exercise all intelligent people.
6. Studying the siddur can be an exciting experience when conducted in a totally safe environment.
7. The participation of supervisory personnel signals that efforts to enhance *t'filah* are of high priority.
8. The nature of the participation of supervisory personnel is helpful when those personnel participate as peers.
9. Teachers are more motivated to participate in workshop-seminars when they have a voice in determining the agendas of the study.
10. Successful demonstration lessons with pupils enhance the credibility of the consultant and the perceived value of the lesson plans being demonstrated.
11. Teachers feel "liberated" when they realize that they are not expected to "know the answer" to the complex questions addressed by religion.

12. It is important to break down the walls that keep teachers apart by encouraging peer observations of lessons in *iyun t'filah* and prayer services.
13. Prayer services are enhanced significantly when they include elements of depth.
14. The aesthetic quality of the spaces used for prayer can affect the mood and the quality of the prayers.

What was required was a change in the culture of prayer in the school. This would involve, first and foremost, changing teacher attitudes and helping them develop more knowledge and skills. The fundamental strength of the school and the loyalty and professionalism of its faculty and administration were crucial factors in allowing for an intervention with any chance of success.

The goals set down by the administrator and the consultant included the following:

1. Establishing a zone of complete safety for the exploration of prayer and its related topics.
2. Helping teachers address their own memories and issues that impinge on the teaching of *t'filah*.
3. Demonstrating that the siddur addresses perennial issues that all thinking people must confront at some point in their lives.[13] Demonstrating that pupils in the elementary school are capable of thinking deeply and engaging in *iyun t'filah*.
4. Encouraging teachers to cooperate in developing and evaluating lesson plans in *iyun t'filah*.
5. Introducing experiences of depth into daily prayer.
6. Encouraging the teachers to "grow" the prayer service so that pupils constantly feel growth in their movement toward prayer literacy (skills and understanding).
7. Sensitizing teachers to explore ways of creating *pinot kodesh* (corners of holiness) in their classrooms that would focus the attention of the pupils on the prayer experience through the nexus of *k'dushah* (holiness) and *yofi* (beauty).

Work with the teachers' own relationship with prayer took on a central role. The consultant's work was guided by ideas of transformative learning.

TRANSFORMATIVE LEARNING

Transformative learning is connected to the search for meaning in life. It was taken as axiomatic that one cannot come to terms with something as a professional unless one comes to terms with it as a human being. Teachers are motivated to participate in learning experiences when they believe that these experiences can help them understand themselves better and increase the competence and comfort they feel in their work. Mezirow studied this area in the 1970s and listed phases through which people go in experiencing transformation. These include experiencing a disorienting dilemma, self-examination, critical assessment of assumptions, recognizing that others have gone through a similar process, exploring options, formulating a plan of action, and reintegration. Central to this process is self-reflection, which takes three forms: reflection on the content of what is being studied, reflection on the strategies that may be employed in seeking to solve the problem, and reflection on the assumptions, beliefs, and values that underlie the problem.[14]

Transformative learning is more likely to occur when

- there is a shared awareness of one or more problems and a motivation to find solutions;
- the participants have a role in determining the agenda of learning and the priorities that govern the process of learning;
- time and other resources are made available to work on the problematic area;
- supervisors combine support for and expectations of those involved in the process;
- a climate of safety and mutual respect is established within the learning environment.

Transformative learning is less likely to occur when

- those involved deny or minimize the severity of the problems or lack motivation to tackle the problems;
- fear and defensiveness are present;
- outsiders (e.g., consultants) are seen as lacking in knowledge of the setting and/or empathy for the participants.[15]

People approach an experience of change with memories and experiences that can trigger resistance. In the case of prayer and prayer teaching, this resistance is both personal and professional. People cannot come to terms with something as professionals until they come to terms with it personally. Therefore, the first steps in facilitating change involve helping teachers take a fresh look at prayer and at the liturgy. A key element in this is helping them see the relevance of the ideas in the prayer book to their own lives. Motivation is in the learner. If subject matter touches deep needs, it will deeply involve the learner.

The liturgy is the book of values of the Jewish people. All of the teachers involved in this experience have Jewish commitments of one kind or another; if they come to see the connection between the prayers and their own values, one barrier will be removed.

COMPONENTS OF THE T'FILAH ENHANCEMENT PROCESS

In order to develop vibrant, participatory, and meaningful prayer services, supported by a curriculum of *iyun t'filah*,[16] the first step in this case was to begin with study sessions for the educators in which prayer texts could be analyzed from literary and rhetorical perspectives. At the same time, these sessions acted as springboards for discussion of theological issues that, for some, represented real obstacles to addressing prayer seriously. The goal was to help transform teacher attitudes, understandings, and practice in the teaching of prayer and in facilitating prayer services.

Study Workshops

At the beginning and throughout the process, the visits of the consultant (four to six times a year) were planned cooperatively by the administrator and the consultant. Teachers were actively involved in the process as well, and their suggestions and recommendations were key factors in determining the agenda items for these visits. Having a sense of ownership over the process strengthened their motivation to address the project with respect and professionalism. In the first stage, the consultant studied selections from the siddur with the teachers with the goal of promoting awareness that the prayers address living issues and that their study could be engaging. Almost from the beginning, theological questions emerged. In the first stage, teacher might frame these questions in terms of their students (e.g., "But the pupils will ask…").

Gradually, this was replaced by personal statements and questions that pointed to the dilemmas that can arise when the theology of the liturgy seems to be in conflict with the experiences of life.

The participation of the administrator was critical because it pointed to the priority placed by the school's leadership on the project. More than that, however, was the nature of that participation. The administrator (who was present at every session) would share her own questions with the group. Since she was known to be an Orthodox Jew, this made it easier for teachers to do the same without fear or embarrassment. The consultant also shared life experiences that threw the assertions of the liturgy into doubt, and so a sense of peerage was established that undoubtedly helped create a sense of safety for all concerned. The faculty also appreciated the fact that this project was being conducted "on school time" (with all the attendant logistical challenges this entailed), and this too contributed to their growing enthusiasm for the seminars. A learning community was established, and this proved to be meaningful to all concerned.

Lesson Plans and Model Lessons

The second stage involved distribution of lesson plans designed by the consultant to illustrate *iyun t'filah* with pupils. This was followed by demonstration lessons by the consultant with "postmortem" critiques with the faculty members who observed these lessons. Where pupils responded enthusiastically to a lesson, this enhanced the credibility of the consultant and of what was being proposed. Where the lesson proved less than totally successful, teachers had an opportunity to make suggestions and thus to teach the consultant. These suggestions were received with respect and appreciation, further engendering a climate of professional and personal peerage among the participants.

Observation of Prayer Services

In the lower school (grades 1–5) *t'filah* generally took place in the classrooms. Over the course of several years, the consultant spent part of his visits to the school observing *t'filot*. Four goals guided these visits:

- To determine the extent to which services were more than an exercise in liturgical skills and the extent to which they included moments of real depth

- To determine whether there were adequate transitions into and out of services or whether they were abruptly added to the daily regimen
- To assess the extent to which pupils grew in their exposure to the liturgical texts from month to month and year to year
- To assess the aesthetic quality of the prayer spaces and the extent to which the visual stimuli enhanced the sense of *k'dushah* that, ideally, characterizes worship

Fortunately, on the last of these points one of the teachers was a model. Her classroom was exceptionally beautiful in its creation of a *pinat kodesh* (a part of the classroom that serves as the focal point for prayer). In general, the project encouraged teachers to visit each other's classrooms, observe each other teach, and observe each other's prayer services. Thus the example of this teacher's classroom encouraged others to pay attention to the aesthetic quality of their prayer spaces.

Outcomes: Linking Liturgy and Meaning Making

In 2009, the researcher was invited to assess the degree to which the intervention project met its goals. He received excellent cooperation from the faculty and administration. The researcher utilized observation of classrooms, questionnaires, focus groups, and individual interviews to determine perceived outcomes. The overall theme that emerged from these interviews and observations had to do with adding elements of meaning making and relevance to the students. For example,[17] one teacher noted, "This year, for the first time, I asked the pupils on the first day, *Lamah mitpal'lim* [What is the purpose of prayer]?" Another asked the students "to choose their own prayer spot in the classroom during the *Amidah* and after... [to] tell the class why they chose that spot." She reported "the strong impression that the choice is a thoughtful one."

Importantly, teacher's efforts to promote meaning making were often linked to specific elements of the liturgy. For example, one teacher described using the specifics of the liturgy as a springboard for personal relevance:

I taught *Mah Tovu*.[18] We focused on the words for "dwellings." The pupils noted that some were simple and others quite elaborate. When I asked why they thought the opening prayer of the service listed five of these words, several answered that it showed that one can pray to God in a classroom or in a fancy chapel and feel confident that God hears the prayers.

Another teacher used a discussion of personal prayer as a framework through which to analyze the liturgy:

Months ago, I asked the pupils, "If you could ask one thing of God for yourself or the family or in general, what would you ask?" They wrote their answers and I collected them. I then distributed a worksheet containing the structure and general contents of the *Amidah*. Over the course of the year, we studied [*iyun t'filah*] all of the *b'rachot* of the *Amidah* and also noted where this *Amidah* differs from that of Shabbat. Later, I asked the pupils to prioritize the *bakashot* [petitions] in the *Amidah* of weekdays. They did this in writing. I then asked them to write down their own *bakashah*, repeating the exercise that I had given them months earlier. I then distributed the cards on which they had written the original exercise. They were able to compare the two exercises. Those who wished to (most of the pupils) told the rest of the pupils about the two answers. In most cases they were quite different. I then pointed out that while the order and content of the *b'rachot* doesn't change, their mood and sense of what is needed on any particular day do. One child then said, "That's why we need them all!"

A final extended example comes from an observation of a third-grade teacher engaged in *iyun t'filah* and illustrates the intersection of meaning making and gratitude:

The teacher was sitting in front of the class. She bent her head and shoulders and said, "*Ani k'fufah* [I am bent over]." She straightened up and said, "*Achshav, ani z'kufah* [Now, I am erect]." After repeating this a few times, she invited the pupils to join in with the statements, "*Anu k'fufim* [we are bent]" and "*Anu z'kufim* [we are erect]." She then asked them, "Have you ever felt *kafuf*?" (treating the word metaphorically as "bent out of shape"). When no one answered, she proceeded to tell them that, as a young girl growing up in Israel, coming to a new school, she was snubbed by a lot of the other girls and felt very "bent out of shape. I would walk with my head down." A boy who was considered to be a star in her class in Israel came over to her and said, "I'd like to be your friend." This led to her being accepted by the others as well. The pupils she was teaching were fascinated by this personal vignette. One said, "But you're so pretty and so nice, how could the kids not like you?" She said, "Thank you. I didn't feel pretty or nice. I just felt *k'fufah*, bent out of shape, and I walked with my head bent. After this boy became my friend, I felt *z'kufah*. I walked with my head high. A few pupils shared moments when they felt "*kafuf.*" She asked the class, "What do you think the author of this *b'rachah* had in mind when he said that God is *zokeif k'fufim?*" The pupils offered different answers. The teacher continued, "These are thoughtful answers. I really like it when we have deep discussions. Let me suggest another possibility. I think that we are being told that we too are supposed to do the things we praise God for doing. It's not just that we praise God. We also are taught to try to imitate the things we praise God for doing. So if God is *zokeif k'fufim*, we can try to do that too." Then the teacher said to them, "We Jews have a lovely idea called *hakarat hatov*. It means to recognize when someone does something good to you and to express your appreciation. If ever you were feeling *kafuf* and someone said something or did something that made you feel *zakuf*, the way that boy did for me, I want you to find that person and say *todah* [thank you]. Or, if you know someone who is *kafuf* and you think you can say something or do something that will help that person feel *zakuf*, I want you to try to do that. We can talk about it tomorrow."

Conclusions

One may wonder if the emphasis on *iyun t'filah*, elements of meaning making, crowded out issues of the skills and competencies needed to participate in a prayer service. It is our contention that this is a false dichotomy. Rather, building personal connections enhances motivation to participate and provides a context for skill learning. The following "unanticipated outcome" serves to illustrate this point.

When the intervention began, prayer instruction did not exist in the middle school (grades 6–8). There was much turnover in teachers and administration. The consultant did not work with the middle school except for an occasional meeting to satisfy the curiosity of some of the staff there about what was happening in the lower school. Work with the middle school began in earnest in 2007. Since then the faculty has been stable and is very cohesive. *Iyun t'filah* is now a staple of the curriculum, and pupil behavior (which in the past had been problematic, particularly in the seventh and eighth grades) has greatly improved. The middle school is blessed with many talented and creative teachers, and the prospects for the future are bright. Because work has been limited in the middle school, it is not easy to determine to what extent the improvements are in any way connected to my work with the lower school and the middle school. One anecdote is encouraging. In April 2008, the consultant received a call from the coordinator of *t'filah* in the middle school. It seems that the eighth graders were inadvertently left without adult supervision in the *beit midrash*, as both supervisors were, unbeknownst to each other, called away for legitimate reasons. When this was realized (about twenty minutes after the service was supposed to start), a teacher was dispatched to fill the supervisory gap. She found that the pupils had organized themselves, had chosen a *sh'liach tzibur* (prayer leader), and were davening with a good deal of spirit and behaving entirely appropriately. These were the first pupils to have been exposed to the intervention in the third grade in 2002. Perhaps, their exposure to the intervention and/or the new approach to *t'filah* in the middle school or both had some influence on the way they chose to respond to an unprecedented situation. It is also possible that, given the opportunity to assume ownership over the situation, the pupils took responsibility for ensuring that the quality of the experience would not be diminished.

Just as a school culture with regard to prayer is difficult to change, individual attitudes, beliefs, skills, and behaviors related to *t'filah* are likewise hard to impact. Just as schools need to exhibit readiness for change, those interested in enhancing the *t'filah* experience in Jewish educational settings need to foster the readiness among teachers, and students, that serves as an entry point to prayer. The ability to find personal meaning and to express personal doubts can be the gateway to this journey.

11

Kesher v'K'hilah:
Community, Friendship, and Jewish Engagement among Reform Youth

LAURA NOVAK WINER AND DANA SHEANIN

*F*EELING A CONNECTION *to and engagement with community and creating deep friendships are just two of the vital components of social-emotional health in youth. This chapter will explore the lessons learned by the Reform Movement regarding the role community and friendship play in building Jewish commitment for elementary through high school learners. It will chronicle the research the Union for Reform Judaism undertook from 2006 to 2009, including findings from the 2007 NFTY Survey and a review of literature on teens and Jewish engagement. We will highlight key lessons from the research and share implications for keeping youth meaningfully engaged and connected to Jewish community and Jewish life.*

The Reform Movement and its umbrella organization, the Union for Reform Judaism (URJ), have long been admired for their deep commitment to children, adolescents, and building vibrant communities. Many senior members of the Movement's professional and volunteer leadership in congregations and in Movement-wide institutions attribute their deep and abiding Jewish identity to time spent in North American Federation of Temple Youth (NFTY) or URJ camping and Israel programs as children and adolescents.

In spite of this, in 2006, the URJ leadership determined with its Portraits of Learning congregational survey that Reform Movement programs serve only 20 percent of the 65,000 eligible adolescents after they become *b'nei mitzvah* at age thirteen. Committed to raising that number exponentially, the leadership of the then-Lifelong Jewish Learning and Youth Departments undertook a series of research projects and exploratory studies to learn more about what teenagers are seeking during these critical years for Jewish identity and faith development and how our Movement might provide it.

The results of these studies pointed to the critical role of social-emotional learning (SEL) in our youth programs. In recent years, the term SEL has become popular in education circles. Through the URJ's research and development efforts, we have come to define SEL as the process of helping children develop fundamental skills for life effectiveness. Our definition evolved from the work of several experts in the field, including Ron Berger, Rachael Kessler, and Jeffrey Kress. Our understanding of SEL employs a "whole child" approach to learning. Frequently also referred to as 'character education' or 'building resilience', this approach prioritizes affective influences on learning. URJ staff came to realize that the development of strong friendships and enduring community matter deeply for Jewish identity development, perhaps more than any other aspect of our programming. The implications of this and the concrete relevance to individual congregations are the focus of this chapter.

Learning about Ourselves

Portraits of Learning

The URJ's data-gathering effort began with the 2006 Portraits of Learning study, which surveyed our full network of almost nine hundred congregations, achieving approximately a 3 percent response rate among congregations with schools. Portraits of Learning primarily considered classroom learning opportunities for children and families within congregational life. The study considered gender balance, teacher training and retention, outreach to interfaith families, and use of URJ curricula, among other areas.

One of the most significant findings of the study was the confirmation that the majority of teens in Reform congregations do not continue their involvement with congregational life beyond the age of *"bnei mitzvah."* While the rates of participation after age thirteen were higher in experiential educational settings, it became clear that the Movement needed to learn more about precisely what teenagers were seeking from Jewish involvement in order to better provide it.

In reviewing the Portraits of Learning results, Dr. Jonathan Woocher wrote:

> Beyond additional research I would suggest that the challenge for the Movement and for the entire community is to re-envision adolescent Jewish engagement and learning. We live in a time when teens lead very different lives than they did when most of our current frameworks were created. Although we certainly have tried to adapt these frameworks to the demographic, social, cultural and technological changes that have affected all of us, we still need to think far more radically than we have, both substantively and structurally, if we are to find effective ways to keep the vast majority of teens Jewishly engaged throughout their high school years.[1]

NFTY SURVEYS: 2006 AND 2010

Taking its cue from Dr. Woocher, as a logical next step, the URJ posed additional questions regarding our adolescent population. In 2006–7 the Movement undertook a survey of participants in its NFTY group, ages fourteen to eighteen, that sought to understand "how NFTYites experience the relationships, activities and community environment in their temple youth group." This survey produced rich data too varied in scope to fully recount in this chapter. However, among its key findings were the following:

- Teens who believed that many adults care about what happens to them tended to have higher scores on questions measuring future orientation. Researchers Michael Ben-Avie and Roberta Louis Goodman note in their analysis of the survey findings that such future orientation helps teens develop and articulate a sense of meaning and purpose to their life.[2]
- Fifty-six percent of teens surveyed agreed that there is at least one adult in their congregation to whom they can ask an embarrassing question.
- Only 5 percent agreed or strongly agreed that they try to hide their feelings from others in their temple youth group (TYG).
- Sixty-six percent of teens agreed that actively participating in t'filot (prayer) in their temple youth group is important.
- Fifty-eight percent of teens agreed that services in their temple youth group are run in a way that allows them to learn how to pray.

In an interpretive essay on the NFTY survey results, Ben-Avie and Goodman) conclude:

Temple youth groups provide an environment where teens can grow socially and emotionally, strengthen their identity as Jews, form relationships with peers and adults and feel part of a Jewish community. . . .. TYGs serve as a social network in which youth feel that the congregation is a place where throughout their lifetime they can safely seek support for their well being.[3]

In addition to social bonds, support for youth well-being also involves the ability to participate in worship experiences through which they can explore their relationship to the world around them, and think more about their own faith development—critical components of social-emotional growth.

In many ways, this assessment confirmed what URJ staff had long believed to be true. In an attempt to learn more about programmatic interests for long-range planning purposes, a follow-up NFTY survey was conducted in 2010, which echoed the previous survey's findings. Narrative responses to a question regarding why teens participate in NFTY elicited similar themes, such as the following:

- All my friends are in NFTY.
- I make my strongest friendships in NFTY.
- It is a place that I know I can just be myself and not be judged.
- I learn about myself and about my Judaism.

When asked about their interests for targeted summer programming, high school teens responded with strong levels of interest (approximately 50 percent) in programs that address their spiritual needs, Jewish identity, and desire to be with friends. They were less interested in programs such as entrepreneurship, Red Cross training, or university-level academic courses. To staff, it is clear that these interest areas indicate the teens' needs to articulate a sense of purpose to their lives and a way to engage in activities with friends who will support them in clarifying their values.

Respondents to the 2010 survey also included adult professionals and staff in congregations. When asked what they felt NFTY had to offer to its participants, again the narrative responses conveyed similar themes:

- Community of peers
- Socialization
- Acceptance
- Reform Jewish identity[4]

All of these findings regarding what teens are seeking from participation in NFTY have been considered in the creation of NFTY's Strategic Plan, completed in 2010.

Literature Review and Expert Interviews

Parallel to the analysis of the 2006 NFTY survey results, the URJ also began to explore the broader context in which adolescents live and experience congregational life. Staff sought to answer two primary questions:

1. Who are Jewish teenagers in 2007?
2. How can they best be served by the Reform Movement?

A two-stage process was developed to answer these questions. In stage 1, staff conducted an extensive review of literature on adolescents in both the Jewish and secular realm between the years of 2006 and 2007. More than thirty-five studies were reviewed, covering topics including mental health, school, time use, faith development, friends, family, and classroom and experiential education. The themes elicited from these studies were then used to design interview questions for stage 2. During this second stage, staff interviewed fifteen experts on adolescenc—both within and outside the Reform Movement including rabbis, educators, congregational youth professionals, camp directors, and mental health professionals, to elicit their perspective on critical issues facing Jewish adolescents.

KEY LESSONS FROM THE RESEARCH

From the information collected in the literature review and the expert interviews, five common themes underscoring the importance of attending to social-emotional learning emerged. These are as follows:

1. Many teens lack the skills to become *resilient*, identify their own strengths and weaknesses, and maintain self-confidence and excitement about the future.
2. Individuals born into Generation Y (and by extensions their parents) expect to be able to *tailor all academic and extracurricular experiences* to their specific needs, schedule, and interests.
3. A majority of teens (both Jewish and non-Jewish) say that *religion* is important to them, but a minority of them feel they are able to successfully access religious life.
4. The influence of *friends* is likely the most important factor in teen decisions about how and where to spend time. The second most important factor is parents.
5. Needs of middle and high schoolers vary not only by age but also by *gender identification*.

The lessons learned from the research effort have led the URJ to sharpen its focus on the task of nurturing the social-emotional development of youth. We began by confirming that a "whole child approach" aimed at building resilience and life skills should be a cornerstone of the Movement's education programs.

Over the past four years, staff has increasingly articulated that the programs and services provided to Reform congregations are prime opportunities to address critical developmental issues with our youth, and that the Movement can lead by example in doing so. The URJ came to understand that *how* we teach our young people is just as important as *what* we teach them, regardless of age. Finally, while the research focused primarily on teens, staff across departments realized that the implications of the research apply to serving younger children as well.

If we are to be successful in engaging our teens post–*b'nei mitzvah* and raising Jewish adults characterized by *menschlichkeit*, changes must be made to elementary and pre–*b'nei mitzvah* learning and engagement to strengthen the social-emotional health and skills of youth from early childhood forward. As Melissa Frey, director of URJ Kutz Camp and associate director of NFTY, has articulated during staff training, "Every child is the most important person in the world to someone." This message bears repeating through all stages of program development.

Social-Emotional Learning as a Cornerstone

To be sure, the URJ employs a wide range of strategies to engage and retain youth in our Movement and to build Reform Jewish identity. As a result of our research efforts, we are convinced that proactively attending to the social-emotional development and well-being of our learners must be a cornerstone of each of our core strategies: (1) classroom education, (2) camping, (3) NFTY, and (4) professional development.

CLASSROOM EDUCATION

The URJ's *CHAI Curriculum: Learning for Jewish Life* is a curriculum core that explores big ideas about Torah, *avodah* (service), and *g'milut chasadim* (works of loving-kindness) through twenty-seven lessons at each grade level. The lessons include various modes of small group learning, to allow learners to get to know one another and develop relationships through the religious school years. Levels K–7 were developed prior to 2007. However, both the structure and content of *CHAI* Level 8, which was piloted during the 2010–11 school year, have benefited tremendously from the URJ's new familiarity with the tools of social-emotional learning theory.

From the outset, URJ staff and curriculum authors articulated that *CHAI* 8 needed to adopt an entirely different structure, both from the levels that came before it, and from those that will come after, in acknowledgment of the unique needs of eighth-grade learners.

Recognizing the critical role of autonomy at this developmental stage, *CHAI* 8 offers learners more control over how their classes are organized and taught, and over what topics they study. It is structured in units, each with a "Launch lesson" to help educators become attuned to developmental needs and explore learner interests for further study. The introductory launch lesson, "Building Bridges," "is designed to create a classroom environment that will help the teacher establish learner input, show the learners their input will be taken seriously, and assist in putting forth possible topics for study."[5]

The launch lesson titled "Bless" provides an illustration of the approach taken by the URJ's new materials. In this lesson, the educator is asked to introduce "three areas of theological thought: spirituality, faith, and belief" and is provided with background information regarding James Fowler's six stages of faith development. The stage of a typical eighth-grade learner is described in the background material, and educators are encouraged to use the "Bless" launch lesson to provide age-appropriate opportunities for learners to see options, raise questions, and think through ideas about faith. The intent is to enable learners to feel comfortable thinking and talking about these issues with trusted adults and peers in their congregation, and to see the congregation as a safe place to explore ideas they are already wrestling with in their daily lives.

Furthermore, in a departure from prior curricular materials, the *CHAI 8 Guidebook* contains a detailed introduction exploring the intellectual, social, emotional, and physical development of eighth graders. It also includes suggestions for teachers adapted from the secular literature on social-emotional learning, addressing how to help learners learn cooperatively, find relevance in what they study, decompress from their daily lives, and build relationships to establish classroom community.

For many years, eighth grade has been a challenge for Reform education. Viewed as post–*b'nei mitzvah*, and generally categorized with high school programs, yet often not specifically geared to the needs of learners who are not developmentally ready for high school. Initial response to our new *CHAI* 8 materials has been positive, and the potential exists for the curriculum to reshape the way Reform congregations think about the social-emotional needs of middle school learners over the next several years. With the introduction of *CHAI* 8, congregations are encouraged to consider not just Jewish content, but the total experience of learners at religious school.

Following publication of the new curriculum, the URJ plans to offer training for congregational educators, designed to support their facility with the material. Topics planned for training include: how and why these materials differ from previous curricula, how to create a safe and effective learning environment that encourages learners to fully engage, techniques for building classroom community, and how to identify, recruit, and retain appropriate teachers for middle school learners.

CAMPING

The Reform Movement's network of thirteen summer camps serves close to ten thousand children and teens across North America each summer. The camps have begun to make changes to their programs and staff in order to better attend to the social-emotional needs of their campers. These innovations reflect several of the key lessons learned from the research.

Camper Reflection

Several camps now have designated time each week—often on Shabbat afternoon—for campers to engage in personal reflection on their experience and about the week that has passed. At Camp Newman in California, campers complete an age-appropriate reflection page that helps them articulate to the staff what challenges they are facing at camp and, what successes they have experienced and seek guidance on questions they may have. Younger campers who may not be able to articulate their feelings in words complete smiley faces to express how they are feeling. Older campers are given the time and space to write out their reflections and feelings in narrative form. Senior staff members review the camper reflections and follow up with individual campers who may have expressed challenges or issues of concern. At the same time, cabin counselors complete their own set of reflections on an "Each and Everyone" sheet. The combination of the camper and counselor reflections helps the senior staff anticipate problems or identify issues that may be brewing before they become too intense. There is a commitment from the staff that every individual concern is addressed, each in a manner appropriate for that unique situation.

At Camp Harlam in Pennsylvania, Shabbat morning incorporates a similar exercise. At the conclusion of Shabbat *Shacharit* services, each *eidah* (session) engages in an age-appropriate Torah study. Following Torah study, each cabin breaks away for its own *sichah* (conversation) time in which they continue the Torah discussion as well as spend time reflecting on the week that has passed and the week that lies ahead. Campers have the opportunity to share with their cabin mates and counselors concerns or challenges they may be facing. This provides an opportunity for the cabin to work through any relationship issues, group dynamics issues, or other challenges they may be facing.

Exercises such as these help campers learn to identify and articulate their own successes and challenges. They also help build resilience in the campers by giving them permission to ask for help, resolve problems, and celebrate successes.

Niche Programming

As indicated by the research, the youth attending camp today have many choices and expect to be able to tailor each summer experience to their unique needs and interests. All of the URJ summer camps have—and have had for many years—a component of their programs that cater to the individual interests of the campers, such as *chugim* (electives), or specific time slots in which campers can choose from a number of different types of activities.

The URJ Kutz Camp in New York has structured its high school summer program to mirror a university-based model in which campers choose both a major and a minor for their learning time at camp. Major choices have expanded in recent years to include newer interest areas such as digital media design, *Hagshama* (mind, body, and soul), and *Teva* (outdoor adventures), while still maintaining traditional offerings such as youth group leadership training, Judaic studies, song leading, and creative arts. Campers learn independence and responsibility by managing their time during the day. During the evening they participate in cabin or all-camp programs that bring teens together as a community and allow friendships to flourish across differing interest areas.

Recent years have also seen the expansion of specific niche pro-grams for campers. Summer 2010 marked the opening summer of the Six Points Sports Academy in North Carolina, the Movement's newest camp. Six Points offers both high-level sports training and a Reform Movement camping experience much like other URJ camps. In es-tablishing a sports camp, the Movement is now able to serve campers who might not have previously chosen a Jewish summer camp because of a greater degree of commitment to their advancement as athletes. Whereas in the past families might have had to make a choice between a sports camp and a Jewish camp, now they do not. This enables youth to honor multiple interests and parents to offer the access to Jewish com-munity and learning they seek for their children.

Gender-Focused Programming

Almost all of the URJ's summer camps incorporate some aspect of age-appropriate gender-based programming. Some camps have introduced separate gender groupings for worship once or twice during a session. Most camps offer an evening of single-gender programming during each session in which girls engage in learning together with their female staff while the boys engage in parallel learning with their male staff. Often supported by visiting rabbinic and education faculty, these programs provide a safe venue for the campers to discuss some of the messages from mainstream culture they grapple with about what it means to be a girl/woman or boy/man and learn what counter-messages Judaism has to offer. Teen campers may have the opportunity to talk about chal-lenges they face in developing relationships with peers of both genders. Several camps make use of the URJ's highly regarded *Sacred Choices: Adolescent Relationships and Sexual Ethics* curriculum, which includes a variety of approaches to addressing these topics. Senior camp staff note that a key challenge of gender-based programming is ensuring that staff are sensitive enough to the emerging gender identification processes that campers are experiencing to avoid potential for miseducation or feelings of exclusion among youth questioning their gender identity.

Camp Coleman in Georgia has been at the forefront of addressing the gender issue, particularly with its male staff. The leadership of Coleman has developed a unique training for its staff that helps male counselors consider what it means to be a man and explore how to be effective role models for their campers. Since 2004, Coleman has run a program for male staff in which they select a group of leaders among the staff to participate in Jewish text study and personal storytelling. The environment is one in which all participants are encouraged to "authentically communicate" and tell their story about their growth into manhood. In telling their stories to each other, these young men challenge and reconsider not only how they behave but also how they see themselves. They are "given permission to be real, to show emotions, to make mistakes, to reset cultural norms and expectations for what it means to be a man."[6]) A parallel program is run for the female staff in which the young women focus on shedding and resetting cultural expectations about what it means to be a woman and developing a sense of acceptance for oneself. After participating in these programs and hearing each other's stories, staff are strongly encouraged to tell their stories to their campers as a way of modeling these newfound understandings about identity to the younger campers who look up to them.

Animals at Camp

In many Reform camp settings, campers have regular opportunities to interact with camp pets, such as dogs, horses, and other farm animals. We have found this type of interaction to be particularly meaningful for campers experiencing homesickness. At Olin-Sang-Ruby Union Institute in Wisconsin, campers have responsibility to help care for animals in camp, including goats, sheep, chickens, and rabbits. Campers help feed and water the animals, and clean out their pens. This has helped the homesick campers feel a sense of purpose to being at camp and to distract them from homesickness.

In 2009 Camp Newman in California partnered with a non-profit animal rescue organization that helps place abandoned animals in foster or permanent homes. The camp adopted two puppies, with the goal of teaching the campers about fostering, and hopefully finding permanent homes for the puppies at the end of the summer. At the beginning of the summer, campers helped name the puppies. Throughout the summer, campers had the opportunity to play with the puppies and encounter them over the course of the day. Camp Newman associate director Ari Vared explains that "simply being around the dogs helped change a camper's day. Dogs don't judge. All they do is love. Homesick or troubled campers, when given time to play with the dogs simply opened up back to them."[7] At the end of the summer, camper families who expressed interest in adopting the dogs participated in a lottery to determine who would adopt the dogs.

Designated Camper Support Staff
Several camps have developed staff or faculty positions specifically focused on addressing the mental health needs of the camp community. The primary goal of these faculty members is to help all children be successful at camp, given varying strengths, abilities, and challenges. While called by different names in the various camps (*Nefesh* faculty, Camper Care team, inclusion coordinators), those who hold these positions are primarily professionals with training in social work, psychology, and other mental health professions, or younger exceptional staff who are pursuing careers in the mental health fields. These faculty members assist the camp staff in addressing challenges they may be facing with campers, including group dynamics in the cabin or friendship issues. They may also meet with individual campers facing specific challenges and monitor campers who have special learning needs or developmental disabilities. If camp staff ultimately determine an individual camper cannot remain at camp, these faculty members are appropriately trained to help the camper recognize the successes they have accomplished in spite of being unable to complete the camp session. Such professional support provides a level of expertise that can be invaluable to the counseling and programming staff at camp, many of whom do not yet have the life experience or professional skills to effectively deal with challenging situations such as these.

Residential campers have the daily opportunity to learn many of the life skills they need to successfully navigate the real world—truly social-emotional learning at its best. The Reform Movement camps recognize the impact the camp experience can have on each individual camper and thus takes these learning opportunities very seriously. As T-shirts provided by one Movement camp have aptly expressed it: "Camp is life, the rest is just details."

NFTY

As the research described above indicates, friendship is at the heart of NFTY. However, for teens who seek new or deepened involvement, the road to belonging is not always easy. The rituals, language, and culture associated with NFTY can be taken for granted by veteran participants, who are not always aware of the exclusionary environment that may result. With the URJ's heightened awareness of the need to attend to our teens' social-emotional development has come intentional focus on creating a more open and welcoming NFTY community for all teens, regardless of level or length of involvement.

Senior NFTY staff has begun to work closely with youth leadership to raise awareness of these issues and explore how each region can ensure that teens are welcoming. Regional youth boards and advisors have discussed how to balance the needs of the individual with those of the community, and the teens have begun to use new language in discussing these challenges. As a result they are more open to increasing participation, and more thoughtful about how to do that, including, in some regions, integrating rising eighth-graders into end-of-year NFTY events.

PROFESSIONAL DEVELOPMENT

In what is arguably the most significant impact of the Movement's efforts to date, the theory behind social-emotional learning has now become part of the lexicon of Reform professional development. Today, many congregational educators, youth professionals, camp directors, and others throughout the system who were not previously familiar with the concept of SEL understand this term, and have begun to consider what it means in their unique institutions. The URJ has provided training for these individuals in a variety of settings.

NFTY has begun to think differently about the staff they employ and how to train them to be sensitive to helping youth form and nurture their friendships. The NFTY system employs regional advisors for each of its nineteen geographic regions and strategizes carefully about their training both in terms of orientation of new staff and ongoing skill building. A recent effort to update NFTY regional advisor job descriptions included the articulation of core competencies, several of which speak directly to the role these advisors play in supporting the emotional needs of youth. Core competencies on which advisors are evaluated annually include honesty and integrity, a positive and joyful attitude, and the ability to be a team player. The intent is to identify staff members who have the ability to be approachable, and to ensure that they serve as positive role models. Additionally, URJ leadership has made a commitment to hiring staff with stronger professional training and to creating full-time positions that enable these staff members to devote more hours to building sustainable relationships over a teen's middle and high school years.

URJ director of teen engagement (and coauthor of this chapter) Rabbi Laura Novak Winer writes:

> We need to be paying greater attention to who we hire to serve in these key roles and how they are trained to do their jobs. While vital, youth programming is not only about fun, making friends and building a youth community. . . . It is also about learning and growth. It is about education. It is about, among other things, learning what it means to be a member of a Jewish community and to live a life guided by Jewish ethics, values and the teachings of our tradition. When we consider the developmental impacts of our youth programming, . . . we see that those who work with our youth would benefit from training in child and adolescent development, Jewish education, group dynamics and related fields in order to better provide the richest environment for our youth to learn and grow through their engagement. The *NFTY Survey* showed that "only 53 percent [of teens] agreed that 'my advisor pushes me to accomplish more than I had ever thought possible.'" We need the adults who work with our youth to educate, inspire and support our youth. We need to train them in how to do that effectively and appropriately.[8]

In order to reach beyond youth professionals, during 2008–9 several of the URJ's youth and education specialists implemented workshops across the country on incorporating the theory behind social-emotional learning into various learning environments. On the West Coast, congregational educators participated in a full-day seminar that adapted secular materials on character education and introduced numerous tools for creating a classroom environment that nurtures the growth of teens and pre-teens. Educators worked in teams, and left the seminar with specific approaches they wished to try, including *chevruta* study, journaling, and exploration of *midot* (character measures). Variations on this workshop were also conducted for rabbis at the Central Conference of American Rabbis (CCAR) and Pacific Association of Reform Rabbis (PARR) conferences during that year, as well as for the National Association of Temple Educators (NATE).

Also in 2009, the URJ hosted a national think tank for eighty congregational educators, titled "Reach High," designed to encourage conversation about and innovation in post–*b'nei mitzvah* education. A primary goal of this conference was to familiarize our educators with the utility of social-emotional learning theory, and to give them a chance to explore with their colleagues how to apply it to their teaching environments. In addition to learning more about the needs of adolescents in general, and about Jewish identity formation, educators were exposed to new approaches to post–*b'nei mitzvah* education incorporating key components designed to nurture the social-emotional development of learners, such as recognition of important life-cycle events, curricular choice, and thoughtful relationship building with mentor adults.

Already, attendees of the event have begun to develop innovative programming to help build resilience among their youth. For example, at Temple Beth Elohim in Wellesley, Massachusetts, after the conference:

> We began to ask whether our ideas about creating holy community work for teens....We began to formulate an idea to create a system to provide us with tools to foster and maintain relationships, to enhance our students' sense of belonging, and our staff members' ability to get to know teens really well. As part of our new Jewish Journey process, each teen, ideally beginning in sixth grade, will have at a minimum a one-on-one connection with at least one other adult staff member at TBE who will meet regularly with the teen to learn about his or her Jewish journey....This process will continue through high school or perhaps through college.[9]

In recognition of the critical role parents play in helping children build relationship, and the importance of honoring life-cycle events, Congregation Achduth Vesholom in Fort Wayne, Indiana, realized the following:

> The most important message [we] walked away with is that we need to engage our families at a much earlier age....A few of the suggestions...[that] have been brought back to my congregation [include] sending a weekly email to families to give them something to discuss on the way to religious school, hosting a parent breakfast with the rabbi once a month...organizing a ceremony to celebrate with fourth graders

and their parents, presenting them with their own copy of *Mishkan T'filah* (the new Reform Movement prayer book).[10]

Finally, in 2010 the URJ developed a new *Planning Guide for Teen Engagement* as a resource for congregations interested in exploring the strengths and weaknesses of their post–*b'nei mitzvah* program. The *Planning Guide* includes a series of six discussion modules, that enable a congregation's volunteer and professional leadership to look critically at a wide variety of programmatic components. One of these modules focuses entirely on opportunities for social-emotional learning. Through a series of detailed questions, this module asks congregations to assess the following:

- How much deliberate attention is paid to the social-emotional needs of learners in congregational programming
- How the congregation actively supports friendship building among learners
- How adult mentors among clergy, teachers, and lay leadership are identified and nurtured

FUTURE AREAS TO ADDRESS

While our progress has been steady in the areas above, we have also identified three areas in which work is still needed. These include the following:

- Revision of our existing *CHAI Curriculum: Learning for Jewish Life* K–7 materials, to incorporate elements of social-emotional learning theory
- Strategic evaluation and redesign of junior youth groups, to effectively encourage friendship building
- Development of support and education networks for parents during the elementary through high school years

Conversations are already under way about each of these areas, as staff strive to learn from congregations about efforts presently under way, while also experimenting with new programmatic initiatives.

Implications for Educational Settings

It is through cooperation (working together in groups), companionship (coming together as friends), compassion (revealing sympathetic concern for others and desire to help them), and communion (moments when we let go of preconceived ideas about each other and communicate as openly and authentically as we can) that spirituality is nurtured in the classroom[11]

The lessons learned by the URJ can be applied to many of the institutional settings in which Jewish youth engage in Jewish learning. The URJ hopes congregations and other educational settings will consider implementing some of the following approaches in congregational, formal, and experiential learning settings in order to support the development of healthy, happy, youth.

BUILD COMMUNAL CONNECTIONS

- **Create opportunities for youth to connect with adults who are not their parents.** As was suggested by the findings of the NFTY surveys, youth who can connect with adults other than their parents find valuable role models, mentors, and teachers. They identify safe people to talk to about their fears, concerns, challenges, and successes. Invite youth to interact with adults in the congregation/community through intergenerational programs, Torah study, *chavurot*, or even a Jewish Journeys program such as the one described above. Create mother/daughter or father/son book groups, retreats, or movie nights through which youth can connect with their own parents and guardians as well as other adults in the community.
- **Help younger youth and families build friendships.** These relationships need to be nurtured by the congregation. They do not grow organically. Develop extended family learning opportunities, *chavurot*, and social programs for families in specific grade levels.
- **Incorporate community service.** *Tikkun olam*,[12] a value in and of itself, also provides outstanding modeling of compassion and fairness. These values can be linked back to classroom relationships. Consider your definition of community. It can be as simple as

the classroom or as broad as *Am Yisrael* (the people of Israel). Be aware that to build empathy, community service should invove: preparation, action, reflection, and demonstration of learning.

- **Create opportunities for youth to share their passion and skills with each other and with the congregation.** Youth with musical skills can be invited to participate in the congregational music ensemble, or the choir. Youth with an affinity for Torah chanting should be encouraged to do so often. Those with a passion for social justice, serve on the social action committee. Web design, videography and blogging are all skills that youth may show greater proficiency in than adults; invite them to work on the congregation's website, digital media, and social networking.

- **Strengthen and support youth groups for upper elementary, middle school, and high school youth.** Provide more opportunities for youth to engage in socialization activities and make friends, beginning in elementary school. Build Jewish experiential learning programs into youth group events. Be aware that youth groups that incorporate Jewish learning and conversation into the socialization activities help youth create deeper connections with each other and with Judaism. Be mindful of the benefits of youth groups for young learners, as well as teens.

CLASSROOM/CURRICULAR ENHANCEMENTS

- **Create learning options in the curriculum.** Create Jewish independent education plans for learners. Allow youth and families to choose from among learning options. Offer *chugim* during religious school. Break the learning year into trimesters and allow learners to rotate subjects or teachers a couple times during the year. Broaden the types of options of congregational engagement that "count" toward learning credit, such as attending worship services, participating in a NFTY regional conclave, participating in a congregational social action program and so on.

- **Develop a class mission statement and framework of expectations.** Involve each class in the writing of a class mission statement. Different than rules, this allows learners to explore their purpose for being in class. Learners may also write individual mission statements, which can be a basis for journaling.

Invite big questions about what has meaning to learners: Why am I here? What am I passionate about? What do I wonder about?

- **Utilize learner check-in.** Allow learners to decompress about their day or week at the start of each class. Invite them to share "what's great and what's not so great," keeping in mind that the things that may seem inconsequential to adults are crucial to them. Ask learners to share joyful events, to celebrate them, and to express gratitude about them, even if they have to talk first about what they are not grateful for. Provide an "attitude book,", a place in which learners are invited to drop a note before class telling the teacher what attitude they brought with them today— and follow up as needed. Or let them sit quietly to consider (in a developmentally appropriate way) how they are doing physically, intellectually, spiritually, and emotionally.

- **Focus on *midot* (character measures).** Consider focusing units of time on exploration of character measures or habits: a virtue a week, a month, or a yearly theme. Use *midot* to reinforce developmental tasks, for example, orderliness in kindergarten learners, effort first grade, kindness second grade and so on. Use biographical material to raise questions such as: What strengths of character enabled them to achieve what they did? What obstacles were faced? Display an inspirational quote at the front of the room each day.

- **Engage in peer-facilitated learning in small groups around Jewish texts.** Give a group a text to study, guidelines for conversation, and an outcome to produce (e.g., a sentence, a cheer, a skit, a poser...). Studying Jewish texts together creates a level playing field that does not exist in a math class, on the soccer field, or during recess at school. When young people are asked to share in depth their thoughts and feelings about Torah, God, Jewish values, or prayer, they create meaningful connections with each other. While it is beneficial for adults to monitor the conversation, it is important to give the youth space to engage with each other in a peer-directed manner.

- **Hold class meetings.** Begin each day with a class meeting where successes are shared and conflicts are explored and resolved by the class. Use the class meeting to explore *midot*. Consider structuring the meeting with four components including: a greeting activity, individual sharing, a group song or reading, and a daily message.

- **Provide time for journaling and other artistic expression.** Give learners space to write regularly about something that matters to them. Provide a journaling queston, or theme, such as a particular *midah* the class is working on. Use journaling to allow learners to address qualities they believe are essential to good character, or to a good learning experience. Ask learners to write on: what they did well today, what they wish they had done differently, what was hard to talk about, whether someone said anything to upset them. Allow learners to create themed original work through fiction, poetry, illustrations, computer presentations, photography, drama, or movement.
- **Allow for project-based learning.** Look for opportunities for learners to engage in individual or collaborative learning based on their own interests. This is a particularly useful tool for middle school learners who are seeking independence.

REFRAME ADULT ROLES

- **Consider carefully the qualities desired in the adults selected to work with youth.** The adults who work with youth as teachers, youth group professionals, and others should be those who can simultaneously act as mentor, coach, listener, trusted advisor, and guide. Select people with whom youth can easily connect, talk openly, and trust for support and direction. Provide ongoing training and professional development to the teachers and professional staff of the congregations to enable them to increase their skills and expand their resources in these areas.
- **Model listening and questioning skills.** Practice questioning learners ahead of time about key issues, and if they don't have an answer, or have an incomplete answer, suggest they take a few minutes to think about it and come back to them. Allow silence after questions have been asked. Let silence stir the learners to think and pay attention to what they are feeling. Develop a classroom culture that values participation and effort—make it cool to raise your hand and care about the conversation.

- **Pay attention to transitions.** Be aware of learners' needs and interactions immediately before and after class, during breaks, and during small group time. Share the agenda each day: What are we going to learn today? Why is it important to learn? How are we going to study it? Invite learners to share with you what you are doing as a teacher that supports them, or makes it hard for them to be part of the community. Be aware both of the idea that souls cannot thrive at rapid speed, and of the reality that our learners lives allow for very little transition time. Address peer cruelty immediatey—take social concerns seriously.
- **Be attentive to life events.** Make an effort to be aware of what is happening in learners' home lives and to check in with them at difficult times; keep other congregational staff informed about them. Consider a school or class *r'fuah sh'leimah* committee, and create a culture of outreach to learners who are absent, sick, or facing challenges. Create a compliments box in which learners are invited to place anonymous compliments about others, to be read aloud at the end of class. Find opportunities to meet with children individually to talk, either during individual project time, before or after class, or at recess.

Conclusion

As the URJ's professional and volunteer leadership come to understand more about the theory behind social-emotionl learning, the role of friendship building in Jewish identity, and the rapidly changing needs of modern adolescents, we are reminded of the text from Psalms 1 v. 22: "The stone that the builders forgot has become the cornerstone." Certainly prior to the Portraits of Learning study in 2006, the Reform Movement had not forgotten the role it plays in building thoughtful, emotionally mature, Jewish adults. However, the research effort has given us new language and created a new context that acknowledges, as Ben Avie and Goodman write, "everyone is a child developer."[13]) With this new reminder before us, the URJ hopes to redouble its efforts to engage, inspire, and enrich the children of today's congregations, who will become tomorrow's Jewish leaders.

12

Ask Jethro:

Two Chicago Campus Initiatives to Reach and Assess Jewish Emerging Adults

Scott Aaron,
Josh Feigelson,
and Daniel Libenson

EVER SINCE the 1990 National Jewish Population Study[1] showed a record high percentage of intermarried Jews coupled with a record low percentage of affiliation, serious efforts have been made toward better understanding the sense of Jewish identity and community of the current Jewish young adult generation, often referred to as the Millennials.[2] Research shows that life experiences, rather than institutional engagement, are the portals to reaching these Millennials, who place a greater emphasis on Jewish meaning rather than membership. Three important contemporary fields of study have come to the fore of our understanding why this is the case: emerging adulthood, experiential education, and Jewish peoplehood. These fields have changed the way we understand the stage of adult life that encompasses ages eighteen to thirty, and Jewish organizations have begun to adapt their work to meet young adults where they are rather than wait for them to affiliate with the larger community. Knowledge gleaned from these fields has impacted training and programming provided to its affiliate staff by Hillel: The Foundation for Jewish Campus Life, the largest agency to serve Millennials in North America).[3] This chapter will focus on two local programs that have been incorporating the lessons learned from these fields to reaching and impacting the Jewish Millennials they serve on their respective campuses. These initiatives, at the Hillels at the University of Chicago and Northwestern University, will be used as a basis from which to draw lessons for the field of Jewish education as a whole.

Emerging Adulthood

Emerging adulthood is a substratum of developmental Psychology, a field that developed over the course of the twentieth century. Along with foundational theories of development that span the life course, such as Jean Piaget's stages of cognitive development, Erik Erikson's stages of psychosocial development, and Lawrence Kohlberg's stages of moral development, theoreticians, including Arthur Chickering and William Perry, among others),[4] have specifically focused on the developmental stage of young adulthood, encompassing roughly the ages of eighteen to thirty). In 2000, a refined theory of development for this age group was introduced by Dr. Jeffrey Jensen Arnett of Clark University, who coined the term "emerging adulthood" and explained

> Having left the dependency of childhood and adolescence, and having not yet entered the enduring responsibilities that are normative in adulthood, emerging adults often explore a variety of possible life directions in love, work, and worldview.[5]

Arnett noticed that in technologically advanced societies such as North America's, increased amounts of education are required to advance in the workforce. Hence, adults who once entered the workforce at age twenty-two with a bachelor's degree now tend to extend their time in school to pursue master's degrees and even doctorates. They are accordingly delaying traditional life experiences that accompany full adult independence such as marriage, child-bearing, home acquisition, and membership in religious and cultural institutions. They are not embracing commitment in the same way as previous generations, and this transience is leading to less of a personal interest in affiliation with mainstream communal institutions such as houses of worship, social/fraternal organizations, and political parties. Emerging adults are more reflective than previous generations, seeking more personal meaning for their lives, a characteristic exemplified in an increase in social justice activities. They also seek a spiritual understanding of the world but are reticent to be bound by a religious system. Socially, they seek intensive, intimate relationships with a diverse range of peoples and are skeptical of broad moral assumptions and large cultural and political institutions. They think in shorter time-spans—academic cycles and amount of hours expected of them to achieve a goal—and are generally unwilling to make long-term commitments beyond the completion of their academic milestones. In short, in contrast to those in this age range in previous generations, the longer path to maturation of today's emerging adults is marked by more intensive social and personal experimentation, change, and risk than previous generations, with an emphasis on short-term impact rather than long-term consequences. It is important to note that there is currently little data published in this area specifically focusing on Jewish emerging adults, and what does exist often addresses religious, as opposed to ethnic or cultural, aspects of Jewish identity. Hence the work being done with Jewish emerging adults based on developmental theory is based on extrapolated information rather than a solid amount of tested and specific data.

Experiential Education

Experiential education has been recognized as an important mechanism for education in general over the last century, but the Jewish community has intentionally embraced it as such in only the last two decades.[6] In 1991, Dr. Barry Chazan published an influential article titled "What Is Informal Jewish Education?" in which he demonstrated how informal education is applied in the Jewish community and proposed how it could be improve).[7] His article was published just as the results of the 1990 National Jewish Population Study mentioned earlier were being absorbed by the community. After much soul searching, the community attributed these results to decades of poor supplementary Jewish education, and a flurry of resources and effort was put into alternatives to supplementary education, including informal Jewish education experiences that were always known to be impactful but were not necessarily understood as educational, namely, camping, youth groups, and Israel travel. In 2003, Chazan updated his theory in an on-line article titled "The Philosophy of Informal Jewish Education."[8] In this article, Chazan laid out eight defining characteristics of successful Informal Jewish educatio.:

1. Person-centered Jewish Education
2. The centrality of experience
3. A curriculum of Jewish experiences and values
4. An interactive process
5. The group experience
6. The culture of "Jewish" education
7. Education that engages
8. Informal Jewish education's holistic educator

Synthesizing these characteristics, Chazan refined his definition of informal Jewish education:

> Informal Jewish education is aimed at the personal growth of Jews of all ages. It happens through the individual's actively experiencing a diversity of Jewish moments and values that are regarded as worthwhile. It works by creating venues, by developing a total educational culture, and by co-opting the social context. It is based on a curriculum of Jewish values and experiences that is presented in a dynamic and flexible manner. As an activity, it does not call for any one venue but may happen in a variety of settings. It evokes pleasurable feelings and memories. It requires Jewishly literate educators with a "teaching" style that is highly interactive and participatory, who are willing to make maximal use of self and personal lifestyle in their educational work.

While Chazan's theoretical construct was initially applied to Jewish educational programming for youth, it was not until 2004 that a major endeavor was specifically designed around this theory for emerging Jewish adults, through the implementation of the Birthright Israel program. This effort, with Dr. Chazan as the founding education director, sought to connect Jewish emerging adults to Israel through a free ten-day travel experience to Israel. While the actual long-standing impact of the trip on participants' long-range Jewish and Zionist identity is still being analyzed and debated, it is clear that there is a positive behavioral and attitudinal effect from the trip experience on the participant.[10] Jewish communal agencies that work with large numbers of Jewish emerging adults now understand the value of training their staff in informal education theory and techniques and actively craft their programmatic work as informal education experiences.

Jewish Peoplehood

Jewish peoplehood is also a relatively new sociological prism through which to view today's Jewish community. Drs. Ezra Kopelowitz and Ari Engleberg, leading researchers on Jewish peoplehood, note:

> The idea of "the Jewish People" is ancient, but the concept of Jewish Peoplehood is new, both to the English and Hebrew languages.... The intensive use by Jewish organizations of the Peoplehood concept and intellectual interest in the topic in almost all cases began no earlier than 2004.... [I]t is enough to note that major organizations such as the United Jewish Communities, the UJA New York Federation, the Jewish Agency for Israel, the Israel Ministry of Education, the Diaspora Museum, the Avi Chai Foundation, the American Jewish Committee and many other smaller organizations are either making the Peoplehood concept into an organizing principle in their organizations or initiating high profile programming with an explicit focus on Jewish Peoplehood—all since 2004).[11]

What exactly Jewish peoplehood entails is debated among scholars, but Kopelowitz and Engleberg have described three principles that are generally accepted as definitive criteria.

1. **A multi-dimensional experience**—The concept of Jewish peoplehood assumes an understanding of Jewish belonging that is
   multidimensional.
2. **Rejection of strong ideology**—Strong ideological frameworks that
   overemphasize one dimension of the larger Jewish experience are
   not an acceptable starting point for understanding how individuals
   connect to the Jewish people.
3. **Connections between Jews, not Jewish identity**—Those concerned with the Jewish peoplehood concept do not focus on the
   identity of individuals, but rather on the nature of connections
   between Jews. The concern is with common elements and frameworks that enable Jews to connect with one another both emotionally and socially.[12]

Critics of Jewish peoplehood often dismiss it as a secular concept
that rejects religious identity, but we see that as inaccurate. Rather
peoplehood expands the concept of the Jewish people to encompass
all theologically Jewish identities as well as non-theological identities,
and reorients the Jewish community on a social spectrum rather than
a religious hierarchy. It is allowing the community at large to envision
itself as holistic and organic rather than dichotomous (e.g., observant/
non-observant, Israeli/Diaspora, left/right,) so that the entirety of the
Jewish community is equalized. This can help the Jewish community
contextualize historical arguments of the last century such as denomi-
nationalism, intermarriage, support for Israel, and gender roles into
part of a larger communal gestalt rather than litmus tests for authentic
communal membership. In terms of Jewish emerging adults, Jewish
peoplehood has allowed Jewish educational and social institutions to
reframe their work with this population so that Jewish observance is
not the primary filter for Jewish identity processing and growth.

The development of the two program models described here has been
influenced by lessons learned from these three fields of study. As the
reader will see, both programs have incorporated the developmental
reality of emerging adulthood, the creativity of experiential education,
and the permission of Jewish peoplehood to craft unique and successful mechanisms to meet and support Jewish emerging adults on their
respective campuses where they are in their life course. While neither
program is a universal solution for every Jewish emerging adult's needs,

they both offer pertinent entryways for Jewish emerging adults under-going their own personal definition process.

The Ask Big Questions Initiative
at Northwestern University

One of the leading thinkers in moral development for emerging adults, Sharon Daloz Parks has persuasively written that the years of emerging adulthood are marked by an exploration of some of life's biggest questions: Who am I? Where do I come from? Where am I going? Who will be my partners? Who or what will be my legacy?

> Typically, in the years from seventeen to thirty a distinctive mode of meaning-making can emerge, one that has certain adult characteristics but understandably lacks others. This mode of meaning-making includes (1) becoming critically aware of one's own composing of reality, (2) self-consciously participating in an ongoing dialogue toward truth, and (3) cultivating a capacity to respond—to act—in ways that are satisfying and just.

The Ask Big Questions (ABQ) Initiative was developed with the vision that Hillel could contribute to a campus culture in which these questions animated campus life. If the university were a place where *all* students were asking these questions, then Jewish students would be more likely to engage with Jewish tradition—either through their own initiative or through active engagement strategies implemented by Hillel professionals. As students unpacked the big questions of their lives, they would look for sources of meaning to help them, and Hillel would be the place for them to find guidance and partnership. In this sense the inspiration for the initiative was none other than Moses, who had the presence of mind to look at the Burning Bush and ask a question about it. The initial aim of ABQ was simply to help students ask the questions that Jewish tradition is ready and able to help them explore.

The story of ABQ begins in 2005, when Fiedler Hillel at Northwestern University began a new method of public engagement with the university and the Jewish community. Hillel staff started hanging banners on its building ann around campus. The banners literally asked big questions, and were usually timed to be meaningful within the context of the Jewish, secular, or university calendar. For instance, at Rosh Hashanah (which was also fell near the beginning of the academic term) a banner asked, "What will you do better this year?" At Thanksgiving a banner read, "What are you thankful for?" And during fraternity and sorority recruitments a banner inquired, "Who do you belong to?"

The purpose of the banners was to position Hillel as an asker of meaningful questions. Hillel's web address was printed on them, but there was no specific follow-up to the banners on the Hillel website or through programming. As time went on, the banners gained notice and attention on campus and began to provoke conversation. In 2007, Hillel International partnered with the Jewish Outreach Institute (JOI) to promote "public space Judaism" projects and offered grants to individual campuses for initiatives along these lines. Under the guidelines of the grant program, initiatives needed to create opportunities for Jewish engagement in public spaces on campus—quads, coffee shops, student centers and so on. The banner campaign seemed like a natural fit, and JOI awarded Northwestern University Hillel a grant to develop the banner campaign into a larger initiative, Ask Big Questions, complete with print media, a website, and live events.

The grant proposal was submitted in May, and awarded in July, after students had already left campus. The website and the whole initiative were scheduled to launch in the fall when students returned. Thus the initiative was developed over the summer, largely independently by the campus rabbi. In October the rabbi engaged a number of students to create a student leadership team. These students were drawn from both traditionally engaged populations and from among the newly-created Campus Entrepreneurs Initiative (CEI), which was composed of Jewish students who had previously been uninvolved in institutional Jewish life on campus. CEI was aimed at developing participating students as Jewish social entrepreneurs and engaging their uninvolved friends in Jewish life.[14]

The grant and the process that led to it shaped ABQ in three significant ways. First, the grant enabled the design and creation of a website that would develop and complement the questions asked on the banners. Instead of pointing students to www.nuhillel.org, which at that point featured no content to follow up on the questions, students would be directed to www.askbigquestions.com, which would feature short video interviews in which students provided answers to these questions, a short blog post contextualizing the question in Jewish terms, and links to Jewish explorations of the questions.

Second, the banners were integrated with the website and other print materials, including stick-on notes and posters, to create a unified print culture that sparked interest and established a brand identity for the initiative as both meaningful and fun—and public. Third, and perhaps most significantly, events were held at the Starbucks in the student centers, and featured the campus rabbi interviewing popular professors, of whom many, but not all, were Jewish. The inclusion of professors in the initiative was critical to student participation, as their presence was intended to communicates that these conversations were "safe spaces in which they would not be proselytized to and that would adhere to campus norms of intellectual honesty. At the same time, the events created alternative spaces for students and professors to interact outside the classroom and for professors to speak beyond their academic discipline.

Between October and December 2007, six questions were asked on campus, online, and in "fireside chats" with professors:

- "Where do you feel at home?"
- "Would you die for a cause?"
- "What are you thankful for?"
- "What do you say no to?"
- "What is the best advice you've ever receive?"
- "What day in your life would you live over"

In keeping with JOI's emphasis on Jewish engagement through public space projects—with the goal of further Jewish engagement in more identifiably Jewish spaces—students at each event were asked to fill out a small information card indicating their interest in different types of programming. These cards were to be used in following up with participants, either by Hillel professionals or student groups.

Northwestern Hillel funded the initiative independently once the grant funding expired in December 2007. In February 2008, the student leadership team and the campus rabbi informally evaluated the effectiveness of the initiative. Among the successes of the initiative were the website, which, though not as robust as desired, was still remarkable in integrating video, writing, and comments. The print materials were viewed as successful in creating a playful yet serious feeling.

But the evaluation also revealed a point of significant tension around both the events and the website. According to anecdotal feedback, in many students' minds it was not clear what ABQ was trying to be. Was it aiming to be a Jewish initiative open to the general public? Or was it a secular initiative (as indicated by the presence of the professors in the events), with a Jewish twist? In either of the cases, the Jewish students organizing the initiative felt discomfort and tension: either ABQ should be more unabashedly Jewish, with discussions taking place in Hillel and the Jewishness prominently featured as part of the advertising for the events, or it should become fully open to all points of view, not just Jewish ones. This tension was expressed by both the students from more institutionally affiliated backgrounds and those in CEI.

An example helps to illustrate the case. In January 2008, the rabbi and the student leaders decided to develop a new print product, a booklet of ten cards, each of which would feature a big question on the front and follow-up questions on the back. The cards could be used by individuals or groups to create their own ABQ conversations. In keeping with the Jewish engagement aims of the original grant, the rabbi included quotes from Jewish sources along with the follow-up questions on the back of the cards. When one of the student leaders saw the draft, she commented that it didn't make sense to her: either the cards should feature quotes from a number of different spiritual and religious traditions, or they shouldn't feature Jewish quotes. In her mind, ABQ needed to be either no-faith or multi-faith, but it could not be only Jewish, at least not if it aimed to have a public profile. (While the student leaders ultimately liked the idea of including quotes from multiple traditions, time constraints forced them to proceed with cards without the quotes altogether.) In addition, though the rabbi's facilitation and reflections were valuable, the centrality of the rabbi to the conversations and the writing of the blog posts on the website generated suspicion among the students as to whether there was an ulterior religious motive to the overall program.

In light of this, the student leadership team opted for a change: ABQ would become independent of Hillel, and would instead aim to engage the entire breadth of the university community. With help from the rabbi, the group secured funding from the university provost and the department of philosophy, which enabled the student leaders to re-design the website and build an infrastructure for growth. The rabbi became an informal advisor, the chair of the philosophy department was engaged as an additional advisor, and the initiative continues to be run by a student board (still disproportionately Jewish, but including a more diverse representation of the student body than when the initia-tive was part of Hillel). Additionally, while ABQ continues to sponsor public events with professors, students on the board now also organize "wine and cheese" events in student living rooms for students to talk to other students.

Lessons Learned From ABQ

Ultimately Hillel, other religious institutions, cultural organizations, and even academic units such as the philosophy department, benefit from a campus culture that promotes students' exploration of big ques-tions. A rising tide lifts all boats. ABQ has more credibility as a univer-sity entity—with Hillel as a key partner—than as one solely sponsored by Hillel. And while the public events of ABQ may no longer feature Jewish conversation as readily as they did in the initiative's early days, the methodology and philosophy of big questions have come to strongly influence Jewish conversation within Hillel. These points are discussed below

Jewish Emerging Adulthood:
Jewish students are no different from their peers in being interested in the big questions of emerging adulthood. These questions matter to them, and when they have safe spaces in which to discuss them, they respond. But as evidenced by ABQ's ultimate move away from Hillel, many of them can be quite sensitive to where and how they integrate Jewish tradition into their exploration. The students who pushed for a clearer identity for ABQ—either fully Jewish or fully non-sectarian—felt literally out of place discussing Jewish values in a public setting. In their minds, that kind of discussion was more appropriate for a more clearly Jewish setting, such as the Hillel building or a Hillel-sponsored event that was clearly Jewish in its advertising and public image. ABQ did not mention anything about Jewish explorations in its advertising, and thus the Jewish students felt that when other students showed up to

an ABQ event and found the rabbi emceeing, they would feel surprised. Whether non-Jewish students actually felt this way is less important than the perception among the Jewish student organizers that they would; it reflected their own notions about where Jewish life was appropriate and where it was not, specifically that Jewish life needs to be conducted in Jewish space, or, if conducted in public space, needs to be clearly and unabashedly Jewish. These tensions are emblematic of the struggle among emerging adults to find personal guidance and meaning from social structures such as religion while still being mistrustful of them as limiting or exclusive of others.

Experiential Education:
Northwestern Hillel's educational philosophy has become rooted in big questions. Northwestern Hillel staff have become accustomed to engaging students in such questions, and students themselves have become increasingly comfortable using big questions (e.g., "What's the best advice you've ever received?") in place of small questions (e.g., "What's your favorite flavor of ice cream?") to introduce a group to one another. This is in keeping with person-centered practice as identified by Chazan. Asking big questions like this as part of the communal culture has stimulated a broader student interest in studying traditional Jewish texts as sources of life lessons. Text study now regularly begins with a personal question and then moves to a big question, which frames the study of text. Text study at first blush is assumed to be a formal educational tool, but it fits quite well into experiential education in the right context. Text is rarely if ever presented as a stand-alone entity, but is instead framed by personal and collective exploration of big questions. Thus, for example, a text study on the Creation narrative of Genesis would be framed by an exploration of a big question: "Where do you feel at home?" or "What is our purpose in the world?" This would be preceded by an immediate, personal question that engages students iertheir own experience, for example:, "Think of the place you feel most at home. Jot down a few words that describe it, or draw a picture of it,"—followed by communal sharing of responses. This preparatory work situates Jewish text learning within the personal narrative of the student, and creates a level playing field for all participants when studying the text. It also helps them to understand traditional texts within a larger context of human life. Text thus becomes an interlocutor in the student's personal

narrative, which furthers an educational vision in which every student is writing the story of his or her life in dialogue with the enduring story of the Jewish people.

Jewish Peoplehood:
Central to both the discussion approach and the larger conceptual framework of ABQ is a replacement of dogma or *Truth* (with a capital T) at the center of the conversation with *truths* espoused by the individual participants and articulated in a context of community. ABQ changes the paradigm of dialogue from one in which there is only one truth to a pluralistic acknowlegement of multiple truth claims. A discussion in which participants answer the question, "Where do you feel at home?" and such follow-up questions as, "What defines home?" and "Can we have homes together?" is very different from a discussion on the question, "Do Jews have a historical claim to the Land of Israel?" While the latter is the kind of question on which we have tended to focus— not only with regard to Israel, but with our religious lives in general (think: "Intermarriage—right or wrong?" or "Who is a Jew?")—educators working with emerging adults have long known that such either/or discussions are frequently non-starters at best, and damaging at worst. An ABQ approach thus takes an entirely different tack, aiming for rich conversation that is at once anchored in personal narrative and a larger sense of peoplehood. ABQ's approach exemplifies the connective nature of Jewish community rather than an ideological one, and it allows student participants to express a multiplicity of truths that could all be understood as Jewish. ABQ provides emotional and social connectivity while also understanding the holistic nature of Jewish identity and community.

The Jethro Initiative at the University of Chicago

In 2006, Newberger Hillel at the University of Chicago began to design a new approach based on the understanding of emerging adulthood as a distinct developmental and educational phase of life. Reasoning that a new developmental phase called for a new institutional structure the Jethro Initiative was launched. The initiative was so-named because it drew inspiration from the story in chapter 18 of the Book of Exodus describing the visit to the Israelite camp of Moses's father-in-law, Jethro, the priest of Midian.

Traditionally, Hillel's work had been accomplished largely through a "club model"—with Hillel functioning as the "Jewish club" on campus—and through "programming." The generally implicit theory behind Hillel's work was that students came to college with relatively well-formed Jewish identities that could be sustained through college if Hillel provided regular Jewish events and a physical space in which Jewish activity was comfortable and encouraged. As more and more Jews arrived at college without well-formed Jewish identities in the 1990s, various experiments were tried to "engage" these students in Jewish activities, but the underlying model was not changed very much. Hillel still tried to attract students to a central Jewish location by putting on and marketing a variety of events and by focusing on Shabbat and holiday services and meals in the central location.

At the same time that University of Chicago Hillel began to rethink its model, Hillel's Schusterman International Center (SIC), based in Washington, D.C., and the main support institution for campus Hillels, had recently adopted a strategic plan that grew out of a national survey of Jewish students that highlighted just how different Jewish students were in 2006 compared to the 1960s and 1970s, or even the 1980s and 1990s. Working in parallel, the SIC and University of Chicago Hillel converged on the idea that relationships, rather than programs, were the key to the Jewish engagement of these students.

To paraphrase Tolstoy, committed Jews are all alike, but every disengaged Jewish student needs to be engaged differently. Of course, committed Jews are not really all alike, but their commitment often means that their needs can be met within the existing structures, which is not true for disengaged students. As many Jewish organizations have discovered, especially through efforts working with emerging adults, mass marketing and mass programming are not effective with a population of individuals used to servicing their particular niche interests through the Internet. That emerging adults are particularly self-focused only exacerbates the issue: emerging adults take it as a point of pride that they would not stoop to participating in an experience that was not specifically designed for people just like them. It quickly became apparent that a strategy built around a central location that was trying to broadcast from the core to the periphery was not going to be successful.

As the staff of University of Chicago Hillel came to understand emerging adulthood as an extended transition from childhood to adulthood—as Arnett) puts it, "the period of life that offers the most opportunities for identity exploration in the areas of love, work and worldviews"[15]—its leadership drew inspiration from another time of exploration, namely the Israelites' sojourn in the wilderness as they transitioned from being slaves in Egypt to being free people in Canaan. At the beginning of this journey, Moses's father-in-law, Jethro, the priest of Midian, arrives at the Israelite camp and sees that Moses has put into place an ineffective organizational structure. Moses's centralized approach has made the people utterly dependent upon him; worse, the inefficient system exhausts both Moses and the people (who are forced to wait on line all day to talk to him) and is not effective at reaching most of the people most of the time. Jethro advises Moses to set up a broad-based leadership structure, with leaders of groups as small as ten people. Moses is to select capable leaders and train them, and these leaders will do the day-to-day work, leaving Moses to deal with only the most difficult issues.

When this story is applied to Hillel's challenges with emerging adults, two fundamental insights in Jethro's advice are apparent. First, young people need to feel individually known and cared for in order to feel part of something; and second, the organization's central leaders and structures cannot give every individual that feeling, and certainly not while also planning and implementing the institution's broader programming.

The first step, then, was to question how to give every Jewish student on campus the feeling that he or she is personally known and cared for by someone in the Jewish community. From the Jethro story and from experience, it was clear that Hillel's full-time staff—even if it grew substantially—would never be able to accomplish this gargantuan task. Jethro's advice to Moses was to appoint non-professional leaders of tens, fifties, hundreds, and thousands, and this advice was seen as relevant for a campus community as well. With a grant from the Covenant Foundation, University of Chicago Hillel invented an approach of its on, and also built on the SIC's Campus Entrepreneurs Initiative.

The SIC launched the Campus Entrepreneurs Initiative (CEI) in 2006. The idea of this project was to hire a number of student interns (usually between eight and twelve per campus, which is more a factor of limited funding than any kind of magic number) and to train each student to be a kind of Jewish community organizer. Each intern is then responsible for establishing and maintaining sixty relationships with uninvolved Jewish students in their campus community. The interns themselves are generally students who have not previously been involved in Jewish life on campus but are attracted to the internship opportunity, so theoretically these students better understand their uninvolved peers and are likely to be able to relate to them. CEI interns also typically design programmatic initiatives for their peers and also recruit their contacts for Birthright Israel trips and other intensive Jewish experiences.

At the University of Chicago, the CEI model was adapted and modified in a few key ways so that the interns could essentially function as Jethro's "leaders of tens"—that is, the level of leadership closest to the people. A training curriculum was built around Jewish texts so that the interns would start to see the relevance of Jewish ideas to their own lives—they are participating in a leadership education program in order to become effective community organizers, and they discover that these texts are capable of teaching leadership and community organizing—and would become increasingly able to talk to their friends about why Jewish "stuff" was actually interesting and compelling. A set of on-campus experiences were also designed, such as a monthly "Mega-Shabbat" Friday night dinner that took place outside the Hillel building (and thus felt less like an activity of the central Hillel institution), to which interns could invite their peers so that they could have a rhythm of positive Jewish experiences that might start to become a habit. Like Jethro's leaders of tens, the CEI interns' job was getting to know "tens"—that is, each individual student—and making them *feel* known and cared about, and then linking these friends and contacts into a web of Jewish activity and establishing relationships between them and the next group of leaders.

The Covenant Foundation grant allowed University of Chicago Hillel to experiment with that next level of leadership, analogous to Jethro's "leaders of fifties"—more removed from the people's day-to-day experience, but also more able to connect students with substantive and meaningful Jewish content and experiences. Keeping in mind the need for individual attention, the resistance to mass marketing and mass experiences of emerging adults in the Internet age, and their expectation of connecting to others through niche interests, University of Chicago Hillel hired what it called "adjunct educators" to work with small groups of studens, assembled around shared interests. These adjunct educators were post-college adults who were hired to work for ten to fifteen hours per week to connect with twenty or thirty students in the context of small-group activities and one-on-one interactions. Where the CEI interns were previously uninvolved in Jewish life, the adjunct educators were people living adult lives in which being Jewish was well integrated into their other interests. As such, they could serve as role models for students, establishing plausibility structures for the students to imagine their own Jewish adult lives.

As the CEI program and the adjunct educator program have co-evolved, University of Chicago Hillel has found that the winning strategy is to connect one or two CEI interns with an adjunct educator who shares an interest with them. Based on this shared interest, interns are able to connect their friends with the same interests to the adjunct educator, who is able to offer a deeper and more substantive Jewish experience than the intern can. One illustrative example involves an adjunct educator who is both an experienced informal Jewish educator, stemming from long experience in the Jewish camping world, and a certified yoga instructor. The adjunct educator connected with a CEI intern who had a passion for yoga, and together they quickly built a Jewish yoga community of about twenty students that meets weekly. Students who come to yoga every week—many of whom started off as the interns' friends or part of their target engagement group—grew close with the adjunct educator and had frequent coffee dates and conversations about their lives and concerns. These conversations allowed the adjunct educator to raise Jewish questions and to discuss Jewish issues. Over time, many of these previously uninvolved students applied for Birthright trips and other high-impact experiences, attended Mega-Shabbat and other regularly occurring activities, and even applied to become CEI interns.

During the execution of and experimentation with these projects, University of Chicago Hillel also began to develop a model of Jewish emerging adult development that was based on a traditional Jewish text. It became apparent in the course of these projects that students move through three phases of Jewish engagement. In the first stage, students who begin with little to no interest in Jewish matters can be connected through CEI interns and initial positive experiences and, after regular participation in low-intensity experiences like Mega-Shabbat or intern-created initiatives, can become more open to more content-rich experiences, such as a Birthright trip or an adjunct educator's small groups. After these experiences, students enter the second stage, becoming more active seekers of Jewish experiences—engaging in what looks like a kind of "dating"—until they develop a sense of themselves as Jewishly committed. In the third stage, this internal sense of commitment must be nurtured and maintained, as even committed students are still emerging adults—a developmental stage in which non-commitment is the norm—and backsliding or outright rebellion and abandonment of prior commitments are not unusual.

University of Chicago Hillel developed a conceptual model that maps these phases onto the four children described in the Passover seder—the child who does not ask questions, the simple child, the rebellious child, and the wise child (see illustration on page 217). While no two students go on precisely the same path, this conceptual model is broadly applicable and helpful in describing where a student currently is and what sorts of experiences might help him or her move toward increasing interest in or commitment to Jewish life. The conceptual model is used to train new staff and to design specific educational experiences targeted at helping students move from one stage to the next, as opposed to simply creating "positive Jewish experiences" aimed at an undifferentiated mass audience.

For example, the recognition that a period of alienation (the rebellious child) is normal and common led to an evaluation of what sorts of experiences could be made available to students when they are feeling alienated. University of Chicago Hillel staff realized that, because alienated students would by definition be uninterested in attending programs, the only tool available would be relationships with other people. At that point, Chicago Hillel began to design a mentoring program that would try to establish mentoring relationships between trained volunteers—Jewish adults from the community—and students before the students entered the "rebellious" phase so that when students became alienated, they would still be in close contact with someone who could help them reconnect when the time was right.

For both funding and demographic reasons, Chicago Hillel's focus to date has been the engagement of uninvolved students and those at the earlier stages of Jewish exploration. As it has succeeded in engaging more and more of these students, it has recently begun to focus more

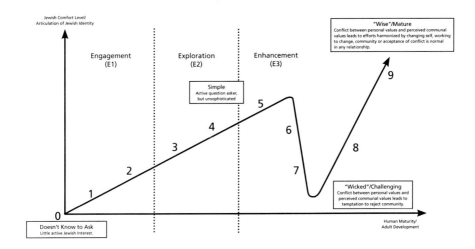

on building more content-rich experiences that help students engage more deeply and begin to build mature adult identities as committed Jews, understanding that this commitment will manifest itself very differently for different students. While students who develop a strong interest in exploring Jewish life are more open to programs aimed at an undifferentiated large audience, an individualized approach—or at least a small-group interest-based approach—is still far more effective. A key challenge is to design approaches that can provide this individualization in a cost-effective and affordable way. Recently, for example, University of Chicago Hillel has begun to experiment with a new internship in which it will train more engaged and knowledgeable students to design substantive and innovative Jewish experiences for their peers. This project balances the affordability of interns with the greater depth needed to satisfy and maintain the interest of students who have entered the second stage—the simple child—described above.

As the Jethro Initiative continues to develop, University of Chicago Hillel is moving rapidly toward accomplishing its goal of inspiring and empowering every Jewish student at the University of Chicago to make an enduring commitment to Jewish life.

LESSONS LEARNED FROM THE JETHRO INITIATIVE

Jewish Emerging Adulthood

The Jethro Initiative used the knowledge the emerging adults exhibit two seemingly disparate behavioral trends, namely, that they are narrowly focused on their own experience while not secure enough in themselves as they transition from childhood to adolescence to feel completely independent in their self-identity. By creating a programmatic process that allowed for exposure to secure Jewish adults who are experts in specific areas that individual students find of personal value, Jethro could work with the developmental conditions of the students to provide role models and mentors for the students' own developmental journey. Chicago Hillel was also able to place its observations about Jewish student development in a specifically Jewish context, using the parable of the four children from the Passover seder.

Jewish Experiential Education

The Jethro Initiative recognized that a fundamental point of reaching students at a developmental level was to lead with experience in order to create conditions of acceptance for identity development stimulus. Whether the experiential medium was music, yoga, cooking, or others, all of them provided a common experience for the participants with the potential Jewish role model who both empowered the student to master a personally valuable skill set and created a trusting relationship to explore a common Jewish identity through the prism of the shared medium. The experience itself was truly a self-learning one through the hands of a skilled teacher and role model.

Jewish Peoplehood

By intentionally not prioritizing or focusing on religious or theological rubrics of Jewish identity and instead placing the priority on common interests among Jews rather than on Judaism as the common interest, the Jethro Initiative implemented an intentional peoplehood approach to Jewish identity. Theology and practice were never addressed unless raised by the students and there was no expectation that they would ever come up otherwise. Of course, as expected, students did raist such issues with the adjunct educators, who were trained to allow the students to lead the conversation and not respond with any answer that was not authentic to the educator's own identity. Judaism became part of the discussion, not its focus, and students could come to whatever point they were ready for with it on their terms and at their own pace. In other words, they came to it when it suited their developmental interest and process.

Conclusion

The common lessons of both the Northwestern and the University of Chicago Hillel programs is that a theory-based approach and an understanding of a specific population and its dynamics can be valuable tools in designing and implementing impactful educational programs that succeed in reaching this population in depth. Both programs were designed for individuals to find their own meaning within them, to access them at their own pace, and to see them as a resource in their own Jewish growth in whatever way the individuals were ready to develop their personal Jewish adult identity. This approach can be modeled not just on campuses like those in Chicago, but on campuses around the Jewish world.

13

Carrying the Burden of the Other:
Musar and Adult Development

ARIELLE LEVITES
AND IRA F. STONE

MUSAR is a traditional Jewish practice that aims to narrow the gap between the *knowledge* of ethics and the *practice* of ethics. *Musar* provides a clear regimen for cultivating an ethical life, as well as a language for understanding spirituality and human development that is both authentically Jewish and psychologically sophisticated. Using the Philadelphia Mussar Leadership Program (MLP) as a case study, this chapter explores how traditional texts and educational methods can be used in contemporary settings to promote the spiritual and social-emotional growth of adult learners. We consider the philosophical rationale for emphasizing the social-emotional dimension of

Jewish education, the personal goals that lead Jewish adults to seek out these kinds of settings the impact on Jewish practice, and the pathways through which participants understand their own development.

Musar and the Development of a Fine Soul

> Our Sages taught: One of the methods by which Torah is acquired is by carrying the burden of our fellows. Each of the [48] steps that they enumerate there [*Pirkei Avot* 6:5] are like preliminary goals, achieved by following each step, in order to bring about the ultimate goal. All of them taken together instill in one a new nature—that of being "master of a fine soul"—one fit for Torah and wisdom to be attached to, as a result of which one's soul is bound up with the bond of eternal life.
> —RAV SIMCHA ZISSEL ZIV, *Hochmah u'Musar* 1:1

One of the perennial questions of educators of all stripes is, "How do we help students translate knowledge of ethics into ethical actions?" This question preoccupies religious educators as well as secular educators. It has been an especially central question throughout the ages of Jewish education precisely because Jewish education is so filled with what amounts to an ethical curriculum: the biblical narratives and laws, the corpus of Rabbinic narrative and law. Moreover, the emphasis placed on activity in Jewish education, that is, educating for the purpose of fulfilling mitzvot, blurs the distinction between knowledge and action insofar as it is too easy to judge the enactment of mitzvot as being the end goal—the value action—that we are striving for when, in fact, such actions, in the ritual domain at least, can be performed with little or no consciousness of ethics. In fact, the tension between law and ethics, law and narrative, is one that characterizes Jewish thought as represented in its literature from the earliest times. For example, soon after the publication of one of the earliest halachic codes, known as the Alfasi, Bachya ibn Pakuda's *Duties of the Heart* was published.

The Hebrew word *musar* means "discipline" in the same sense that we use that word in English. That is, it describes an area of study, like the "discipline" of chemistry, as well as a practice of behavior, like the "discipline" of yoga. It likewise contains the sense of correction and instruction, as in the case of a parent disciplining a child. Thus, while *musar* was intended to serve as a corrective for ethical lapses consequent to focusing merely on the practice of the letter of the law, it eventually became the common Hebrew word for ethics itself and is mostly used that way today. This is somewhat unfortunate, since the more accurate Hebrew word for ethics is really *k'dushah*, or holiness. Thus we understand *musar* as a discipline intended to correct our behavior such that the pursuit of holiness is understood to be the intention of the law, while the law itself is understood to be instrumental to the pursuit of this goal.

The first of the great *musar* works was *Duties of the Heart*, composed by Ibn Pakuda in eleventh-century Spain. Ibn Pakuda argued that while the law was concerned with the duties of the body, the duties of the heart, the ethical duties that undergird the achievement of a holy community, were being neglected. This division of literature and of vision persists through the entirety of the medieval period and continues into the modern period. Throughout these centuries an entire genre of Jewish literature known as *musar* developed in tandem with the legal literature, although clearly viewed by the religious establishment as secondary to the legal corpus.

The irony of this tradition of ethical instruction is precisely the fact that it continues to be needed. Regardless of how much *intellectual* support there is for living life according to an exacting standard of ethical/holy behavior, the very nature of human beings seems to militate against achieving it. It is this discrepancy between knowing what to do and acting ethically from which the Musar movement developed. It is this psychological challenge inherent in promoting ethical action that necessitated that the study of *musar* grow from a genre of Jewish literature into a movement in Jewish life.

Israel Salanter's Musar Movement

It was the insight of Rabbi Israel Lipkin of Salant (Lithuania), known as the Salanter Rav, that precipitated this transformation from literature to comprehensive pedagogical approach. Rav Israel was struck by the lack of ethical concern among his contemporaries, who represented some of the most learned and observant Jews in history. He lived in the nineteenth century at a time when the Jewish world was being assaulted on all sides. Intellectually it was being challenged by the Haskalah, the Jewish Enlightenment, whose various supporters were united in their condemnation of the traditional Jewish community for its lack of concern with ethics. Spiritually it was still recovering from the assaults of the rise of Chasidism in Ukraine and Poland and now spreading into Lithuania, which portrayed the Lithuanian Jewish community as being spiritually stale and overly concerned with theoretical Rabbinic learning rather than the pursuit of holiness.

Rabbi Salanter addressed these multiple problems by creating a Musar movement out of the traditional literature of *musar*. That is, he devised a program of spiritual/ethical discipline that addressed these problems in turn. But most importantly he responded to the problem of internalizing the goal of religious education and the observance of mitzvot by creating a new analysis of the human soul (psyche) and a practice aimed at impacting people at the level of the soul rather than merely at the level of intellect. The theological structure underlying this practice begins with the idea that each human being is created with a *yetzer ra* and a *yetzer tov*, an evil inclination and a good inclination, and that these inclinations are at work beneath the conscious surface, controlling our behavior.

Salanter explained that the reason the accumulation of texts and exhortation to ethical behavior had not succeeded was the fact that human beings were controlled by internal forces of which they were often not aware. These forces, or "soul roots," needed to be revealed and then transformed by the application of particular methodologies that were precisely not intellectual, but rather had the emotional power to pierce the veil of unconsciousness. This required, for example, not merely studying exhortative texts, but studying them "with lips aflame." He strove to use these exercises as the catalyst for an emotional breakthrough, often driving the student to the point of tears as he recognized himself in the words of correction contained within the traditional *musar* texts.

In addition to this ecstatic use of texts, the student would be directed to engage in a period of verbal confession by which the events of each day, measured against a set series of character traits known in the traditional *musar* literature as *midot*, would be evaluated. This would take the form of what might be called a verbal journal of the day's events in light of the particular trait under consideration. For instance, if a

CARRYING THE BURDEN OF THE OTHER   225

student were working on the trait of *savlanut*, or patience, he would verbally review every situation in which the student had found himself during that day so that he might "rate" the extent to which he had succeeded or failed in enacting the characteristic.

Salanter instructed his students to form small groups during which they would evaluate one another's behavior. In these groups students who believed that they had indeed met the highest expectations for ethical behavior would be challenged. These students, along with those who admitted that they were having problems escaping the unconscious forces that caused them to act counter to their highest aspirations, would receive advice and solace and sometimes chastisement in order to goad them into working harder and delving deeper into their souls to find a solution.

The Mussar Leadership Program

In the contemporary American Jewish community *musar* is enjoying a resurgence of interest, particularly among the non-Orthodox segment.[1] This chapter focuses on Rabbi Ira Stone's approach to *musar*, as outlined in his book *A Responsible Life* and in his commentary to *M'silat Y'sharim*.[2] The Mussar Leadership Program (MLP) began ten years ago with one cohort of ten adult participants. It presently, and for the last few years, consists of three cohorts of adult learners, now facilitated by people trained in the program totaling close to forty participants. In addition we have expanded to include three off-site groups and one web-based group.

The practice consists of the following elements rooted in Salanter's curriculum: *chevruta, cheshbon hanefesh, shiur, vaad,* mitzvah, *Torah lishmah*:

1. *Chevruta*: Each student agrees to pair with another student in order to prepare the central text of the program, *M'silat Y'sharim*. This eighteenth-century ethical treatise by Moses Chayim Luzzatto was one of the best known and best loved of its time. It was selected by Rav Israel Salanter as the chief text of his *musar* program and continues to be an invaluable resource for contemporary *musar* students. The *chevruta* partners also discuss and

support each other regarding the *midah*, or character trait, being "worked on" that week. The *chevruta* meets once a week for at least thirty minutes.

2. *Cheshbon hanefesh*: Literally, "an accounting of the soul," this is the daily practice of *musar* and the heart of the program. Students spend five to ten minutes every day, preferably at a fixed time, reviewing their activities and actions during the previous twenty-four hours focusing on the ways in which the *midah* of the week appeared in their day and evaluating whether or not they were able to use the *midah* to better serve the needs of another or whether their own self-absorption caused them to obscure the needs of another. Then the participants "journal" about one such situation, asking themselves: Who was the other? What caused my *yetzer ra* to be triggered? What was I afraid of? Was it a legitimate fear? If not, can I constrain my impulse and learn to act in a different way if and when a similar situation occurs?

3. *Shiur*: This is the class that begins the once-a-week program taught by Rabbi Stone and focusing on *M'silat Y'sharim*.

4. *Vaad*: The *vaad* is a peer group for processing the work being done on the *midot*. Among the *midot* that are used in this process are order (*seder*), patience (*savlanut*), equanimity (*m'nuchat hanefesh*), and humility (*anavah*). A student working on the *midah* of patience, say, would be asked to monitor his or her behavior during the course of the week and record how this he or she encountered this *midah* in the course of daily activity. During the *vaad*, the student would share some particular instance. The *vaad* is facilitated by one of the trained *madrichim* (facilitators) of the program.

5. **Mitzvah**: Each participant agrees to take on two traditional mitzvot, one *bein adam lachaveiro* and one *bein adam LaMakom* (literally, "between man and his peer" and "between man and God," referring to two classes of commandments).

6. *Torah lishmah*: This is learning Torah for its own sake. We ask each participant to spend five minutes daily learning Torah of their own choosing. It may be the Bible, a book of Rabbinic wisdom, even a book of contemporary Jewish thought. The idea is to maintain the connection between *musar* practice and its

source in Jewish life and literature and thus avoid a disembodied spirituality unrelated to Jewish community.

Insights for Educators from MLP

We, the authors, have been actively engaged in the Mussar Leadership Program in the position of founder and teacher (Rabbi Ira Stone—ten years) and participant-observer (Arielle Levites—one year). In an attempt to supplement our own perspectives about MLP, we conducted a series of interviews with people enrolled in the on-site program. A number of themes emerged that shed light on the experiences of adults in Jewish educational settings that promote social-emotional and spiritual development. Our analysis focuses on what MLP *means* to its participants, how they understand their own development, and to what source they attribute any changes. We have tried both to provide insights that may be of practical use for those curious about implementing such a program and to raise questions that will stimulate discussion for stakeholders in the field of Jewish education.

We should note that our discussion may seem to focus disproportionately on the social-emotional rather than the spiritual. This is because within the theological framework of MLP the two elements are inseparable: one serves God through ethical treatment of others. What is particularly interesting about MLP is its ability to relate Jewish practice in a way that resonates among participants with starkly different beliefs about God and spirituality. While some participants spoke about their *musar* practice as strengthening their relationship with God, others rejected a belief in a "supernatural" God at all. The *process* of *musar*, which insists that holiness is best achieved through service to others, allowed for tremendous diversity in conceptions of the divine.

"Getting in the Game:"
Jewish Practice through the Lens of MLP

MLP participants are, by and large, educated consumers in the marketplace of adult Jewish education. Those interviewed were not new to the kinds of programming offered by the Jewish community and were somewhat cynical about those opportunities and their deficiencies. Other adult education programs were seen as limited by their more formal and largely content-oriented approach. These programs were, as one woman put it, "strictly informational," whereas MLP offered a more comprehensive "daily practice." This kind of feedback suggests that adult education programs that model themselves after more formal education settings, like a university course, may not be accurately reading the breadth of motivations that adults bring when seeking Jewish education. In contrast, the MLP program utilizes a highly varied assortment of educational practices. Most significantly, participants were asked to monitor and reflect on all of their daily interpersonal interactions. The theology of *musar*, which frames mitzvah practice as an instantiation of service to others, became an entry point into a new way of understanding the place of Jewish practice in their daily lives. There was a palpable sense of discovery as participants encountered a theology that reframed much of their earlier Jewish knowledge. What came before *musar* was now understood as shallow or episodic; puddles of Jewish experience became oceans. This was described, in the words of our interviewees, as the difference between "knowing about football and actually getting into a football game" and entering into "24/7 Judaism." This new understanding of Jewish practice seemed to affirm a previously held belief of what Jewish life *should* look like: deep, continuous, rigorous, and coherent.

By far, the most dramatic claim we heard in our interviews, again and again, was how *musar* impacted participants' daily interactions. In particular we heard about children, spouses, and parents and how these primary relationships were understood as profoundly transformed. One woman shared that since her participation four years ago she has become "a better friend, a better wife. I think that my life has changed tremendously for the better." Another framed the change using the traditional Hebrew phrase *sh'lom bayit*, "peace in the home," offering that *musar* for her has been about "looking first and foremost with the people in my family."

Yet MLP participants were engaged in what might be understood as idiosyncratic Jewish practice. Their observance of the new mitzvot they had taken on as part of their participation in the program waxed and waned at various points in their involvement in MLP. Often mitzvot were discussed in terms of something the participants had been, but no longer were, practicing. Instead, MLP participants focused on the *midot* through careful attention to interpersonal behavior rich in the vocabulary of traditional *musar* texts. Adam explained his observance this way:

> I now carry around a copy of Luzzatto or another small religious text. My usual practice [of reading books]) is to mark them up with colored pencils but these [*musar* books] I don't [mark up]. The practice of pulling these out and reading them on the bus or when I'm traveling or when I'm waiting—it, in some ways, becomes a religious act in that it calls me to attention to what I'm doing in the day and the moral commitments I've been making through *musar* and my own life.

Adam offers a challenge to Jewish educators about how we might measure programmatic success. His observance of mitzvot may be somewhat sporadic, but his commitment to ethical Jewish living is informed, rigorous, and, by his own account, deeply meaningful to him.

In their study of the Melton Mini-Schools, Grant and colleagues noted that participation allowed adults to deepen their "understanding of themselves as Jews"[3]—but not to "change their behavior."[4] One question this analysis raises is what kinds of behavioral changes we as Jewish educators should seek. Is more ethical treatment of others, informed by a rich Jewish vocabulary, but not necessarily within the context of regular mitzvah observance, a success? Certainly *musar* developed in a milieu that never doubted the centrality of halachic practice. Are we satisfied with Adam's claim that he is willing to observe a few mitzvot, but that core to his practice is the frequent reading of a classic, but non-canonical, Jewish text?

As Jewish educators, we are necessarily interested in how education impacts traditional measures of communal membership and practice. Horowitz complicates this approach, suggesting that such measures attend to

> only a narrow set of traditional Jewish ritual, religious and communal practices, without allowing for a wider range of variations in Jewish practice. In effect, this accounting strategy gives higher marks to a more homogeneous traditional Jewish population, and lower marks to a population characterized by a wider variety of less traditional Jewish behaviors."[5]

The reports of MLP participants suggest that there may be other variables we want to measure when considering programmatic success. Interestingly, a concept such as *sh'lom bayit*, which is consonant with traditional Jewish practice and belief, is often not included among the stated curricular goals of many Jewish learning endeavors. Attention to the social-emotional and spiritual dimensions of education may demand a reassessment and, perhaps, an expansion of the goals we have articulated for our educational programming.

Shining a Light: The Vaad and Reflective Relationships

When asked how MLP accomplishes its goals and what elements of the program they understood as responsible for their own growth, the people we spoke with credited the relationships they had formed through the program.

Classically *cheshbon*, or self-accounting, has been understood as the key ingredient of Salanter's Musar program. Participant responses suggest that while journaling and daily self-accounting were shared ideals, they often did not live up to these ideals in their daily practice. The rituals of *chevruta* and *vaad* seemed to be most consistently adhered to by participants. Because there is already a small and growing body of literature about *chevruta* learning,[6] we thought it would useful to focus on the *vaad* experience with the understanding that small groups can be powerful tools that are often underutilized in education settings.

When asked about what she understands as the definitive MLP experience, Susan offered this story:

> One of the moments that really stands out for me is during our *vaad* when we're sharing our work about the *midah* and I was talking about my relationship with my son....I was interacting with my son in a way that I thought was consistent with the *midah*. And I realized through the feedback that I got that it was *yetzer hara* that was guiding my action and that was *huge, huge*, because I completely misunderstood what I was doing and it really, it's given me pause now in everything I do.

We heard a number of stories like this one, which highlighted the difficulty in accurately reflecting on one's life in isolation. While many prominent theories of education have emphasized the role of a social context for skill and content mastery,[7] here we see illustrated the impact of social relationships on affect and behavior, through acting as a more accurate mirror.

Self-reflection has been much heralded in educational and psychological contexts for its importance in providing feedback about one's own learning and behavior. *Musar* practice is somewhat more complicated because it requires not only reflection about oneself and one's own behavior but reflection about the needs, or burden, of the other. Reflective functioning is the awareness of one's own mental state as well as the awareness of the mental state of others.[8] Slade explains that "the capacity to think reflectively means not only that an individual acknowledges or recognizes mental states but also that he or she can reason about his or her own and others' behavior in light of mental states."[9] In the language of *musar* this might be expressed as conceptualizing the burden of the other—their needs, desires, and intentions.

In the last five years, reflective functioning has been identified as perhaps a central element in social-emotional development, impacting how the quality of relationships are passed from generation to generation.[10] In MLP, peers play an active role, both modeling reflective sharing for others and critiquing one another's reflections. Thus MLP could be understood as a program that promotes the development of reflective functioning through peer modeling and critical feedback.

The MLP *vaad* uses trained facilitators to guide participants through their self-account and the group critique. Each week one or two *vaad* members are asked to share an interpersonal challenge for peer feedback. MLP facilitators carefully model constructive forms of *tocheichah*, or rebuke, and will often stop and redirect conversation when they sense the feedback is not productive. Often facilitators intervene because they feel that the *vaad* is being too easy on a fellow participant and not doing a thorough enough job of holding him or her accountable to the other.

It is important to note that group feedback is not always perceived as helpful. One participant offered that occasionally he "felt somewhat attacked by the *vaad*." To insist that a participant present him- or herself up for group critique can lead to potentially negative consequences, and educators who wish to employ MLP techniques should be alert to this possibility.[11]

Participants were also careful to draw a line around the kind of intimacy they were comfortable with in the *vaad*, what one woman called building "a fence around the sharing." Interestingly, all of the participants brought their *vaad* experience into conversation with group therapy, unprompted by the interviewer, carefully outlining the ways *musar* was different from their own perception of what happens in group therapy. They stressed the need for the facilitator to be careful to ensure that the group's conversation focused on productive rebuke and not "over sharing."

One might imagine that Americans in the age of Oprah and reality TV would embrace the confessional elements of the *musar* program. But while they credited the *vaad* with promoting their own development, some participants also found this to be the most uncomfortable element of the program. As one man offered, "We often don't have forums in modern American middle-class life for critique and rebuke…it's just not civil.…We don't have very friendly contexts in which that happens." Americans, perhaps, have only models of "oversharing," and for the participants we spoke with, *musar* was as much about critique and responsibility as it was about sharing.

Conclusion

Sociologists of contemporary American religious life have noted an increasing emphasis on personal meaning over communal commitments.[12] This quest for meaning often looks highly individualized, raising concerns that American religiosity has devolved into a form of narcissism. In his extensive study of support groups in American civic life, Wuthnow points to the emergence of such groups as "thoroughly American,"[13] part of a larger cultural landscape in which traditional religious doctrine is appropriated to fit contemporary American conceptions of the sacred. From this perspective "a divine being is one who is there for our own gratification, like a house pet, rather than one who demands obedience from us, is too powerful or mysterious for us to understand, or who challenges us to a life of service."[14] Similar trends have been observed in the American Jewish community, as the image of the "sovereign self" has emerged as emblematic of post-modern Jewish identity.[15] As personal spirituality gains currency in Jewish settings, educators and researchers need models that respond to this impulse while addressing concerns about commitment to Jewish traditions and community.

We believe that MLP both illuminates and complicates this portrait of contemporary American culture. In particular, MLP offers a more culturally nuanced picture of what "service" might look like in the diversity that is American religious life. For practitioners of *musar*, the "closer other," usually immediate family, becomes understood as the primary venue in which religious obligation plays out. *Musar*, in fact, suggests that religious obligation is best served by a *retreat* from the larger civic landscape, which may distract one from more immediate obligations. Certainly a theology that privileges domestic concerns over expressions of larger group membership challenges many assumptions about how one performs Jewish identity in twenty-first-century America. As one participant put it, "[The] paradox [is] this is not self-help. This is supposed to be about others. But to be for others we have to figure out our own mess and our own virtues. So in a way it's self-help for the other."

Engagement with *musar* literature reminds us that much of the purpose of Jewish education is *affective*. Interviews with participants in MLP suggest that more traditional adult educational enterprises, which privilege the intellectual, may be leaving some serious learners dissatisfied. Reimer offers a critique of Jewish educational programs that are "a warm bath of meaningful experiences and good feelings."[16] In this he echoes Wuthnow's concern that some supportive educational group settings may contribute to a kind of cultural erosion. Certainly there may be many Jewish educational programs that capitalize on the generation of good feeling while asking very little from participants. Programs like MLP suggest that "meaning" and "feeling" can happen in the context of serious demands on a person intellectually, emotionally, and religiously.

The more we learn about learning, the more we understand that the cognitive, social, and emotional domains work in concert with one another. Jewish adults both think and feel; their educational programs should acknowledge that. For those Jewish educators interested in social-emotional development within a context of intellectual rigor and personal responsibility, programs like MLP point to some of the benefits and pitfalls of such curricula.

14

Social-Emotional and Character Development and Jewish Parenting:

Exploring the Spiritual, Research, and Practice Synergy

MAURICE J. ELIAS
AND MARILYN GOOTMAN

P ARENTHOOD is an endless series of small events, periodic conflicts, and sudden crises which call for a response. The response is not without consequence: it affects personality for better or worse. Our teenager's character is shaped by experience with people and situations. Character education requires presence that demonstrates and contact that communicates.

> We want our teenager to be a "mensch," a human being with compassion, commitment, and courage, a person whose life is guided by a core of strength and a code of fairness. To achieve these humane goals, we need humane methods. Love is not enough. Insight is insufficient. Good parents need skill.[1]

In this brief quote, Ginott accurately anticipated research on the necessity of promoting the social-emotional, character, and spiritual development of children[2] and the role of parents in doing so. He spoke about how young people need the skills to respond to numerous daily conflicts and hassles and the character to be a good person and strive for a meaningful and moral life.[3] Ginott also was among the first to state unambiguously that parents require more than intuition and good intentions to help their children become mensches.

In the current, hectic, digitized world in which young people are growing up, the role of parents is becoming more nuanced and complex. Parents need strong relationship skills, knowledge of child development, and family building and management skills. They need to be good problem solvers and decision makers and effective, positive role models in many areas. As implied above, one of the areas now seen as essential by many is the spiritual domain. Staton and Cobb take the position that while there is no basis for endorsing religion as a developmental necessity, the same cannot be said for spirituality.[4] They would concur with Seymour Sarason, who refers to a universal yearning for transcendence as "a belief that one is part of a larger scheme of things in two respects: that the scheme of things impacts on you and you somehow do or will impact on it."[5] Staton and Cobb note that it is unlikely that spirituality takes on the kind of cognitively driven stage sequence posited by Fowler,[6] but it is certainly related to how we reflect on our experiences over time.[7] Still, as Gordis and Gardner suggest,[8] spirituality is not inherently connected to verbal-linguistic competence and is strongly shaped by a variety of experiences and senses:

> Some of us do our spiritual journey through religion while others find music, nature, or art more compelling. But deep down, I believe that

almost all people wonder about the world, think about what happens after they die, and desperately want to believe that their lives have meaning.[9]

From our point of view, the research on social-emotional learning and character and spiritual development have many implications for parents and parenting. Here, we focus on three areas of parenting whose importance can be viewed as a direct consequence of emerging research on social-emotional competence:

1. Reflecting on one's views of spirituality and how it evolved from childhood until the present
2. Reflecting on one's own social-emotional and character competencies and how they evolved from childhood until the present
3. How to use the insights from the above reflections to create a family environment oriented toward building a positive sense of personhood and spirituality/meaning over time.

Reflecting on Spirituality

The emergence of literature in clinical and personality/identity development fields pointing to the importance of storytelling for positive growth and healing[10] has been accompanied by a reconceptualization of the role of storytelling in the development of Judaism, as well as individuals' spirituality.[11] The notion that spirituality is not only to be acquired by didactic instruction or directed experiences is not universally accepted within the Jewish world, but it is consistent with emerging research in neuroscience and the multiple intelligences, as well as on spiritual development. Gillman described three models for spiritual development within the Jewish tradition: (1) intellectual, in which spirituality is acquired by studying Torah and related texts as a way to understand God and God's will, leading to a life of holiness/spirituality, (2) behavioral, in which fulfilling mitzvot and halachah (Jewish law) and engaging in social action lead to a sense of spiritual satisfaction, and (3) pietistic, which posits that spirituality involves a connection to the awe and wonder of creation, to transcendence, purpose, and meaning, and that this is best communicated via aesthetics.[12] While there is connection between these models, Wachs believes that the last is the most accessible to the largest number of people and especially to teenagers. He also notes that all three elements can be combined but that individuals are not equally attuned to each one.[13] That said, and in light of Gardner's work on the multiple intelligences,[14] we believe that aesthetics will help ensure that the largest proportion of children of all ages are reached, including many of those who may be deeply immersed in formal religious education.

Parents want their children to have lives with meaning and to develop good values and a sense of caring about the world around them. Accordingly, it behooves parents to reflect on their own pathways of spirituality and consider these questions:

1. When do you find yourself filled most with feelings of spirituality, connection to the world, transcendence?
2. What, when, and/or whom is it that awakens or touches this spirit within you?
3. What do you think were the most important influences on you in developing your spiritual sense?

Parents sometimes have a hard time putting into words their beliefs about spirituality and related "transcendent" ideas. Often, it is easier for them to relate to real or fictional stories of others' experiences. In the same way, it is through the narrative of one's life, rather than specific, formal training experiences, that parents can communicate spiritual values to their children. Indeed, children benefit from parents' reflecting about the "big questions" of life and the meaning of what the family is doing, because this is missing from much of their daily lives. Sometimes, parents may find adolescents more responsive to their being prompted with interesting questions that actually capture what is often on their minds but difficult to bring up in conversation. Some of these questions are as follows:

• When or with whom are you at your best, and what does that feel like?
• What is lying dormant within you, waiting for a chance to flower?
• How does the "divine" (however one wishes to refer to it) express itself in everyone, in the world around us, in you?

The more that family life includes opportunities to reflect on these kinds of questions, the more in touch with their own spirituality children can become. Yet ultimately, the spiritual is carried out in the context of day-to-day family life. And in that context, social-emotional competencies are essential for children (and adults) to accomplish their goals.

Reflecting on Character and Promoting Children's Social-Emotional Competencies

Thanks to Dan Goleman's best-selling books on emotional intelligence[15] and the Collaborative for Academic, Social, and Emotional Learning's seminal volume that coined the term "social-emotional learning,"[16] social-emotional competencies are in the consciousness of people from all walks of life and from various professions, including clinicians, educators, members of the business community, and the military. Social-emotional learning is based on advances in brain research[17] and has benefited from extensive research showing its connection to education and mental health.[18]

There is no doubt that parents must be aware of their children's social-emotional competencies, and accomplishing this requires awareness of their own competencies and how they encourage and model growth of social-emotional skills in their children. While there are many definitions and lists of social-emotional competencies, Table 1 is designed specifically for use with parents as a practical way of helping them understand how the skills are essential aspects of everyday interactions.

Elias, Tobias, and Friedlander) identified a set of competencies that parents need to facilitate social-emotional competencies in their children.[19] Rooted in best practice research, these guidelines are organized in Table 1 in the form of a self-assessment to allow parents to identify their strengths in parenting, as well as areas needing improvement, to promote children's emotional intelligence. Most helpful to parents is to identify several areas where they have strengths that they want to continue to employ, and one or two areas rated 4 or 5 that they will focus on improving. Looking at the list, one can see clearly how parents lacking in even one of the abilities in Table 2 to an extreme and visible degree may inadvertently send messages at odds with children's developing a sense of spirituality.

TABLE 1

Rate each of the following as Definitely True; Sometimes/Sort of True; and Rarely, If True:

Does Your Child:

___ Know lots of words to describe his or her feelings

___ Easily talk about emotions

___ Have empathy and sympathy for others

___ Have an optimistic attitude

___ Enjoy laughter and humor

___ Wait patiently for something he or she really wants

___ Have goals reasonable for his or her age and some thoughts about how to reach those goals

___ Listen attentively

___ Know what he or she needs and how to ask for it

___ Know how to solve problems independently

___ Handle him- or herself well in a group of kids his or her own age

Displaying Our Character

Relatedly, children know parents mainly from the words and behaviors that parents display. While there might be a lot "more" to parents than who they are and what they do in family life, children typically are not aware of this. Parents benefit from realizing that they can infer the kind of character they are imparting and modeling for their children by reflecting on how they act when their children are around them, and especially in their interactions with them. Table 2 presents a set of character dimensions we find that parents often display with their children. As parents review these items, they have an opportunity to consider the character and moral messages they are presenting to children during their interactions. However, from an ecological and developmental perspective, the wider context of these interactions both shapes them and conveys broader thematic messages to children about how to live a life of meaning. When we observed earlier that spirituality is often enhanced by storytelling, we were presaging our larger point: the way in which family life and routines are organized tells the most powerful story of all, and exercises great influence over the nature of interactions, the opportunities to build social-emotional competencies, and the ways in which parents help children develop values and meaning in their lives. In the section that follows, we present ways that Jewish wisdom can guide parents in setting up family routines and rituals that will foster children's spirituality.

Creating a Jewishly Informed Family Environment That Promotes Children's Spirituality

> Good as well as faulty character traits can only be acquired or become embedded in the soul if one repeatedly practices the acts that result from these character traits over a long period of time.... No one is born with innate virtues or vice... and everyone's conduct from childhood on is undoubtedly influenced by the behavior of relatives and countrymen.
> —MAIMONIDES, *Eight Chapters*, chapter 4

Purpose, meaning, and caring develop less from direct instruction than as an outgrowth of authentic, regular practice. Judaism offers specific guidance to parents for creating homes where this practice becomes second nature. This guidance for how to raise a child to become an ethical, caring, generous, and emotionally intelligent adult with a strong identity is applicable for families who come from a wide variety of Jewish orientations and beliefs. Jewishly informed routines and rituals for daily living, coupled with conversations that encourage reflection and perspective taking, provide a powerful way for parents to cultivate character and spirituality. These conversations go beyond modeling and direct experiencing of rituals and practices by providing dialoguing opportunities that stimulate deeper cognitive processing of the events and their meaning on the part of children).[20] Asking open-ended questions, using imagery and analogy, and putting oneself in the place of others all create deeper learning and identification with the concepts underlying what is being experienced than would be the case without such mediation.

Next, we focus on three areas where the ongoing environment created by parents generates a powerful, continuous positive influence on spirituality that provides a synergistic context for the approaches mentioned earlier: celebrating Shabbat, performing deeds of loving-kindness, and expressing gratitude. These are three among many similar areas linked to Jewish routines and rituals).[21]

CELEBRATING SHABBAT: OPPORTUNITY FOR PROVIDING SECURITY AND DEEPENING RELATIONSHIPS

Celebrating Shabbat provides parents with multiple opportunities for cultivating meaning and values. While the idea of a Sabbath was put forward millennia ago, it is as relevant today as ever—maybe even more so. We live in a fast-paced, hectic society; parents' jobs are demanding, and their children are often in formal after-school care and/or extensive programming. Often, there is not even a time when everyone can sit down and eat dinner together. Yet, there is strong research evidence that when families dine together, children are better adjusted socially, get better grades, and have less drug use).[22] When families eat together, they learn how to socialize with each other and build stronger bonds; family meals also provide opportunities to share reflections on their day and to help one another solve problems.

The conceptual core of a Friday evening Shabbat dinner is to ensure that at least once a week, families sit down and eat dinner together, providing consistency and security for children. If the dinner was set for another day of the week, inevitably, it would be postponed and maybe even eventually phased out. Judaism creates a context where Shabbat cannot be postponed. So the benefits of a strong commitment to a weekly dining ritual were anticipated correctly by ancient sages.

Routines are comforting to children, especially when unexpected and bad things happen. Lives can quickly get disrupted by sickness, death, and natural disasters, which may seem overwhelming and frightening to children. Too many children today see their parents beset by financial problems or, worse, see their parents having to deal with difficult circumstances related to their own parents' health. Their world suddenly seems out of control. Establishing routines and rituals like Shabbat to which children can return provides children with stability and security and thus facilitates their adjustment. Shabbat can provide healing for the soul in times of trouble.

The Shabbat dinner can provide an ideal opportunity for parents to enhance the social and emotional skills of their children through rich conversations. Since this requires that everyone be mentally as well as physically present, in the spirit of Shabbat, it would be wise to enforce a moratorium on all forms of electronic communication. With no distractions, family members can focus on each other and engage in meaningful conversations.

Other aspects of the Shabbat experience are also spiritually enriching. When parents involve their children in designing how to make the Shabbat meal special with special foods, special songs, even special tableware—they further enhance the meaning and delight of the experience. The definition of "special" is unique to each family. For some it may be traditional expressions of Shabbat, while for others it may be eating certain favorite foods and singing favorite songs. However, our point is that one need not study texts and engage in extensive explicit religious observances to accumulate spiritual benefits to one's family from Shabbat routines and rituals.

PERFORMING DEEDS OF LOVING-KINDNESS: OPPORTUNITY FOR ACTUALIZING CARING

Jewish tradition holds that performing deeds of loving-kindness (*g'milut chasadim*) is even greater than giving money to charity. Charity involves only one's money, while bestowing loving-kindness can involve either money or one's personal service; money can be given only to the poor, while bestowing loving-kindness can be done for both the rich and for the poor (Babylonian Talmud, *Sukkah* 49b).

Also significant is the benefit to the giver. The wonderful feelings that result from acts of kindness lead to their repetition. Kindness can become a way of life for children if their parents know how to guide them. "Do good deeds for the doing's sake" (Babylonian Talmud, *Nedarim* 62a) reflects the spiritual-emotional benefit of helping those in need. The link between doing and understanding is forged through practice.

There is an art to being kind and caring. Judaism helps cultivate this art by providing specific guidelines for how to intentionally and consciously perform acts of loving-kindness, rather than just hoping people will perform random acts of kindness. As the Torah says, "You will do and then you will understand." (Exodus 24:7). Parents can use these guidelines to help instill kindness and caring in their children through life experiences, such as welcoming guests and visiting the sick.

Welcoming Guests

The story of Abraham greeting the three strangers in the desert (Genesis 18) provides the basis for traditional Jewish guidelines for welcoming guests. Certainly Judaism is far from unique in recognizing the psychological and emotional importance of greeting, something that has been confirmed in recent research on social-emotional intelligence).[23] Parents can use these guidelines to teach their children how to be kind, caring, gracious hosts, thus generating empathy and thoughtfulness and creating connections to a sense of meaning and purpose.

- **Greet guests eagerly, and welcome them graciously.** The three men looked like poor, weary people. Abraham had no idea who they were or if they could be helpful to him, yet he greeted them royally. We are advised in the Talmud (*Derech Eretz Zuta* 9) that the host should be cheerful when greeting guests and at meals so that the guests will feel comfortable. Parents model hospitality for children by greeting guests with comments like, "Hello, I'm so glad you came. We've been looking forward to your visit." When children hear parents say this often enough, it will become second nature to them to say this also. And they will learn that it's not necessarily meant as an expression of accurate feelings. It's meant as recognition that guests deserve to be treated with dignity, respect, and consideration.

   Parents can inspire empathy and thoughtfulness by such comments as "Remember, when our guests come, let's be sure to smile and welcome them graciously" or "How can we make our guests feel welcome when they arrive?" Even if children are teenagers and have not learned this lesson yet, it's not too late for parents to start.

- **Serve food and participate in the preparations.** As soon as Abraham got the visitors settled, he ran to prepare food. Involving children in preparing food teaches responsibility as well as sensitivity to other people's desires. "What foods do you think Barbara will enjoy?" "Let's remember not to serve anything with nuts because Mike is allergic to them. Instead of pecan pie, why don't we make apple pie?" "Do you think this will be too spicy for Arielle?" "Shall we serve our favorite cake?" are all questions that help children practice being caring. In fact, the Talmud relates that some people in Jerusalem had the custom of putting all the food on the table at once so that a guest could choose what he liked and not feel compelled to eat something he didn't like *Eichah Rabbah* 4:4). (Perhaps this is the origin of bounteous buffet spreads!)

- **Be a considerate guest.** The Talmud sagely advises, "The guests, for their part, should express their appreciation to their hosts, and should not overstay their welcome." (*Derech Eretz Rabbah* 6). Parents can teach children that being a good guest means being attuned to the feelings and needs of one's host.

Visiting the Sick

The Abraham story is also the basis of the commandment to visit the sick. The Talmud tells us that one who visits the sick removes a fraction of that person's pain, and those who visited Abraham did so just at the time that he was recuperating from being circumcised at the ripe old age of ninety-nine. Recognizing that visiting those who are ill is difficult, Jewish values create an imperative to engage in these acts. And guidelines are provided to make those visits more likely to go well and lead children to feel a sense of fulfillment as a result of their actions.

- **Time visits according to the patient's needs.** The Talmud makes a point of saying that visitors should not come early in the day or late in the day or when a patient is receiving treatment (*Nedarim* 41a). Why? Early in the day, patients may not yet be groomed and ready to welcome people. Late in the day, they may be too tired. And most people want privacy during treatment. "Let's think about the best time to visit our friend," "I wonder when she'll feel up to accepting visitors," and "Let's not go too early because he might not be dressed," "Let's not go too late because he may be tire." are all comments parents can make to help their children learn to think about the feelings of others.
- **Talk about positive, interesting topics.** Thought also has been given to conversation, especially to not convey distressing news but rather to "gladden" the sick person (*Shulchan Aruch* 337). "How could we cheer him up?" "What is some good news we can share?" "Let's remember not to talk about anything that will make her stressed, such as accidents or politics," "Let's think

about some things we could talk about that she would find interesting."Ultimately, parental reflections such as these lead children to be empathic, caring people who can put themselves in others' shoes.

Expressing Thanks: An Opportunity for Spiritual Growth

According to the findings of the study of gratitude by Emmons and McCullough),[24] those individuals who participated in daily gratitude exercises where they consciously expressed gratitude, reported higher levels of enthusiasm, determination, optimism, and energy. Additionally, they were more likely to help others and were more likely to feel loved. These researchers noted that gratitude encouraged a positive cycle of reciprocal kindness among people.

Because gratitude inspires character and spiritual development, it is universal to all religions—all include some form of giving thanks. Expressing gratitude is a highly spiritual act that connects people to each other and to God. Jewish teachings emphasize the need to bring gratitude to a conscious level. In fact, the Hebrew expression for gratitude,"*hakarat hatov*," literally means "recognizing the good." Judaism provides the means for bringing the good to consciousness with concrete tools for recognizing and expressing appreciation for the gifts of life, whether it be special moments, the gift of freedom, or the gifts of nature. Parents can use these tools of appreciation to enhance their children's character and spiritual development.

Part of having rituals is having some words to use to express our gratitude, either to oneself or aloud. The *Shehechayanu* blessing heralds joyous primary experiences such as the day people become parents, the first time children take a step, lose a tooth, or ride a two-wheeler (without falling), or when children graduate from high school, college, or beyond. It can be said upon visiting a place for the first time, for the first snowfall of the season, or for the first rain after a drought. Children can also say it the first time they see snow, the first time they see a ladybug, the first time they taste pistachio ice cream, or even the first time they are wearing their bathing suits for the season, for example. Reciting *Shehecheyanu* can inspire family joy, an appreciation of the good, and a deep spiritual satisfaction.

Judaism can also bring spiritual comfort during times when it might be tempting to see a glass half empty rather than half full. If one has suffered a serious illness or escaped danger, sometimes it may be a challenge not to keep focusing on the horrors of what was experienced. But our Rabbis shift our focus to be toward the positive, toward appreciation of the fact that we made it through. The *Gomeil* blessing helps us express appreciation for surviving illness or danger. We are encouraged to say this blessing in front of others, making it a public expression of appreciation. The scripted community response wishing that kindness be bestowed on the speaker can be extremely affirming. Families who institute this practice gain empathy and spiritual comfort by doing so.

The Passover seder is an ideal tool for parents to teach their children in a hands-on way what it means to be free people. The secret of the seder is that every year, the story is more created than told, and this ancient story can come to life by allowing children to appreciate how freedom from slavery is still important and must never be forgotten.

We eat bitter herbs that symbolize the bitterness of slavery: "Can you imagine how hard the Jews must have worked in Egypt? Imagine lifting those heavy blocks in the hot sun all day long. How do you think it must have felt? Have you ever felt that you had to work very hard? When could you stop working? How does it compare to what the Jews had to do in Egypt?"

We dip parsley in salt water that symbolizes the tears shed by the slaves: "Have you ever had to work so hard that you felt like crying? How does that compare with the experience of the Jews in Egypt?"

Even to eat matzah is symbolic because it is meant to remind us that our ancestors had to leave Egypt in a great hurry: "The Children of Israel had to get out of their houses as fast as they could. They couldn't even take the time to let their bread rise. What must it have been like for them to leave their houses so fast they couldn't even cook their food? What would it feel like to be forced to leave your house quickly? How do you think the children must have felt? Have you ever felt that way? How was that different from the Jews coming out of Egypt?"

It's tradition to recline on pillows at the seder table to remind ourselves that now, we are free people. "Isn't it fun to sit on comfy pillows during the seder? Can you imagine not being able to even sit at a table without getting someone's permission? Or not even having a table just getting a little bit of food once a day and having to sit on a dusty or muddy floor? That's what it's like to be a slave."

Many other aspects of Jewish tradition reinforce appreciation of living in a country with freedom of religious practice. "Proclaim liberty throughout the land" (Leviticus 25:10) implies that steps must be taken for freedom, including religious freedom, to exist. Appreciating freedom must be active and sustained by routines and structures. Families benefit from having the means to teach children appreciation of religious freedom and the responsibilities that come along with it. Chanukah and Purim are holidays that create valuable routines for families to promote this kind of gratitude.

Chanukah, when candles are lit and fried foods like donuts or potato pancakes are consumed, and Purim, with its costumes and sweet hamantaschen pastries, are reminders of times when the Jewish people were saved from religious persecution. Indeed, part of the Purim celebration includes an obligation to give of what we have to those who are less fortunate. These active observances lead to opportunities for family reflection and storytelling and can lead to a wonderful discussion of appreciating and accepting differences: "King Antiochus didn't like that we were different from other people and wanted everyone to be the same. We're lucky he didn't get his way. Do you know of other situations where people who are different are being forced to change? Why isn't that right?" Chanukah candles can remind families to show appreciation that we survived Antiochus by being a light to the world, making sure others are not oppressed because they are different, especially in their religious beliefs.

Even the Jewish calendar is based on gratitude for the blessings of nature. The Jewish calendar provides families with a year-long appreciation of Mother Earth, a celebration of nature and its gifts. Each holiday provides opportunities for families to engage in activities and discussions that lead to an awe and appreciation of nature. Passover begins the planting season, while Shavuot celebrates the first fruits of the garden. Then, in the fall, Sukkot invokes rejoicing with the fruits of the harvest. Tu BiSh'vat gives parents the opportunity to teach their children about the importance of trees and to appreciate all that we get from trees.

Judaism guides families to eat in a mindful way, expressing our appreciation for nature by blessing God for bringing forth bread from the earth (and not the grocery store!) and for creating fruits of the vine, the tree, and the earth, among others. These blessings provide a wonderful opportunity to discuss where our food comes from. These traditions force us to think about what we are doing and what it means, as opposed to simply taking it all for granted.

Using the lens of Judaism, raising children to be thoughtful and deeply appreciative makes it more likely that they will carry these same characteristics into their adult lives. Building a sense of positive personhood, that is, *menschlichkeit*, is the result of how parents design daily living experiences rather than of techniques and isolated practices.

IMPLICATIONS FOR PARENTING AND PROGRAMMING

We have seen how living Judaism can teach children how to become kind, responsible people who possess social and emotional skills and good values and how Judaism can provide meaning and purpose in children's lives and a strong sense of identity. This is best accomplished by a collaboration between educators and families so that family life as well as school life becomes infused with Jewish values.

Parental attitudes toward Jewish education may present a challenge to Jewish educators for engaging parents as partners. Many parents have less than positive memories about their own Jewish educational experiences. They may send their children to Jewish schools because their parents did so and because they want their children to know about their heritage. Even in the case of Jewish day schools, parents may send their children because of the general educational reputation. Many parents provide door-to-door chauffeur service yet rarely enter through the Jewish school doors. When parents feel some ambivalence about the subject matter, on top of being stretched for time, it is challenging to get them involved in their children's Jewish education. Yet, we know that preaching without modeling is rarely effective and not a sound pedagogical model. Research shows that when parents are not involved in their children's Jewish education, Judaism is less likely to become an important part of children's value system).[25] However, less is known about what happens when parents consciously imbue their home with Jewish values and rituals, in the ways noted earlier, even if they do not engage in conspicuous formal religious practice).[26]

Accordingly, for those involved with Jewish education, we recommend a gradual approach based in the value of Jewishly informed family decision making, routines, and rituals for creating a harmonious, meaningful household in which their children are more likely to become kind, caring, and responsible. This approach can also offer the promise of general academic success, eventual professional success, and prevention of substance abuse by children, all of which are correlated with children's social-emotional competencies.

Educators, including clergy, can take the first step toward engagement by inviting parents to explore strategies for creating a home inspired by Jewish values and customs that can be easily and pleasantly implemented. However, before they will commit, many parents will require reassurance that there is no hidden agenda, that the goal is not more strict religious observance. Explicit communication that the goal is using Jewish wisdom to make parenting easier and family life more peaceful and spiritual is essential. Inevitably, some families will become more religiously observant as they implement our suggestions, but that will be their choice.

The agenda for the initial get-together could include an overview of what Jewish wisdom has to offer parents as well as the opportunity for them to engage in self-reflection, as described earlier. That will prepare them for the next session, where they will explore how Shabbat can be used to enhance family life and teach children values.

Arranging shared Shabbat dinners can be a good starting point. Families could be divided into groups perhaps by neighborhood or by ages of children, with two to four families in each group. On a rotating basis, once a month, a family will host Friday evening dinner for the other families in the group. Parents and children together could plan these dinners. Preparations would include discussions of food (based on the guests' preferences and dietary needs), songs they think everyone would enjoy, and how each family can make the evening special. Perhaps the hosts could provide the meal, while the guests provide the grape juice and challah. Parents can brainstorm with their children the specifics of how they can be good guests or good hosts, based on Jewish wisdom, as discussed earlier. These shared Shabbat dinners provide an authentic opportunity to learn empathy, caring, kindness, and responsibility through a joyful Jewish celebration.

Ultimately, the challenge for educators is to "package" the parenting procedures in ways that parents will find acceptable and capable of implementing into their family routines. This is a crucial area for research, because until and unless interventions are acceptable, tests of their impact will not be meaningful. Our view is that a focus on Jewish wisdom and its everyday applicability to family life, parenting issues, and the positive upbringing and future of children is a viable strategy for improving acceptability of Jewish education programming for parents. Once interventions are implemented in the context of supplemental and day schools, as well as areas where one can reach parents who are not providing a systematic Jewish education experience for their children, research can be conducted on the impact of the interventions on Jewish identity development in children and adolescents.

Judaism offers exquisite tools for social-emotional and character development within a spiritual context. Programming that integrates Jewish values and spirituality into everyday family routines provides authentic, meaningful experiences for "living Jewishly." This requires engaging parents in the education of their children; the promise of joyful, successful parenting can be the lure. Such an approach would generate new and viable research opportunities to study how these authentic experiences contribute to Jewish identity over time.

TABLE 2

Parental Self-Assessment for Facilitating Children's Social-Emotional Competencies

To what extent would you say that you:

a. Are aware of kids', spouse's feelings:
   This is: Definitely Me   Sort of Me   Definitely Not Me
              1   2   3   4   5

b. Show a high degree of self-control with your children:
   This is: Definitely Me   Sort of Me   Definitely Not Me
              1   2   3   4   5

c. Possess a strong sense of empathy with your children:
   This is: Definitely Me   Sort of Me   Definitely Not Me
              1   2   3   4   5

d. Are great at seeing other family members' points of view:
   This is: Definitely Me   Sort of Me   Definitely Not Me
              1   2   3   4   5

e. Set positive goals for your children, family:
   This is: Definitely Me   Sort of Me   Definitely Not Me
              1   2   3   4   5

f. Do organized, detailed planning around parenting tasks:
   This is: Definitely Me   Sort of Me   Definitely Not Me
              1   2   3   4   5

g. Act in highly effective, comfortable ways with your children:
   This is: Definitely Me   Sort of Me   Definitely Not Me
              1   2   3   4   5

h. Resolve household conflicts peacefully:
   This is: Definitely Me   Sort of Me   Definitely Not Me
              1   2   3   4   5

i. Use creative problem solving around parenting issues:
   This is: Definitely Me   Sort of Me   Definitely Not Me
              1   2   3   4   5

j. Find time to laugh with your children:
   This is: Definitely Me   Sort of Me   Definitely Not Me
              1   2   3   4   5

TABLE 3

| Showing Parents' Character to Children |

For each attribute below, ask yourself how often you tend to show this to your children. It's useful to calculate this separately for each of your children. Also influential is how you treat your spouse/partner, so you may want to reflect on that separately, as well:

	Always	Regularly	Once in a While	Rarely	Never
Loving	1	2	3	4	5
Proud of Others	1	2	3	4	5
Fun	1	2	3	4	5
Compassionate	1	2	3	4	5
Respectful	1	2	3	4	5
Understanding	1	2	3	4	5
Interested in Others	1	2	3	4	5
Angry	1	2	3	4	5
Disappointed in Others	1	2	3	4	5
Frustrated	1	2	3	4	5
Annoyed	1	2	3	4	5
Embarrassed by Others	1	2	3	4	5
Anxious	1	2	3	4	5
Withdrawn	1	2	3	4	5

As you reflect on your responses, consider the balance between positive and negative feelings. Consider how similar or different your responses are to different children and to your spouse/partner. Also important is whether you believe your displays of character are aligned with your feelings. Often, parents feel more positively, and believe they act more positively, than in fact they do. Remember, children only know what you show. Are you modeling a decent emotional range, especially for teens? What feelings would you like to display differently? How might you accomplish this?

CONCLUSION

Setting the Stage for Spiritual, Social, and Emotional Growth

JEFFREY S. KRESS

THE AUTHORS in this book have drawn from their experience to provide important insights about conceptualizing—and working to foster—the spiritual, social, and emotional as part of Jewish education. Perhaps the key message to be gleaned from these chapters is that social, emotional, and spiritual growth should not be left to chance. These elements are central goals of Jewish education and should be actively cultivated. The work of the authors represents a diversity of denominations and educational settings, underscoring the broad relevance of these issues.

That being said, it often seems difficult to stretch our construct of *education* to encompass the promotion of growth in these arenas. It is challenging enough to think about how to teach Hebrew language, foster a familiarity with Bible stories, or promote a working knowledge of the siddur. *Now, an educator may wonder, I am supposed to deal with social, spiritual, and emotional issues!* Of course, educators constantly address such issues in their work, intentionally or not (and sometimes by omission). Looking across the chapters of the book, one can draw some broad conclusions about key elements in educating for inter- and intrapersonal development.

Becoming a Developmental Coach

It is important not to let the inadequacy of language derail our efforts. Of course, we do not "teach" spirituality or social-emotional competence in the same way that we might teach academic subjects. We can, however, help to promote underlying competencies and attitudes that make the achievement of spiritual, social, and emotional more likely and create environments conducive to development in these areas. We might put friendship, for example, at the forefront of what we want our students to achieve, but we cannot teach friendship in the same way that we can teach the multiplication tables, or that 2 + 2 = 4, or that pressing a particular set of piano keys produces a C chord. Rather, we help learners develop the skills and attitudes that underlie the desired outcome (e.g., conversation and listening skills, a value placed on the importance of friendship), provide scaffolded opportunities to practice these skills (e.g., group work that encourages mixing among cliques), and reflect on the experience as a way not only of building and reinforcing the skill, but also to bring the desired outcome more centrally into a sense one's identity. Though the spiritual (or social or emotional) whole is certainly more than the sum of these component parts, building the parts makes the whole more likely to emerge, particularly when there are meaningful opportunities in the environment to put these skills into practice. This two-pronged approach—readiness plus opportunity—is consistent with Shire's ideas about encounter, reflection, and instruction in chapter 1. As with any outcome in the social and emotional domain, we keep our vision on broad outcomes while educating for small steps ahead.

In some ways, the process is similar to that of coaching a sport. A coach might introduce basic skills (e.g., ways to pass the ball most effectively) and strategies (e.g., if you are throwing the ball to someone who is running, throw a few steps ahead of them). These skills and strategies are practiced in controlled situations of increasing complexity (e.g., drills in practice to start with, progressing to games like scrimmages) with continuous feedback given. The coach will also likely model the skills. I will use the coaching metaphor to trace some themes that emerged from my reading of these chapters and that I have gleaned from my own work in the field.

Although the chapters span the developmental continuum, I position my comments from the standpoint of youth development. I have divided my reflections into three categories: environmental approaches, direct approaches, and approaches related to the adults with whom youth interact. These categories are not mutually exclusive and intersect at many points. This approach is consistent with *ecological* approaches[1] that emphasize the developmental potential of a broad range of roles and relationships—some in which an individual is a direct participant (e.g., a classroom) and some in which he or she is not (e.g., a faculty meeting at school). One can think of these categories as addressing both the *macro* (environmental) and *micro* (direct) elements of education. I sometimes modify an adage and say that successful education in social-emotional realms requires attention to *both* the forest *and* the trees; looking at either "environment" or "instruction" in isolation is insufficient.

ADDRESS SPIRITUAL, SOCIAL, AND EMOTIONAL SKILLS ENVIRONMENTALLY

We all know that the people and places with whom we come into contact influence us greatly. Environmentally based approaches to promoting spiritual, social, and emotional development can be powerful but are not without limits.

Modeling and Messages

The environment provides cues for norms and expectations, whether intentionally planned or not. Are emotional issues treated as distractions

from learning or as opportunity for growth? How do adults in the setting speak to one another? Are teacher interactions thoughtful and respectful? How about interaction with the custodian and secretaries?
When learners violate rules, is the reaction punitive discipline or consequences that might help shape future behavior? The difference is far
from semantic; rather it determines the direction of the powerful influence that the environment can play. The chapters that open this book
are particularly useful in providing central themes around which environmental messages can be organized (e.g., Ingall and Heller's focus on
transcendence in chapter 2, Scheindlin's on sensitivity in chapter 3, and
Levingston's on moral education in chapter 4). Educators serving as
developmental coaches might take inventory of the ways in which these
themes are evident throughout their setting. How might a visitor know
that the spiritual, social, and emotional are valued in this place?

Modeling is an important aspect of coaching, particularly for setting
norms, providing reinforcement, and as will be discussed further, opening unforeseen ranges of possibilities. Modeling has its limitations—I
can watch a highly skilled swimmer, violinist, or Torah reader but make
little progress on developing my own abilities. The limitations of modeling are particularly pronounced in the intra- and interpersonal arenas,
which have many elements that may not be fully visible. If an educator
is practicing self-control, for example, how might a learner see that?
One implication is that educators should make some of these invisible
elements more visible to students. Just as educators often *think out loud*
to demonstrate, say, the solution to a math problem, they can also *feel
out loud* to share with their students their emotional experiences, moments of spiritual connectedness, and so on.

Prompts and Opportunities

Much of the work of a coach involves structuring opportunities for practice and providing prompts for what he or she expects to happen during
these practices (and beyond). While often framed as a passive influence, the environment can also be proactively structured by educators
to promote Jewish developmental outcomes. The work of the Chicago
Hillels (chapter 12) provides an example of educators modifying the
environment to prompt reflection on issues of meaning. Educational
settings can and do provide opportunities for encounter with spiritual,
social, and emotional issues within experiences authentically rooted

in the Jewish tradition. Prayer (e.g., chapter 10) is a particularly salient example. Likewise, settings are increasingly embracing work with *tikkun olam*, often in the form of service learning activities that have been shown to build a variety of social and emotional competencies.[2] Opportunities to connect with nature and the outdoors can also be important. Settings that promote positive development are marked by communal celebration of significant milestones,[3] and these can be strongly linked to Judaism, as is the case regarding *Shabbatonim*, communal retreats for the celebration of Shabbat.[4]

Coordinate Developmental Contexts

Youth, now more than ever, are exposed to multiple developmental influences with potentially conflicting norms and messages regarding spiritual, social, and emotional issues. We live at a time when a learner can easily be physically located in one environment (e.g., school) while simultaneously be peering into, or even participating in, another environment (e.g., texting or chatting online). One way to address this issue is to think not just about individual settings, but about intentionally linking the norms of the various developmental contexts in which a young person participates. How, we might ask, can a similar set of Jewish developmental messages be powerfully linked between, say, a supplemental school, a youth group, a camp, and synagogue-based Shabbat services? Similar questions can be asked within each individual setting as well. Is the school's vision for Jewish growth being reinforced only in certain teachers' classrooms and not others? In class but not at recess? Even though Wertheimer introduced us to the phrase some time ago,[5] there are still many silos to be linked both between and within educational organizations. The work of the Union for Reform Judaism (URJ), as reported by Winer and Sheanin (chapter 11) represents an ongoing effort at looking at the experience of youth not just in one setting, but in multiple arenas of participation.

Relationships

The bedrock of coaching is the relationship between the coach and the learner. The centrality of caring relationships as a foundation for positive youth development has been a consistent research finding. It is one, however, with which Jewish communal organizations might struggle. In Smith and Denton's landmark study of spirituality in youth,[6] Jewish respondents indicated some startling points of disconnection. For example, when asked for the "number of adults in a religious congregation or religious youth group attending teens can turn to for support, advice, and help (not including parents)," 72 percent of the Jewish respondents answered "zero" (compared to 39 percent overall).

Smith and Denton conclude that successfully engaging youth in religion will require the strengthening of relationships. They see this as manifesting in small steps

> through simple, ordinary adult relationships with teenagers. Adults other than family members and youth ministers could be intentionally encouraged to make better efforts to learn teens' names, to strike up conversations with teens, to ask them meaningful questions, to be vulnerable themselves to youth in various ways, to show some interest in them, to help connect them to jobs and internships, to make themselves available in times of trouble and crisis, to work toward becoming models and partners in love and concern and sacrifice.[7]

Jewish educational settings present strong opportunities for developing such relationships.

Environment, Motivation, and Plausibility

Environmental initiatives may be particularly useful in building motivation. In fact, one shortcoming of the coaching analogy is that on a sports team, players may have a high level of motivation to begin with, giving the coach a head start in comparison with the developmental educator. While it may be the case that any one coaching practice or drill may not be greatly motivating (participants may grumble about running yet another set of laps around the field), there is a sense of purpose, a broader goal that is valued by the community and acknowledged by the participant ("OK, I don't like running laps, but I really want to be on the starting team this year so I will run hard").

For many—perhaps most—Jewish youth, messages about the importance of growth in the spiritual, social, and emotional realms are unclear at best. Role models in the broader society—entertainers, athletes, and so on—might provide motivation for pursuing fame and fortune. Excellent Jewish role models provide a counterbalance to this. Role models and environments that embrace the spiritual, social, and emotional hold the potential to show youth new possibilities for Jewish outcomes. To noted sociologist Peter Berger, the environment is crucial in showing what *can* be and in providing *plausible* pathways for finding meaning in the world that is "built up in the consciousness of the individual by conversation with significant others (such as parents, teachers, 'peers'). The world is maintained as subjective reality by the same sort of conversation."[8] While plausibility is not the same as motivation, it may be seen as a prerequisite and highlights the importance of the environment as an active element in youth development.

ADDRESS THE SPIRITUAL, SOCIAL, AND EMOTIONAL DIRECTLY

To complement environmental approaches, educators must attend to the inter- and intrapersonal skills of those who make up that environment. Just like members of a sports team, members of an educational community bring with them capacities, habits, or skills in these realms that are potentially quite divergent. Taking the spiritual, social, and emotional growth of youth seriously requires planful thought about how to actively promote development in these arenas. We encounter both

- youth who are very emotionally aware and those who are less so;
- youth who tend to ask "big questions" about their world and those who do not;
- youth who demonstrate self-control and those who struggle to do so;
- youth who are comfortable connecting in the community and those consistently disconnected;
- youth who are more reflective and contemplative and those who are more impulsive.

The environment provides a crucial context but can be complemented by a more active approach to promote social, emotional, and spiritual outcomes.

When we consider desired educational outcomes, we think about how we can scaffold movement of each learner closer to a particular goal (or more than one goal). The expected outcomes may differ among students, but there is an overall sense that education is about providing stepping-stones along the way. When we think of this process in, say, math or reading, we refer to this planful approach of moving toward desired outcomes as a *curriculum*. It may seem strange to think about curricularizing outcomes in the spiritual or social-emotional realm. However, we can think of a curriculum as a structured, thoughtful, intentional, and planful approach to achieving educational (or developmental) outcomes, as opposed to a fixed set of lessons through which an educator provides information. In this way, application of the notion of a curriculum to the intra- and interpersonal arenas makes sense. A good coach has a general plan that is flexible enough to be tailored to individual strengths and needs. He or she can keep focused on this overall plan while still leaving room to address unexpected issues that might arise at any given moment.

Jewish developmental curricula, dealing as they do with emotional reactions and social interactions, would by necessity involve experiential elements—role-play, reflective discussions, and so forth. The Facing History and Ourselves and Open Circle programs (chapters 5 and 6) both contain curricular elements, the former as a stand-alone set of lessons (which, as the authors discuss, overlap with central Jewish values) and the latter as integrated into content areas such as social studies or history. The PassageWorks program (chapter 7) likewise contains structured components for implementation. However, to describe these programs solely as a set of lessons would ignore major aspects of each of them. In each, educators work to create a language that permeates the setting and to reinforce the skills and values of the classroom. Curriculum should not imply rigidity—the experiential elements of the implementation of these programs mean that class discussions and other activities can move in unpredictable ways. A curricular approach, though, means that issues in the developmental realm cannot be addressed only when they "come up" but rather they must be thought about planfully and developmentally.

While we sometimes think about social and emotional functioning as immutable character traits (e.g., "That boy is just awkward"), research has shown that growth in these arenas is possible. A developmental coach might need to work on spiritual, social, and emotional capacities and competencies directly, working with learners to enhance emotional awareness and language, self-control, communication skills, or reflectivity, to name a few examples. These skills might be practiced in the safety of a role-playing situation and in natural opportunities throughout the day.

A coach would also help prepare learners to use skills under adverse conditions, for example, to throw a basketball past a flailing opponent. It is difficult enough to be able to maintain one's spiritual, social, and emotional competencies day in and day out. Even under normal conditions, everyone slips, as it were. We miss opportunities for spiritual engagement, lose our self-control, or engage in inappropriate communications with peers (I, for one, have often managed this trifecta in the span of one day). There are, however, times when staying true to our spiritual, social, and emotional ideals is particularly difficult. Educators need to be proactive in preparing themselves and their students to confront difficult issues such as bullying (chapter 8) and bias (chapter 9). Further, educators should be ready for the inevitable and invaluable questions that arise during moments of prayer or of spiritual challenge (such as the loss of a loved one or confronting the atrocities of the Holocaust, as in chapter 5). Further, even the most skilled professional athletes have coaches. The process does not end but rather is one of continuous growth.

Finally, knowing how to play a sport (that is, having the skills and knowing the strategy) does not guarantee that one will enjoy the game or even choose to play the game. This challenge calls for the strong intersection of the direct coaching approach with the broader environmental approach described above. That is, a coach and learner must have opportunities to express these skills and capacities in meaningful and challenging ways that are valued by the community.

ATTENTION TO THE NEEDS OF THE EDUCATORS AND OTHER ADULTS

The theme that perhaps most infuses the chapters of this book relates to the importance of addressing the spiritual, social, and emotional needs of the adults who work with youth. Several chapters touch on the issue of working with educators on their own spiritual and social-emotional growth, and Levites and Stone (chapter 13) and Elias and Gootman (chapter 14) focus specifically on work with adults.

Even when our specific level of intervention has to do with program implementation for youth, we must keep in mind that the success of this endeavor is mediated by an educator. Education is often discussed in lofty terms as a calling or a sacred task. Many educators will tell you that while they believe this to be true, it sure doesn't *feel* like it on a moment-to-moment basis. The question of who helps the helper is a pressing one. A good coach constantly works to improve his or her own craft!

Educators' concerns about discussing spiritual, social, and emotional issues with their students might fall under the general category of discomfort with dealing with gray areas for which they do not have *the* answer to the questions asked by the learners. However, these areas of "no correct answer" or perhaps "many correct answers" are not peripheral matters in Jewish education but are, rather, the core foci: What do I believe? What course of action should I take? And so on. For some educators, overcoming a reluctance to address ambiguity is in itself a major personal and professional achievement that comes with great effort and calls for support on the part of those who seek to promote such growth in practice.

Issues of faith and spirituality are further complicated by their very personal nature and, as has been pointed out in several chapters, the fact that many educators lack a venue for serious consideration of their own beliefs and doubts. The demarcation between the personal and professional is a blurry one in these matters. Even educators who have had the opportunity to explore and be thoughtful about their theology and other beliefs (and such a process of exploration is far from a given) will likely encounter doubts and elements of questioning and confusion. Even if they embrace these aspects on a personal level, they may wonder what it means to be a Jewish "role model" even in the face of these doubts and questions.

It is unlikely that an educator who doubts her ability or otherwise feels uncomfortable will sustain engagement with any new initiative,[9] and this is no exception. Those who aim to promote spiritual, social, and emotional outcomes among youth cannot ignore adults with whom our youth interact. Educators—and parents—benefit from mediated opportunities to explore the broad range of theology and beliefs that Judaism encompasses and to share their doubts and questions in a safe context. They need opportunities to think proactively about, and actively prepare for, how their beliefs will play out in the context of their relationships with the youth with whom they work.

Informal and Experiential Jewish Education

Recently, interest in informal or experiential Jewish education has blossomed, bolstered by reports of the successes of settings like camps and Israel trips in promoting Jewish outcomes. This field has been marked by inconsistently used terminology. Reimer and Bryfman have suggested that the term "informal" be used to refer to nonschool educational settings (e.g., camps), while "experiential" be used to refer to an approach to education that can be implemented in a variety of settings.[10] In this way, one might find experiential education taking place in formal settings (e.g., in a day school).

I have written elsewhere about the overlap between key components of a holistic developmental approach with core concepts of experiential education.[11] As noted above, it is hard to conceive of a developmental approach that is not at its core experiential. It is likewise difficult to imagine an engaging Jewish experience that does not hold the potential to impact upon the social, spiritual, and/or emotional realms.

The chapters of this book should reinforce the notion that holistic developmental education is a complex matter, involving a sustained, intentional focus on youth, educators, and educational settings. While this idea will not surprise those immersed in this work, it does caution against overly simplistic interpretations of the endeavor. One might, for example, see the solution to the challenges of Jewish education as being to "make it more fun." While I certainly endorse the idea of fun, and while fun might be motivating, it is not the case that a fun activity will necessarily, or even likely, result in growth in the spiritual, social, or emotional realms (to say nothing of the cognitive). An alternate conceptualization can be based on Csikszentmihalyi's idea of *flow*,[12] or the holistic immersion that occurs in activities that provide a degree of challenge that is optimal to growth in one's skills. In this way, we might switch from asking, for example, "How can we make *t'filah* fun?" and ask instead how the *t'filah* experience can challenge students to improve skills that they value, perhaps by incorporating elements of drama, music, or movement or by addressing questions that will stimulate thinking and imagination.

A related tendency is to see the panacea for the problems in formal Jewish educational settings—and particularly in supplemental settings—being "add experiential programming" such as a *Shabbaton* or a simulated Israel trip (featuring music, falafel, a mock airplane). Again, I have no conceptual argument with the utility of adding these components to any program. However, efforts to import episodic educational experiences might mask larger and more significant areas for enhancement, such as the quality of relationships within the setting or the ability of educators to think about how the spiritual and emotional experiences of students can be addressed throughout their educational experiences and not just on special occasions.

Further, my research with day school–based experiential education has led me to suggest that in many cases, a dearth of opportunities for spiritual, social, and emotional growth may not be the key educational challenge. Rather, the missing piece of the developmental puzzle might be our efforts to help learners integrate their experiences into their sense of themselves as Jews.[13] Reflection—seen as an important complement to the "experiences" of experiential education[14]—is crucial in the developmental realms. Noted spiritual practitioner Rabbi Zalman Schachter-Shalomi suggests that after "we talk about a wonderful notion, we encourage the class, 'Now daydream for five minutes about that.' Measure yourself to this idea; see how it feels when you put it on."[15]

Finally, one may point out that many of the chapters of the book lean toward applications to formal settings. On the one hand, much of this material is meant to be generally relevant even when framed with regard to one type of setting or another. And there are chapters focusing specifically on informal settings. It is true, though, that informal settings are often viewed as places in which holistic developmental education thrives. Pulling together chapters related to this work in such settings would be a worthwhile future endeavor. For now, the chapters that have a formal education focus can be read that even in settings such as day schools in which "the transmission of knowledge remains a central focus" and where learning has "usually been seen in cognitive terms,"[16] a holistic developmental approach is both needed and possible. Also, by and large, the chapters represent approaches that infuse multiple elements of an educational setting. This should not diminish from the importance of approaches focused around specific topics or venues, such as environmentalism and nature or the arts.

Closing the Loop:
Cognitive and Knowledge Considerations

One may look at the discussion of social, emotional, and spiritual elements of Jewish education and wonder: *Is all of this just a matter of getting kids to feel good about themselves? What about Jewish content? What do they walk away "knowing"?* This is a very important line of questioning, and responding goes beyond pointing to neurological evidence suggesting the intersection of knowing, feeling, and doing.[17] Intra- and interpersonal elements catalyze learning. For example, our ability to sustain attention and focus is not only important to our interactions with others and with nature, but also with our focus on reading and learning facts.

As stated in the introduction, the goals of Jewish education strongly embrace social, emotional, and spiritual outcomes, as well as knowledge. When applied to living a Jewish life, the "educated" Jew roots the inter- and intrapersonal elements of their experience within Jewish knowledge and practice. One can, for example, participate in service learning without making connections to Jewish ideas and ideals. Jewish educators strive to take the next step and to root these actions in the notion of *tikkun olam* by introducing Jewish terms and/or texts. Similarly, discussion of students' spiritual, social, and emotional lives can emerge from, and lead to, engagement with Jewish texts, history, and so on. Biblical stories, for example, provide rich opportunities to practice empathy and emotional awareness in discussing the feelings and choices made by the protagonists. Moments of heroism and pride—as well as crisis—throughout Jewish history can raise questions of meaning.

While it has become a truism that cognition, affect, and behavior are interconnected, educators still must make decisions about where to put their focus during any given educational experience. We can all imagine a lack of balance among these areas—a boring lecture focused solely on the recitation of facts; a "fluff" discussion group that seemed to go nowhere. The challenge posted throughout this book is to imagine an educator who addresses the whole learner and takes with equal seriousness the worlds of the heart, the spirit, and the mind.

Biographies

Rabbi Scott Aaron is the community scholar for the Agency for Jewish Learning for Greater Pittsburgh, where he specializes in formal and informal adult education. Scott is currently a PhD candidate in educational philosophy through Loyola University of Chicago where his academic work focuses on the impact of experiential education on the Jewish identity of emerging adults. He is the author of a number of published articles and stories, including his well-known book, *Jewish U: A Contemporary Guide for The Jewish College Student* (URJ Press: 2010) which is now in its second edition. Scott is also adjunct faculty at Spertus College and the education schools of the Jewish Theological Seminary of America and the Hebrew Union College – Jewish Institute of Religion.

Jan Darsa is director of the Jewish education program at Facing History and Ourselves. She has developed curricula designed for educators in Jewish day and congregational schools, including *Facing History and Ourselves: The Jews of Poland*. She facilitates workshops, institutes, and other professional development programs for teachers across the country and in Israel and provides follow-up consultations for individual teachers and schools. She was a Jerusalem Fellow and received the Covenant Award in 2010.

Maurice J. Elias, Ph.D., is a Professor, Psychology Department and Director of Clinical PhD Training, Rutgers University, Academic Director of Rutgers Civic Engagement and Service Education Partnerships program, and Director of the Rutgers Social-Emotional Learning Lab. Among his recent books are the new ebook, *Emotionally Intelligent Parenting* (via Kindle and Nook). He collaborated with storytellers in the U.S. and Israel, and a prominent Israeli School Psychologist, to create a book for young children: *Talking Treasure: Stories to Help Build Emotional Intelligence and Resilience in Young Children* (www.researchpress.com, 2012). He writes a blog on Social-Emotional and Character Development (SECD) for the George Lucas Educational Foundation at www.edutopia.org.

Dr. Shira D. Epstein is an assistant professor of Jewish education at the Jewish Theological Seminary. She was the founding director of *Evaded Issues in Jewish Education*, and co-creator of the *Educational Jewish Moments* methodology. She has authored several curricula, including Jewish Women International's *Strong Girls, Healthy Relationships: A Conversation on Dating, Friendship, and Self-Esteem* (2006).

Josh Feigelson is a doctoral candidate in the Northwestern University Department of Religious Studies. He served as campus rabbi at Northwestern University Hillel from 2005 to 2011, and now serves as educational director of Ask Big Questions, a national initiative of Hillel: The Foundation for Jewish Campus Life.

Ruth Gafni is Head of School at Solomon Schechter Day School of Bergen County. Previously she served as the school's Lower School Principal. Ms. Gafni served in the Ridgewood public school system as a Director of Special Needs, ESL & Gifted & Talented. During her tenure, she received Educator of the Year Award by Ridgewood Township and was chosen as an Open Circle Trainer in 2001-2002. Ms. Gafni has been instrumental in identifying the need for, and implementing, successful social competency programs in Ridgewood and at SSDS. She graduated from Bar Ilan University in Israel and received her Masters of Science from Adelphi University in New York. She has written several articles for newspapers and educational magazines. She is also a contributing author to the book "Fine Tuning a Listening Heart," ed. Jeffrey

Kress, which will be released this fall. Ms. Gafni lives in Fair Lawn with her husband and enjoys spending time with her two daughters.

Marilyn E. Gootman, Ed.D. is founder of Gootman Education Associates, an educational consulting company that provides workshops and seminars for parents and educators focusing on successful strategies for raising and teaching children. She is the author of *The Loving Parents' Guide to Discipline* (Berkley: 1995, 2000), *When a Friend Dies: A Book for Teens about Grieving and Healing* (Free Spirit Publishing: 1995, 2005) and *The Caring Teacher's Guide to Discipline* (Corwin Press: 1997, 2001), and with Maurice Elias, a forthcoming book on Jewish parenting. Marilyn has over 35 years of teaching experience, ranging from early childhood to university level, both in Jewish and in general settings. Since founding and the running the PJ Library Program in Athens GA in 2007, Marilyn has become the pied piper of young Jewish families in Athens.

Batya Greenwald was born and raised in South Africa, became a teacher in Australia and recently earned an MA in Education from the University of Montana. She currently teaches kindergarten and has previously taught third, fourth, and fifth grade at the Boulder Community School of Integrated Studies. She was the founding Director of the Boulder Jewish Day School and has taught for more than 15 years. Batya has two daughters and is dedicated to empowering the lives of young people by facilitating and co-creating healthy communities in which they can thrive. Ms. Greenwald leads PassageWorks courses, and presents keynote addresses throughout the United States.

Dr. Randi Hirschberg is completing her post-doctoral fellowship in clinical psychology at the Women's Health Project at St. Luke's-Roosevelt Hospital in New York City. Prior to pursuing a career in psychology, she served as a high school teacher in various settings for four years and a Dean of Students for one year. Her research interests include the impact of social-emotional learning on resiliency and interpersonal relationships.

Carol K. Ingall, Ed.D. is the Dr. Bernard Heller Professor Emerita of Jewish Education at The Jewish Theological Seminary. She is the author of *Maps, Metaphors and Mirrors: Moral Education In Middle Schools*

(Ablex, 1997), *Transmission and Transformation: A Jewish Perspective on Moral Education* (Melton, 1999), *Down the Up Staircase: Tales from Teaching in Jewish Day Schools* (JTS Press, 2007), and *The Women Who Reconstructed American Jewish Education, 1910–1965* (Brandeis University Press, 2012).

Jeffrey S. Kress is associate professor of Jewish education and academic director of the Experiential Learning Initiative at the William Davidson Graduate School of Jewish Education at the Jewish Theological Seminary. His interests include developmental issues in Jewish education, program implementation, and social, emotional, and spiritual elements of Jewish educational contexts. He is the author of *Development, Learning, and Community: Educating for Identity in Pluralistic Jewish High Schools* and co-author with Bernard Novick and Maurice Elias of *Building Learning Communities With Character: How to Integrate Academic, Social, and Emotional Learning.* He has published numerous journal articles and book chapters. Dr. Kress has served as chair of the Network for Research in Jewish Education.

Rabbi Judd Kruger Levingston, PhD, serves as director of Jewish Studies at Barrack Hebrew Academy (formerly Akiba Hebrew Academy) in the Philadelphia area. He also has taught at Gratz College, at Temple University, and at the Reconstructionist Rabbinical College. He is the author of *Sowing the Seeds of Character: The Moral Education of Adolescents in Public and Private Schools.*

Arielle Levites is a doctoral candidate at New York University. She holds a BA from Brown University in Religious Studies and an MS Ed from the University of Pennsylvania in Religious Education. She is an alumnus of the Wexner Graduate Fellowship program and a recipient of the Emerging Scholar Award from the Network for Research in Jewish Education.

Daniel Libenson is president of the Institute for the Next Jewish Future, a think tank, leadership education center, and network of laboratory communities dedicated to accelerating the development of a resonant and compelling twenty-first-century Judaism that has the power to attract and serve the majority of American Jews. He also serves as director of the Institute's Jewish U program for college and graduate students on the University of Chicago campus. During a six-year tenure as executive director of the University of Chicago Hillel, Libenson was awarded an AVI CHAI Fellowship and received the Richard M. Joel Exemplar of Excellence award, Hillel International's highest professional honor. He is a magna cum laude graduate of Harvard Law School, where he served as an editor of the *Harvard Law Review*, and a former law professor.

Dr. Rona Milch Novick is the director of the Fanya Gottesfeld Heller Doctoral Program at the Azrieli Graduate School of Jewish Education and Administration at Yeshiva University in New York. She also serves as the co-educational director of Hidden Sparks, a professional development and mentoring program for educators and holds an appointment as attending psychologist at North Shore-Long Island Jewish Medical Center. Dr. Novick developed and served as director of the Alliance for School Mental Health at Long Island where she authored the BRAVE bully reduction program and supervised its implementation in schools across the United States.

Michael J. Schatz is a doctoral candidate in Jewish Education (ABD) at Gratz College, where he also serves as an adjunct instructor and an administrator in the Jewish Community High School. He serves as a vice president of the Jewish Educators Assembly and has been a practitioner in the field of Jewish education for more than twenty years.

Rabbi Laurence Scheindlin is headmaster emeritus of Sinai Akiba Academy in Los Angeles, where he was head of school for thirty-five years. His articles on education, emotions and cognition, and spirituality have appeared in the *International Journal of Children's Spirituality,* the *Journal of Jewish Education,* and elsewhere. He now is a consultant on school leadership and serves on the faculty of the Rhea Hirsch School of Education at Hebrew Union College in Los Angeles. He is a past president of the Schechter Day School Network.

Dana Sheanin, MSW/MAJCS, is an independent nonprofit consultant, specializing in leadership development and long-range planning. She recently completed a seven-year tenure as a specialist on adolescents and experiential education at the Union for Reform Judaism. Dana's

writing on mentorship, recruitment and retention of Jewish professionals, and integrating Jewish values in clinical social work has been published in the *Journal of Jewish Communal Service*.

Rabbi Dr. Michael Shire is dean of the Shoolman Graduate School of
Jewish Education at Hebrew College. Formerly vice-principal and director of education of Leo Baeck College London, he holds a doctorate
in Jewish education from Hebrew Union College in the field of religious development. He gained MA's in religious education (HUC) and
Jewish studies (LBC) and s'micha from Leo Baeck College. He has published widely in the field of religious growth and development as well
as the Jewish theology of childhood most recently in the *International
Handbook of Jewish Education*, eds. H. Miller et al. (Springer). He has
also published four books of creative liturgy with medieval illuminations in association with the British Museum.

Shoshana Simons, PHD, RDT, is chair of the MA Program in expressive arts therapy at California Institute of Integral Studies. Dr. Simons
was formerly training director and director of special projects at the
Open Circle Program, Stone Center, Wellesley College. She is currently involved with a whole systems arts-based SEL partnership with
Glide Memorial Church's Family, Youth and Childcare Center in San
Francisco.

Martin E. Sleeper is associate executive director at Facing History and
Ourselves. His undergraduate degree is from Willams College in history and he holds masters' and doctoral degrees in teaching and curriculum development from the Harvard University Graduate School of
Education. He has extensive experience in teaching at the secondary
and college levels as well as curriculum design and museum education.
From 1979 to 2000 he was principal of the John D. Runkle School in
Brookline, Massachusetts. He is the author of numerous articles on history education and adolescent development.

Rabbi Ira F. Stone is the spiritual leader of Temple Beth Zion - Beth
Israel in Philadelphia, as well as the founder of The Mussar Leadership
Programs. In addition to teaching at the Reconstructionist Rabbinic
College he is the author of *Seeking the Path to Life* (Jewish Lights),

Reading Levinas/Reading Talmud (JPS), *The Responsible Life* (Aviv) and *Messillat Yesharim with a Contemporary Commentary* (JPS).

Saul Philip Wachs, Ph.D. is the Rosaline B. Feinstein Professor of Education and Liturgy at Gratz College where he directs the doctoral program in education and chairs the education department. A native of Philadelphia, his earned doctorate in Education and Jewish studies is from the Ohio State University. He is also an alumnus of Gratz College and the schools of education and music of the Jewish Theological Seminary of America, which also awarded him an honorary doctorate in Pedagogy. Author of almost ninety publications, he has lectured in close to four hundred communities on five continents. His latest publications include a theory of practice for conducting worship for and with children and youth, published by the Solomon Schechter Day School Association, and an article, written with Diane Ruth Cover, on aesthetics and holiness.

Laura Weaver, MA is the co-executive director of the PassageWorks Institute in Boulder, CO. The Institute provides publications, curricular resources, professional development and consulting that supports teachers to integrate social, emotional and academic learning into the classroom and to cultivate their own inner lives. Laura is the co-author of the upcoming book tentatively entitled *The Five Dimensions of Engaged Teaching*, to be published by Solution Tree in spring, 2013.

Rabbi Laura Novak Winer, RJE, has a rabbinate that focuses on Jewish education, teaching, and helping youth develop deep and meaningful connections to Judaism. She recently completed a twelve-year tenure as a specialist in adolescents and experiential education at the Union for Reform Judaism. Laura is the editor of several curricula, including *Sacred Choices: Adolescent Relationships and Sexual Ethics* (2005 and 2007) and has been published in a variety of academic and online journals.

Jonathan S. Woocher is chief ideas Officer of JESNA and heads its Lippman Kanfer Institute: An Action-oriented Think Tank for Innovation in Jewish Learning and Engagement. He served for twenty years as JESNA's president and chief executive officer before assuming his current position in 2007. Prior to coming to JESNA in 1986, Dr. Woocher served on the faculty of Carleton College in Minnesota and Brandeis University, where he taught in the Benjamin S. Hornstein Program in Jewish Communal Service. Dr. Woocher is the author of *Sacred Survival: The Civil Religion of American Jews* and numerous articles on Jewish education, community, and religious life. The Lippman Kanfer Institute and JESNA promote innovation and systemic change in Jewish education aimed at creating a community of passionate, lifelong Jewish learners who use their learning to live more fulfilling, purposeful, and responsible Jewish lives.

Notes

FOREWORD

1. Anna Fuchs, http://www.jewishkidsgroups.com/2/post/2011/07/what-is-the-point-of-jewish-education-anyway.html.

INTRODUCTION

1. J. S. Kress, *Development, Learning, and Community: Educating for Identity in Pluralistic Jewish High Schools* (Brighton, MA: Academic Studies Press, 2012).
2. M. Rosenak, *Commandments and Concerns: Jewish Religious Education in Secular Society* (Philadelphia: Jewish Publication Society, 1987), 261.
3. S. Fox, I. Scheffler, and D. Marom, "Six Visions: An Overview," in *Visions of Jewish Education*, eds. S. Fox, I. Scheffler, and D. Marom (Cambridge: Cambridge University Press, 2003), 33.
4. S. Fox, I. Scheffler, and D. Marom, *Visions of Jewish Education* (Cambridge: Cambridge University Press, 2003).
5. I. Twersky, "What Must a Jew Study—and Why?" in ibid., 19.
6. Fox, Scheffler, and Marom, "Six Visions," 26–27.
7. E.g., J. E. Zins et al., *Building Academic Success on Social and Emotional Learning* (New York: Teachers College Press, 2004).

8. J. S. Kress et al., "Bringing Together Educational Standards and Social and Emotional Learning: Making the Case for Educators," *American Journal of Education* 111 (2004): 68–89.

9. E.g., R. Rothstein and R. Jacobsen, "What Is Basic?" *Principal Leadership* 7 (2006): 14–19.

10. L. Lantieri, "A Vision of Schools with Spirit," in *Schools with Spirit: Nurturing the Inner Lives of Children and Teachers*, ed. L. Lantier (Boston: Beacon Press, 2001), xiv.

11. R. M. Lerner et al., "On Making Humans Human: Spirituality and the Promotion of Positive Youth Development," in *The Handbook of Spiritual Development in Childhood and Adolescence*, ed. E. C. Roehlkepartain et al. (Thousand Oaks, CA: Sage, 2006), 60–72.

12. R. A. Emmons, "Emotion and Religion," in *Handbook of the Psychology of Religion and Spirituality*, eds. R. F. Paloutzian and C. L. Park (New York: Guilford Press, 2005).

13. G. E. Vaillant, "Positive Emotions, Spirituality, and the Practice of Psychiatry," *Mental Health, Spirituality, Mind* 6 (2008): 48–62.

14. L. Scheindlin, "Emotional Perception and Spiritual Development," *International Journal of Children's Spirituality* 8 (2003): 179–93.

15. I. Scheffler, "In Praise of the Cognitive Emotions," in *In Praise of the Cognitive Emotions*, ed. I. Scheffler (New York: Routledge, 1991), 3–17.

16. J. L. Mirel and K. B. Werth, "Study: Our Relationship with Community," in *The Jewish Lights Spirituality Handbook*, ed. S. M. Matlins (Woodstock, VT: Jewish Lights, 2001), 131.

17. S. M. Cohen and L. A. Hoffman, *How Spiritual Are America's Jews?* (Los Angeles: S3K Synagogue Studies Institute, 2009).

18. J. M. Goodman et al., "An Exploration of Spiritual and Psychological Well-Being in a Community of Orthodox, Conservative, and Reform Jews," in *Research in the Social Scientific Study of Religion*, ed. R. L. Piedmont (Leiden, Netherlands: Brill, 2005).

19. C. Kadushin, S. Kelner, and L. Saxe, *Being a Jewish Teenager in America: Trying to Make It* (Waltham, MA: Cohen Center for Modern Jewish Studies, Brandeis University, 2000), 67.

20. W. Dosick, "The State of Faith," in *The Jewish Lights Spirituality Handbook*, ed. S. M. Matlins (Woodstock, VT: Jewish Lights, 2001), 18.

21. RAVSAK is the association of Jewish community day schools.

22. Cohen and Hoffman, *How Spiritual Are America's Jews?*, 9.

23. Ben Harris, "Study: Ethnic Identification on the Wane, Spirituality Rising among Jews," *JTA*, March 31, 2009, http://jta.org/news/article/2009/03/31/1004139/ethnic-identification-on-the-wane-spirituality-rising-among-jews-study-finds.

24. S. M. Matlins, ed., *The Jewish Lights Spirituality Handbook* (Woodstock, VT: Jewish Lights, 2001).

25. This predates and has no relation to the best-selling book of the same name.
26. Rabbis Rachel Cowan, Nancy Flam, Neil Gillman, Yitz Greenberg, Lawrence Kushner, and Yakov Travis.
27. Drs. Richard Davidson, Maurice Elias, Todd Kashdan, and Robert Roeser.
28. Participants: Beverly A. Buncher, Rabbi Rachel Cowan, Dr. Maurice J. Elias, Rabbi Nancy Flam, Ruth Gafni, Dr. Lew Gantwerk (moderator), Rachael Kessler, Dr. Jeffrey S. Kress, Laurence Scheindlin, Dr. Shoshana Simons.

CHAPTER 1: NURTURING THE SPIRITUAL IN JEWISH EDUCATION

1. M. Rosenak, *Tree of Life, Tree of Knowledge* (Boulder, CO: Westview Press, 2001).
2. Bachya ibn Pakuda, *Duties of the Heart* (Jerusalem: Feldheim Publishers, 1986).
3. M. Buber, *Between Man and Man* (London: Fontana Books, 1979).
4. A. Green, ed., *Jewish Spirituality* (New York: Crossroad Publishing, 1987).
5. Z. Bekerman, "Spiritual Exploration: Following My Head or My Heart?" in *The Sovereign and the Situated Self*, ed. J. Boyd (London: UJIA, 2003); E. Gottlieb, "Development of Religious Thinking," *Religious Education* 101, no. 2 (Spring 2006): 242–60.
6. National Curriculum Council, *Spiritual and Moral Development: A Discussion Paper* (York, UK: National Curriculum Council, 1993).
7. J. Fowler, *Stages of Faith and Religious Development* (New York: Crossroad Press, 1991), 56.
8. J. Fowler, *Stages of Faith* (New York: Harper and Row, 1981).
9. J. Fowler, K. Niplow, and F. Schweitzer, *Stages of Faith and Religious Development* (London: SCM Press, 1992).
10. C. Beck, *Better Schools: A Values Perspective* (New York: Routledge, 1989).
11. K. Mott-Thornton, *Common Faith: Education, Spirituality and State* (Brookfield, VT: Ashgate, 1998).
12. M. Shire, "Educating the Spirit," in *Teaching about God and Spirituality*, eds. S. Blumberg and R. Goodman (Denver: ARE, 2003), 121.
13. Buber, *Between Man and Man*.

REFERENCES

Shire, M. (1987). Faith development and Jewish Education. In *Compass*. New York: UAHC.

Shire, M. (1998, Winter.) Enhancing Religiosity in Jewish Education: *CCAR Journal: A Reform Jewish Quarterly*. p74–83.

Shire, M. (2006). "Learning to be Righteous: A Jewish Theology of Childhood." In K.M.Yust et al, (Eds.), *Nuturing Child and Adolescent Spirituality*. Langham: Rowman and Littlefield.

Shire, M. (2011). "The Spiritual child and Jewish Childhood" in H. Miller et al. (Eds.), *International Handbook of Jewish Education*. Berlin: Springer.

CHAPTER 2: TEACHING FOR TRANSCENDENCE

1. R. Kessler, "Nourishing Students in Secular Schools," *Educational Leadership* 56, no. 4 (December 1998–January 1999): 50.
2. R. N. Bellah et al., *Habits of the Heart: Individualism and Commitment in American Life* (New York: Harper & Row, 1985).
3. S. M. Cohen and A. M. Eisen, *The Jew Within: Self, Family, and Community in America* (Bloomington: University of Indiana Press, 2000).
4. R. D. Putnam, *Bowling Alone: The Collapse and Revival of American Community* (New York: Simon and Schuster, 2001).
5. Walker Percy
6. A. J. Heschel, *The Insecurity of Freedom: Essays on Human Existence* (New York: Farrar, Straus and Giroux, 1963), 229, 64.
7. P. Palmer, "Transforming Teaching and Learning in Higher Education: An Interview with Parker J. Palmer," *Spirituality in Higher Education Newsletter* 5, no. 2 (2009): 1–9.
8. Ibid., 3.
9. J. Kahne and J. Westheimer, "In the Service of What? The Politics of Social Learning," *Phi Delta Kappan* 77, no. 9 (May 1996): 593–99.
10. J. Westheimer, *Pledging Allegiance: The Politics of Patriotism in America's Schools* (New York: Teachers College Press, 2007).
11. É. Durkheim, *Moral Education: A Study in the Theory and Application of the Sociology of Education* (New York: Free Press, 1973), 79.
12. N. Noddings, *The Challenge to Care in Schools: An Alternative Approach to Education*, 2nd ed. (New York: Teachers College Press, 2005).
13. Ibid.
14. B. Kirshenblatt-Gimblett, *The Fabric of Jewish Life: Textiles from the Jewish Museum Collection* (New York: Jewish Museum, 1977).
15. M. Kadushin, *The Rabbinic Mind* (New York: Jewish Theological Seminary, 1952), 203.
16. N. Gillman, *Sacred Fragments: Recovering Theology for the Modern Jew* (Philadelphia: Jewish Publication Society, 1992), 122.

17. L. Scheindlin, "Preparing Children for Spirituality," *Religious Education* 94, no. 2 (1999): 199–200; "Emotions in Jewish Education," *Courtyard*, 2000, 121–41.
18. Scheindlin, "Emotions in Jewish Education," 125–26.
19. Ibid., 131.
20. K. T. Talvacchia, *Critical Minds and Discerning Hearts: A Spirituality of Multicultural Teaching* (St. Louis: Chalice Press, 2003).
21. Ibid., 53.
22. A. J. Heschel, *Moral Grandeur and Spiritual Audacity*, ed. Susannah Heschel (New York: Farrar, Straus, Giroux, 1996), 29.
23. Scheindlin, "Preparing Children for Spirituality."
24. E. W. Eisner, "What the Arts Taught Me about Education," in *The Kind of Schools We Need*, ed. E. Eisner (Portsmouth, NH: Heinemann, 1998), 56.
25. O. A. Backenroth, "Weaving the Arts into Jewish Education: Integration at the Blossom School, an Arts-Based Day School," *Journal of Jewish Education* 70, no. 3 (2004): 50–60.
26. Scheindlin, "Preparing Children for Spirituality," 191.
27. Ibid., 191–92.
28. J. Goldmintz, "Response to Michael S. Berger," *HaYidion* (Autumn 2009), 7.
29. C. Smith, *The Religious and Spiritual Life of American Teenagers* (New York: Oxford University Press, 2005), 267–68.
30. K. G. Simon, *Moral Questions in the Classroom: How to Get Kids to Think Deeply about Real Life and Their School Work* (New Haven: Yale University Press, 2001).
31. J. Lehrer, "Don't! The Secret of Self-Control," *New Yorker* (May 28, 2009), 26–32.
32. Kadushin, *The Rabbinic Mind*.
33. H. Kushner, *To Life: A Celebration of Jewish Being and Thinking* (Boston: Little, Brown, 1993), 51–52.
34. C. K. Ingall, "Heroes Great and Small," *Journal of Jewish Education* 64, nos. 1–2 (1998): 22–32.
35. Danny Siegel
36. R. Kessler, *The Soul of Education: Helping Students Find Connection, Compassion, and Character at School* (Alexandria, VA: ASCD, 2000), 17.

CHAPTER 3: SEEING IS CARING, SEEING IS BELIEVING

1. J. A. Frimer and L. J. Walker, "Towards a New Paradigm of Moral Personhood," *Journal of Moral Education* 37, no. 3 (2008): 333–56. Kohlberg cited his own studies (L. Kohlberg and D. Candee, "The Relationship of Moral Judgment to Moral Action," in *Morality, Moral*

Behavior, and Moral Development, eds. W. M. Kurtines and J. L. Gewirtz [New York: Wiley, 1984], 52–73) that attempted to show the contrary. But as we will see, he recognized the problem and sought ways of addressing it.

2. C. Gilligan, "In a Different Voice: Women's Conceptions of Self and of Morality," *Harvard Educational Review* 47, no. 4 (1977): 481–517.

3. My thanks to Dr. Rob Applebaum for supplying this example.

4. Even then it is hard it is to disentangle emotion from reason, which in the student's situation is assessing the likelihood of a decision contributing to or detracting from his emotional pleasure. One could argue that reason or logic, as usually understood and acting alone, could also say, "If we bring Michael into the game, he will feel better," but that only helps make my point: *Why* would the student want to help Michael feel better?

5. I am not at all suggesting that her only choice is to send her patient elsewhere. Full disclosure of the potential for failure and of the alternatives might be enough. The other alternatives may be more expensive, time-consuming, and intrusive, factors that might easily persuade the patient to proceed with this physician's procedure. I'm not trying to find the correct answer for the doctor. I want to point out that whatever her decision, it will result from a rational judgment that is as much emotional as it is "logical."

6. I recognize that motivation and will, while they overlap with emotion, ought to be distinguished conceptually from emotion and from each other. This is not the place to tease them apart, and since they do overlap, in usages such as this one I refer to the emotional element of will and motivation.

7. W. Damon, *The Moral Child: Nurturing Children's Natural Moral Growth* (New York: Free Press, 1988).

8. M. Hoffman, *Empathy and Moral Development: Implications for Caring and Justice* (Cambridge: Cambridge University Press, 2000), 131.

9. Cited in D. Narvaez and J. L. Vaydich, "Moral Development and Behaviour under the Spotlight of the Neurobiological Sciences," *Journal of Moral Education* 37, no. 3 (2008): 289–312.

10. J. Haidt, "The Emotional Dog and Its Rational Tail: A Social Intuitionist Approach to Moral Judgment," *Psychological Review* 108, no. 4 (2001): 814–34; J. Haidt, S. Koller, and M. Dias, "Affect, Culture, and Morality, or Is It Wrong to Eat Your Dog? *Journal of Personality and Social Psychology* 65 (1993): 613–28.

11. M. D. Hauser, *Moral Minds: The Nature of Right and Wrong* (New York: HarperCollins, 2006).

12. Narvaez and Vaydich, "Moral Development and Behaviour"; M. Bennet et al., *Neuroscience and Philosophy: Brain, Mind, and Language* (New York: Columbia University Press, 2007); M. H. van IJzendoorn et al., "In

Defence of Situational Morality: Genetic, Dispositional and Situational Determinants of Children's Donating to Charity," *Journal of Moral Education* 39, no. 1 (2010): 1–20.

13. J. R. Rest, "The Major Components of Morality," in *Morality, Moral Behavior, and Moral Development*, edS. W. M. Kurtines and J. L. Gewirtz (New York: Wiley, 1984), 24–38.

14. J. R. Rest et al., *Postconventional Moral Thinking: A Neo-Kohlbergian Approach*. Mahwah, NJ: L. Erlbaum Associates, 1999). Kohlberg himself developed a set of categories that he himself described as closely paralleling Rest's, which he implicitly endorsed (Kohlberg and Candee, "Relationship of Moral Judgment to Moral Action").

15. K. Oatley, *Best Laid Schemes: The Psychology of Emotions* (Paris: Cambridge University Press, 1992).

16. In all of these cases, self-identity plays an important role as well. One who goes out of his way to help another may be sympathetically motivated, but, as Martin Hoffman has said, "[The] activation of a caring principle and the addition of one's "self" (the kind of person one is or wishes to be) should add power to one's situationally induced empathic distress and strengthen one's obligation to act on principle" (Hoffman, *Empathy and Moral Development*, 239).

17. I. Scheffler, *In Praise of the Cognitive Emotions and Other Essays in the Philosophy of Education* (New York: Routledge, 1991).

18. Ibid., 7.

19. Ibid.

20. Ibid., 8.

21. Ibid., 8–9.

22. M. Fishbane, *Sacred Attunement: A Jewish Theology* (Chicago: University of Chicago Press, 2008).

23. A. J. Vetlesen, *Perception, Empathy, and Judgment: An Inquiry into the Preconditions of Moral Performance* (University Park: Pennsylvania State University Press, 1994).

24. Cited in ibid.

25. Cited in ibid.

26. Empathy itself should be considered a faculty but not an emotion. Empathy is an essential but forked road that can lead to maliciousness as well as to beneficence.

27. Vetlesen, *Perception, Empathy, and Judgment*, 10.

28. A. Colby and W. Damon, *Some Do Care: Contemporary Lives of Moral Commitment* (New York: Free Press, 1992).

29. L. Blum, "Compassion," in *Explaining Emotions*, ed. A. Oksenberg Rorty (Berkeley: University of California Press, 1980), 513.

30. Fishbane, *Sacred Attunement*, 20.

31. Ibid., 33.

32. Ibid., 34.
33. Ibid.
34. Ibid., 22.
35. Ibid., 114.
36. Ibid., 36.
37. D. Marom, "Educational Implications of Michael Fishbane's *Sacred Attunement: A Jewish Theology*," *Journal of Jewish Education* 74 (2008): 42.
38. Ibid., 35.
39. Ibid.
40. A. Storr, *Solitude* (New York: Ballantine Books, 1988), 17.
41. R. Havinghurst and B. Keating, "The Religion of Youth," in *Research on Religious Development: A Comprehensive Handbook*, ed. M. P. Strommen (New York: Hawthorn Books, 1971).
42. J. Berryman, "Teaching as Presence and the Existential Curriculum," *Religious Education* 85, no. 4 (1990): 510–11.
43. D. Hay and R. Nye, *The Spirit of the Child* (London: HarperCollins, 1998).
44. Ibid., 113.
45. Ibid., 114.
46. P. Fisher, *Wonder, the Rainbow, and the Aesthetics of Rare Experiences* (Cambridge: Harvard University Press, 1998).
47. T. Green, *The Activities of Teaching* (New York: McGraw-Hill, 1971), 196.
48. Ibid., 198.
49. It is the distance in understanding that causes childbirth, an obvious source of joy, to be an object of wonder also. Similarly, lovers may wonder at each other's presence; it is the inexplicability of their connection—the fact of its existence even though it was not a necessity, if, for example, they had never met—that is the source of wonder. Wonder may mingle with joy at something that benefits us, but part of wonder's uniqueness is how often it attaches us to that which does not.
50. M. C. Nussbaum, *Upheavals of Thought: The Intelligence of Emotions* (Cambridge: Cambridge University Press, 2001), 54–56.
51. Fisher, *Wonder, the Rainbow, and the Aesthetics of Rare Experiences*.
52. I follow JPS in translating *tzidkat'cha* as "beneficence," but Mitchell Dahood's "Your generosity" together with his translation of *mishpatecha* as "Your providence" brings the point into even sharper focus (*Psalms I: 1–50*, The Anchor Bible, vol. 16 [Garden City, NY: Doubleday, 1965]). For consistency I retain "beneficence" for *tzedakah* in translating the midrash that follows, even though "Your righteousness" might be more fitting to that midrash's intention, but the ambiguousness of *tzedakah* in this context hints at the moral complexity that the midrash sets forth.
53. L. Scheindlin, "Emotional Perception and Spiritual Development," *International Journal of Children's Spirituality* 8, no. 2 (2003): 179–193.

54. Would high school students be "bored" with such a discussion? I can imagine a teacher giving them Darwin's description of the following episode while he was traveling in a South American archipelago: A native saw Darwin's dinner of preserved meat and, intrigued by the novelty, touched it. Darwin's disgust at his food being touched was only rivaled— perhaps outdone—by the native's disgust at the cold, soft, old meat that Darwin was eating! Darwin observed that "a smear of soup on a man's beard looks disgusting, though there is of course nothing disgusting in the soup itself" (Miller 1997, 1). I don't think the teacher would have lost her students at all.

55. Vetlesen, *Perception, Empathy, and Judgment*, 194.

56. None of my curricular suggestions can operate in a vacuum. They require a caring and empathetic classroom and school environment. Programs such as Responsive Classroom are designed to help schools create such an environment but are beyond the purview of this chapter.

57. Scheffler, *In Praise of the Cognitive Emotions*.

58. A much more detailed summary, including teacher questions and anticipated student responses, can be found in Scheindlin.

59. L. Scheindlin, "Emotions in Jewish Education," *Courtyard* (2000): 121–41.

60. Lesson 1 is based on a lesson in the Full Option Science System (Nashua, NH: Delta Education).

61. P. Schram, "An Offspring's Answer," in *Jewish Stories One Generation Tells Another* (Northvale, NJ: Jason Aronson, 1987), 451–55.

62. I am assuming that this lesson would be used in a day school, that the Hebrew text would be used, and that additional lessons would be devoted to the Hebrew. For the purpose of this unit, the students need to understand only a handful of key phrases in order to "get" the essence of the prayer. I suggest waiting to teach the Hebrew of the prayer in a more detailed way later, after a set of ideas and feelings has been established.

CHAPTER 4: SPIRITUALITY AND MORAL EDUCATION

1. A "pluralistic Jewish day school" is a Jewish day school that sees its mission as creating a climate conducive to welcoming and educating students from a wide variety of Jewish backgrounds. Pluralistic schools tend to promote cross-denominational understanding through a historical and cultural study of different movements, through exploring different approaches to prayer, and through academic study of the Bible and Rabbinic literature more focused on understanding than on practice and belief. Students at pluralistic Jewish day schools may range from the fervently atheistic to the fervently Orthodox.

2. Abraham Joshua Heschel, "On Children and Youth," in *The Insecurity of Freedom: Essays on Human Existence* (Philadelphia: Jewish Publication Society, 1966), 39.
3. Ibid., 41.
4. Ibid., 45.
5. Ibid., 47.
6. In her book, *Moral Questions in the Classroom: How to Get Kids to Think Deeply about Real Life and Their Schoolwork* (New Haven: Yale University, 2001), 37–38, Katherine G. Simon identifies four areas as follows:
   - Queries connected to how human beings should act
   - Queries into life's meaning and the human place in the world
   - Queries into the unknown
   - Exploration of universal existential concerns and ways of knowing
   The chief difference between her four areas and mine is that I separate character and issues of dignity/civil rights from ethical practice; I group Simon's last three areas into one area that relates to deep religious questions.
7. Aristotle, *The Ethics of Aristotle*, trans. J. A. K. Thomson (London: Penguin, 1976), 104.
8. *Character Education Quality Standards: A Self-Assessment Tool for Schools and Districts* (Washington, DC: Character Education Partnership, 2003), 5, 8, 9, 12, 15.
9. Jeff Gammage and Kristen A. Graham, "Rally Commemorates South Philly High School Violence," *Philadelphia Inquirer*, December 3, 2010, http://www.philly.com/philly/news/breaking/20101203_On_the_anniversary_of_S__Philly_HS_violence__calm.html; Jeff Gammage, "Calm Year since Attacks on Asians," *Philadelphia Inquirer*, December 4, 2010, B1
10. Maya Rao and Chelsea Conaboy, "Anti-bullying Measure Goes to Governor Christie," *Philadelphia Inquirer*, (November 23, 2010), http://www.philly.com/philly/education/20101123_Anti-bullying_measure_goes_to_Gov__Christie.html.
11. Ibid., 15.
12. Committee for Children, *Second Step: Student Success through Prevention* (Seattle: Committee for Children, 2008), http://www.cfchildren.org/programs/ssp/overview/.
13. Barbara Dixon Ackerman and LouAnne Smith, *Need a Hand with Advising? Here's a Handbook* (Portland, OR: Council for Spiritual and Ethical Education, 2007); CSEE Moral Development Team, *Highly Effective Programs: Character Education in Independent Schools* (Portland, OR: Council for Spiritual and Ethical Education, 2007).
14. Jenna Russell, "A World of Misery Left by Bullying," *Boston Sunday Globe*, November 28, 2010, A1, A18; Emily Anthes, "Inside the Bullied Brain: The Alarming Neuroscience of Taunting," *Boston Globe*, November 28,

2010, K1; Jan Hoffman, "As Bullies Go Digital, Parents Play Catch-Up," *New York Times*, December 5, 2010, 1, 26–27.

15. These observations were made during my dissertation research at "Beacon High School" in the spring of 1998 when I was shadowing a girl whom I called "Felicia Yanes." See my dissertation, "Startlingly Moral: The Moral Outlooks of Jewish Adolescents" (PhD diss., Jewish Theological Seminary, 2002), chap. 8.

16. Judd Levingston, *Sowing the Seeds of Character: The Moral Education of Adolescents in Public and Private Schools* (Westport, CT: Praeger), 2009.

17. Elliot N. Dorff, "Teaching Ethics," *Jewish Educational Leadership* 8, no. 3 (Summer 2010), 63–64.

18. See http://csee.org/ and http://www.facinghistory.org/.

19. See www.movingtraditions.org and Moving Traditions, *Engaging Jewish Teenage Boys: A Call to Action* (Jenkintown, PA: Moving Traditions, 2010), 23–24.

20. Ibid., 34.

21. Ibid., 36–37.

22. Ibid., 45.

23. Romina M. Barros, Ellen J. Silver, and Ruth Stein, "School Recess and Group Classroom Behavior," *Pediatrics* 123 (2009): 434–35.

24. Johan Huizinga, *Homo Ludens: A Study of the Play-Element in Culture* (Boston: Beacon Press, 1950), 3.

CHAPTER 5: WHERE ETHICS MEETS HISTORY

1. For a complete description of Facing History and Ourselves, see Martin E. Sleeper and Margot Stern Strom, "Facing History and Ourselves," in *The Educator's Guide to Emotional Intelligence and Academic Achievement*, eds. Maurice Elias and Harriett Arnold (Thousand Oaks, CA: Corwin Press, 2006), 240–46.

2. Dennis Barr, "Continuing a Tradition of Research on the Foundations of Democratic Education: The National Professional Development and Evaluation Project" (Facing History and Ourselves unpublished paper, 2010).

3. Jan Darsa, *Facing History and Ourselves: The Jews of Poland* (Brookline, MA: Facing History and Ourselves National Foundation, 1998).

4. Margot Stern Strom, *Facing History and Ourselves: Holocaust and Human Behavior* (Brookline, MA: Facing History and Ourselves National Foundation, 1994).

5. Darsa, *Facing History and Ourselves: The Jews of Poland*, 6–8.

6. Based on G. G. Scholem, *Major Trends in Jewish Mysticism* (Jerusalem: Schocken, 1941), 345.

7. Strom, *Holocaust and Human Behavior*, 56.
8. *Pigeon*, directed by Anthony Green (New York: Avoda Arts, 2005).
9. *Illuminations: The Art of Samuel Bak*, collection at Facing History and Ourselves, Brookline, MA.

CHAPTER 6: FINE-TUNING THE LISTENING HEART

1. M. Walker and R. Rosen, eds., *How Connections Heal: Stories from Relational-Cultural Therapy* (New York: Guilford Press, 2004).
2. D. Goleman, *Emotional Intelligence: Why It Matters More Than IQ* (New York: Bantam, 1997).
3. W. Schutz, *FIRO: A Three-Dimensional Theory of Interpersonal Behavior* (New York: Rinehart, 1958).
4. P. Palmer, *The Courage to Teach: Exploring the Inner Landscape of a Teacher's Life* (San Francisco: Jossey-Bass, 1997).
5. A. S. Bryk and B. Schneider, "Trust in Schools: A Core Resource for School Reform," *Creating Caring Schools* 60, no. 6 (March 2003): 40–45.
6. A. Morinis, *Everyday Holiness: The Jewish Spiritual Path to Mussar* (Boston: Shambhala, 2008).
7. Ibid.
8. Traditionally used terms of congratulations, literally meaning "Your strength should be straight, all the respect."

CHAPTER 7: NOURISHING THE SOULS OF STUDENTS IN JEWISH EDUCATION

1. Bev Buncher, a former principal at a Jewish day school, is currently a consultant and coach. All Jewish educators quoted and mentioned in this article have been trained in the PassageWorks approach to social, emotional, and academic learning.
2. Rabbi Nancy Flam is one of the co-directors for programs at the Institute of Jewish Spirituality.
3. By "inner life," we refer to the essential aspect of human nature that yearns for connection, grapples with questions about meaning, and seeks a sense of genuine purpose, authenticity, and self-expression.
4. PassageWorks Institute is a national educational nonprofit based in Colorado: www.passageworks.org.
5. Rachael Kessler, *The Soul of Education: Helping Students Find Connection, Compassion, and Character at School* (Alexandria, VA: Association for Supervision and Curriculum Development, 2000).
6. Joseph A. Durlak et al., "The Impact of Enhancing Students' Social and Emotional Learning: A Meta-Analysis of School-Based Universal

Interventions," *Child Development* 82, no. 1 (January/February 2011): 405–32.

7. Sarah Sparks, "Study Finds Social-Skills Teaching Boosts Academics," *Education Week*, February 4, 2011, 1.

8. Jack Zimmerman and Gigi Coyle, *The Way of Council*, 2nd ed. (Putney, VT: Bramble Books, 2009).

9. Robert Sylwester, *A Celebration of Neurons: An Educator's Guide to the Human Brain* (Alexandria, VA: Association for Supervision and Curriculum Development, 1995), 72.

10. Arlene Fishbein, "Feeling at Home in Their Own Skins and with Each Other," *Jewish Educational Leadership* 5, no. 2 (2007): 2. Fishbein is a middle school English teacher who has integrated the PassageWorks curriculum into her classroom.

11. Randi Hirschberg, a Jewish educator and doctoral candidate in clinical psychology, has taught the PassageWorks curriculum for a number of years in a variety of contexts.

12. Batya Greenwald, founding director of the Boulder Jewish Day School and current elementary school teacher, is a PassageWorks lead trainer who has played a pivotal role in integrating the PassageWorks approach with Jewish education.

13. Fishbein, "Feeling at Home in Their Own Skins," 3.

14. We are aware that there are other Torah references to *Hineini*, including the moment when Abraham is about to sacrifice his son and responds to the angel who calls his name. This Torah story could also serve as rich discussion for adolescents about how to listen and respond to the voice of God.

15. Abra Greenspan is a Jewish educator and *b'nei mitzvah* program director who has integrated PassageWorks practices and principles into her programs.

16. Fishbein, "Feeling at Home in Their Own Skins," 2.

17. Parker J. Palmer coined this phrase in his book *A Hidden Wholeness: The Journey toward an Undivided Life* (San Francisco: Jossey-Bass, 2004).

18. Fishbein, "Feeling at Home in Their Own Skins," 4.

Chapter 8: Evidence-Based Bully Prevention in Jewish Schools

1. S. M. Kardos, "Jewish Day Schools and Their Future Place in American Jewish Life," *Journal of Jewish Communal Service* 85, no. 1 (2010): 84–87.

2. J. Bieler, "Modern Orthodox Jewish Day Schools and Non-Jews, 2010, www.lookstein.org/retrieve.php?ID=-1366240.

3. L. Bond et al., "Does Bullying Cause Emotional Problems? A Prospective Study of Young Teenagers," *British Medical Journal* 323 (2001): 480–84;

A. Nishina, J. Juvonen, and M. Witkow, "Sticks and Stones May Break My Bones, but Names Will Make Me Feel Sick: The Psychosocial, Somatic, and Scholastic Consequences of Peer Harassment," *Journal of Clinical Child and Adolescent Psychiatry* 34, no. 1 (2005): 37–48.

4. S. W. Tremlow, "The Roots of Violence: Converging Psychoanalytic Explanatory Models for Power Struggles and Violence in Schools," *Psychoanalytic Quarterly* 69 (2000): 741–85.

5. T. Vaillancourt et al., "Bullying: Are Researchers and Children/Youth Talking about the Same Thing?" *International Journal of Behavioral Development* 32, no. 6 (2008): 486–95.

6. D. Olweus, *Olweus Bully-Victim Questionnaire*, 1996, http://www2.ed.gov/admins/lead/safety/training/bullying/question.pdf.

7. E. M. Vernberg, A. K. Jacobs, and S. L. Hershberger, "Peer Victimization and Attitudes about Violence during Early Adolescence," *Journal of Clinical Child Psychology* 28 (1999): 386–95.

8. Vaillancourt, "Bullying."

9. P. K. Smith, "Bullying: Recent Developments," *Child & Adolescent Mental Health* 9, no. 3 (2004): 98–103, doi:10.1111/j.1475-3588.2004.00089.x; P. K. Smith et al., "Definition of Bullying: A Comparison of Terms Used, and Age and Sex Differences, in a 14-Country International Comparison," *Child Development* 73 (2002): 1119–33; P. K. Smith et al., eds., *The Nature of School Bullying: A Cross-National Perspective* (London: Routledge, 1999).

10. Smith, "Definition of Bullying."

11. S. Bauman and S. Del Rio, "Preservice Teachers' Responses to Bullying Scenarios: Comparing Physical, Verbal and Relational Bullying," *Journal of Educational Psychology* 98 (2006): 219–31; M. J. Boulton, "Teachers' Views on Bullying: Definitions, Attitudes and Ability to Cope," *British Journal of Educational Psychology* 67 (1997): 223–33; P. Naylor et al., "Teachers' and Pupils' Definitions of Bullying," *British Journal of Educational Psychology* 76 (2006): 553–76.

12. M. J. Boulton, M. Trueman, and I. Flemington, "Associations between Secondary School Pupils' Definitions of Bullying, Attitudes towards Bullying, and Tendencies to Engage in Bullying: Age and Sex Differences," *Educational Studies* 28, no. 4 (2002): 353–70.

13. Ibid.

14. Smith, "Definition of Bullying."

15. T. R. Nansel et al., "Bullying Behaviors among U.S. Youth: Prevalence and Association with Psychosocial Adjustment," *Journal of the American Medical Association* 285 (2001): 2094–2100.

16. R. A. Astor, R. Benbenishty, and J. N. Estrada, "School Violence and Theoretically Atypical Schools: The Principal's Centrality in Orchestrating Safe Schools," *American Educational Research Journal* 46, no. 2 (2009):

423–61; R. Benbenishty, R. A. Astor, and R. Marachi, "A National Study of School Violence in Israel: Implications for Theory, Practice, and Policy," in *Handbook of School Violence and School Safety: From Research to Practice*, eds. S. R. Jimmerson and M. J. Furlong (Mahwah, NJ: Erlbaum, 2006), 481–97.

17. Boulton, Trueman, and Flemington, "Associations between Secondary School Pupils' Definitions of Bullying."

18. D. L. Haynie et al., "Bullies, Victims, and Bully/Victims: Distinct Groups of At-Risk Youth," *Journal of Early Adolescence* 21, no. 1 (2001): 29–49; S. M. Swearer et al., "Internalizing Problems in Students Involved in Bullying and Victimization: Implications for Intervention," in *Bullying in American Schools: A Social-Ecological Perspective on Prevention and Intervention*, eds. D. L. Espelage and S. M. Swearer (Mahwah, NJ: Lawrence Erlbaum Associates, 2004).

19. M. Peeters, A. H. N. Cillessen, and R. H. J. Scholte, "Clueless or Powerful? Identifying Subtypes of Bullies in Adolescence," *Journal of Youth and Adolescence* 39 (2010): 1041–52.

20. W. B. Roberts and A. A. Morotti, "The Bully as Victim: Understanding Bully Behaviors to Increase the Effectiveness of Interventions in the Bully-Victim Dyad," *Professional School Counseling* 4 (2000): 148–55; K. Bjorkqvist, K. Osterman, and A. Kaukianen, "Social Intelligence – Empathy = Aggression?" *Aggression and Violent Behavior* 5 (2000): 191–200.

21. G. Gini, "Social Cognition and Moral Cognition in Bullying: What's Wrong?" *Aggressive Behavior* 32 (2006): 528–39.

22. E. Andreou, "Bully/Victim Problems and Their Association with Machiavellianism and Self-Efficacy in Greek Primary School Children," *British Journal of Educational Psychology* 74 (2004): 297–309.

23. J. Decety et al., "Atypical Empathic Responses in Adolescents with Aggressive Conduct Disorder: A Functional MRI Investigation," *Biological Psychology* 80 (2009): 203–11.

24. D. Pontzer, "A Theoretical Test of Bullying Behavior: Parenting, Personality, and the Bully/Victim Relationship, *Journal of Family Violence* 25 (2010): 259–73.

25. Peeters, Cillessen, and Scholte, "Clueless or Powerful?"

26. J. Sutton, P. K. Smith, and J. Swettenham, "Social Cognition and Bullying: Social Inadequacy or Skilled Manipulation?" *British Journal of Developmental Psychology* 17 (1999): 435–50.

27. N. R. Crick and K. A. Dodge, "A Review and Reformulation of Social Information-Processing Mechanisms in Children's Social Adjustment," *Psychological Bulletin* 115 (1994): 74–101.

28. M. J. Boulton and K. Underwood, "Bully/Victim Problems among Middle School Children," *British Journal of Educational Psychology* 62

(1992): 73–87; P. K. Coleman and C. P. Byrd, "Interpersonal Correlates of Peer Victimization among Young Adolescents," *Journal of Youth and Adolescence* 32, no. 4 (2003): 301–14; B. Kochenderfer and G. Ladd, "Peer Victimization: Causes or Consequences of School Maladjustment?" *Child Development* 67 (1996): 1305–17.

29. D. G. Perry, S. J. Kusel, and L. C. Perry, "Victims of Peer Aggression," *Developmental Psychology* 24 (1988): 807–14.

30. A. G. Carney and K. W. Merrell, "Bullying in Schools: Perspectives on Understanding and Preventing an International Problem," *School Psychology International* 22 (2001): 364–82.

31. D. G. Perry, J. C. Willard, and L. C. Perry, "Peers' Perceptions of the Consequences That Victimized Children Provide Aggressors," *Child Development* 61 (1990): 1310–25.

32. D. Schwartz et al., "The Early Socialization of Aggressive Victims of Bullying," *Child Development* 68 (1997): 665–75.

33. K. Kumpalainen, E. Rasanen, and K. Puura, "Psychiatric Disorders and the Use of Mental Health Services among Children Involved in Bullying," *Aggressive Behavior* 27 (2001): 102–10; S. M. Swearer et al., "Psychosocial Correlates in Bullying and Victimization: The Relationship between Depression, Anxiety, and Bully/Victim Status," *Journal of Emotional Abuse* 2 (2001): 95–121.

34. D. A. Roth, M. E. Coles, and R. G. Heimberg, "The Relationship between Memories for Childhood Teasing and Anxiety and Depression in Adulthood," *Journal of Anxiety Disorders* 16 (2002): 149–64; Swearer et al., "Internalizing Problems in Students Involved in Bullying and Victimization."

35. N. R. Crick and J. K. Grotpeter, "Relational Aggression, Gender, and Social-Psychological Adjustment," *Child Development* 66, no. 3 (1995): 710–22.

36. S. K. Egan and D. G. Perry, "Does Low Self-Regard Invite Victimization?" *Developmental Psychology* 34 (1998): 299–309.

37. F. Aboud and L. Miller, "Promoting Peer Intervention in Name-Calling," *South African Journal of Psychology* 37, no. 4 (2007): 803–19.

38. W. Craig and D. Pepler, "Observations of Bullying and Victimization on the Playground," *Canadian Journal of School Psychology* 2 (1997): 41–60.

39. C. Salmivalli et al., "Bullying as a Group Process: Participant Roles and Their Relations to Social Status within the Group," *Aggressive Behavior* 22 (1996): 1–15.

40. B. Doll, S. Song, and E. Siemers, "Classroom Ecologies That Support or Discourage Bullying," in Espelage and Swearer, *Bullying in American Schools*, 161–83.

41. Salmivalli et al., "Bullying as a Group Process."

42. P. Delfabbro et al., "Peer and Teacher Bullying/Victimization of South Australian Secondary School Students: Prevalence and Psychosocial Profiles," *British Journal of Educational Psychology* 76 (2006): 71–90.
43. Coleman and Byrd, "Interpersonal Correlates of Peer Victimization," 304.
44. D. L. Espelage and S. W. Swearer, eds., *Bullying in American Schools: A Social-Ecological Perspective on Prevention and Intervention* (Mahwah, NJ: Lawrence Erlbaum Associates, 2004).
45. R. A. Astor, "A Light unto the Nations and a Nation Like All Nations: The Contemporary Exemplar of Jews and School Violence," *Journal of Jewish Communal Service* 84, nos. 3/4 (2009): 218–27.
46. S. M. Swearer and D. L. Espelage, "Introduction: A Social Ecological Framework of Bullying among Youth," in Espelage and Swearer, *Bullying in American Schools*.
47. P. C. Rodkin, "Peer Ecologies of Aggression and Bullying," in Espelage and Swearer, *Bullying in American Schools*.
48. A. L. Sawyer, C. P. Bradshaw, and L. M. O'Brennan, "Examining Ethnic, Gender, and Developmental Differences in the Way Children Report Being a Victim of 'Bullying' on Self-Report Measures," *Journal of Adolescent Health* 43 (2008): 106–14.
49. M. Blain and L. Revell, "Patterns of Spiritual and Moral Development in Religious and Public Schools in Chicago," *Journal of Beliefs and Values* 23, no. 2 (2002): 179–189.
50. Astor, Benbenishty, and Estrada, "School Violence and Theoretically Atypical Schools."
51. Ibid., 453.
52. A. H. Fried, "Is There a Disconnect between Torah Learning and Torah Living? And If So, How Can We Connect Them? A Focus on *Middos*," *Hakira: The Flatbush Journal of Jewish Law and Thought* 6 (2008): 11–56.
53. Ibid., 11.
54. Ibid., 13.
55. R. Novick, "Bullying, Harassment and Social Exclusion in Jewish Schools: Unique Opportunities and Challenges to Promote Positive Peer Culture," in *The Azrieli Papers: Dimensions of Orthodox Day School Education*, eds. D. J. Schnall and M. Sokolow (New York: Yeshiva University, 2011), 105–48).
56. R. M. Novick and J. Isaacs, "Telling Is Compelling: The Impact of Student Reports of Bullying on Teacher Intervention. *Educational Psychology* 30, no. 3 (2010): 283–96, doi:10.1080/01443410903573123.
57. R. M. Novick et al., "Emerging Trends in Bullying in Co-educational Jewish Day Schools" (poster presented at meeting of Nefesh International Association of Orthodox Mental Health Professionals, Happauge, NY, December 2009).

58. D. Olweus, "Bully/Victim Problems at School: Facts and Intervention," *European Journal of Psychology of Education* 12 (1997): 495–510.

59. S. P. Limber, "Implementation of the Olweus Bullying Prevention Program in American Schools: Lessons Learned from the Field," in Espelage and Swearer, *Bullying in American Schools.*

60. S. P. Limber, "Efforts to Address Bullying in US Schools," *American Journal of Health Education* 34, no. 5 (2003): 23–29.

61. Limber, "Implementation of the Olweus Bullying Prevention Program in American Schools."

62. D. Olweus, S. H. Limber, and S. Mihalic, *The Bullying Prevention Program: Blueprints for Violence Prevention* (Boulder, CO: Center for the Study and Prevention of Violence, Institute of Behavioral Science, University of Colorado at Boulder, 1999).

63. C. Garrity et al., *Bully-Proofing Your School* (Longmont, CO: Sopris West, 1994).

64. K. W. Merrell et al., "How Effective Are School Bullying Intervention Programs? A Meta-analysis of Intervention Research," *School Psychology Quarterly* 23, no. 1 (2008): 26–42.

65. J. D. Smith et al., "The Effectiveness of Whole-School Antibullying Programs: A Synthesis of Evaluation Research," *School Psychology Review* 33 (2004): 547–60.

66. D. Olweus, *Aggression in the Schools: Bullies and Whipping Boys* (Washington, DC: Hemisphere, 1978).

67. Olweus, *Olweus Bully-Victim Questionnaire.*

68. R. S. Atlas and D. J. Pepler, "Observations of Bullying in the Classroom," *Journal of Educational Research* 92 (1998): 86–99.

69. T. Beran, "A New Perspective on Managing School Bullying: Pre-service Teachers' Attitudes," *Journal of Social Sciences* 8 (2005): 43–49.

70. M. R. Fekkes, I. M. Pijpers, and S. P. Verloove-Vanhorick, "Bullying: Who Does What, When and Where? Involvement of Children, Teachers and Parents in Bullying Behavior," *Health Education Research* 20, no. 1 (2005): 81–91; C. Oliver and M. Candappa, "Bullying and the Politics of Telling," *Oxford Review of Education* 33, no. 1 (2007): 71–86; P. K. Smith and S. Shu, "What Good Schools Can Do about Bullying: Findings from a Decade of Research and Action," *Childhood* 7, no. 2 (2000): 193–212.

71. R. M. Novick, "German Bystander Inaction during the Holocaust: Lessons Learned from Social Psychology and Teachable Moments for Today's Students," *Prism: An Interdisciplinary Journal for Holocaust Educators* 1, no. 2 (2010): 83–86.

72. J. S. Kress and M. J. Elias, "Building Learning Communities through Social and Emotional Learning: Navigating the Rough Seas of Implementation," *Professional School Counseling* 10, no. 1 (2006): 104.

73. "Quality Circles," in *Encyclopedia of Small Business*, http://www.enotes.com/small-business-encyclopedia/quality-circles.

74. Atlas and Pepler, "Observations of Bullying in the Classroom"; Oliver and Candappa, "Bullying and the Politics of Telling"; Novick and Isaacs, "Telling Is Compelling."

75. S. Epstein, "Supporting Our Teachers in Addressing Evaded Curricular Issues" (paper presented at North American Day School Conference, Teaneck, NJ, January 2010).

76. Fried, "Is There a Disconnect between Torah Learning and Torah Living?"

77. M. R. Benjamins and S. Whitman, "A Culturally Appropriate School Wellness Initiative: Results of a 2-Year Pilot Intervention in 2 Jewish Schools," *Journal of School Health* 80, no. 8 (2010): 378–86.

78. M. Buber, *Between Man and Man*, trans. R. G. Smith (London: Kegan Paul, 1947), 104.

79. Ibid., 117.

CHAPTER 9: EDUCATIONAL JEWISH MOMENTS

1. R. Barth, *Learning by Heart* (San Francisco: Jossey-Bass, 2004).

2. L. Shulman, "Knowledge and Teaching: Foundations of the New Reform," *Harvard Educational Review* 57, no. 1 (1987): 1–22.

3. M. O'Hair and J. Blase, "Power and Politics in the Classroom: Implications for Teacher Education," *Action in Teacher Education* 14, no. 1 (March 1992): 10–17.

4. Ibid.

5. L. M. Brown, *Girlfighting: Betrayal and Rejection among Girls* (New York: New York University Press, 2003).

6. R. S. Charney, *Teaching Children to Care* (Turners Falls, MA: Northeast Foundation for Children, 2002); L. Koplow, *Creating Schools That Heal* (New York: Teachers College Press, 2002).

7. Brown, *Girlfighting*.

8. Koplow, *Creating Schools That Heal*, 58.

9. AAUW Educational Foundation, *How Schools Shortchange Girls: A Study of Major Findings on Girls and Education* (Washington, DC: Wellesley College Center for Research on Women, 1992).

10. S. D. Epstein and N. Less, eds., *Evaded Issues in Jewish Education: A Resource Guide for Jewish Educators* (July 2010), http://mayan.org/knowledge/programs_for_jewish_youth_professionals/evaded_issues/resource_guide/eir_guide

11. S. D. Epstein and N. Less, *Educational Jewish Moments: The Training* (2009), 3.

12. N. Less, Siegal College Summer Institute 09, panel discussion at the Maltz Museum, 2009 [Video file], http://www.youtube.com/watch?v=crnbNEb5nEY.

13. Koplow, *Creating Schools That Heal.*

14. Epstein and Less, *Educational Jewish Moments: The Training,* 6.

15. M. Brydon-Miller, "Education, Research, and Action: Theory and Methods of Participatory Action Research," in *From Subjects to Subjectivities: A Handbook of Interpretive and Participatory Methods,* eds. D. L. Tolman and M. Brydon-Miller (New York: New York University Press, 2001), 76–89; Cammarota and Fine, 2008; P. Lather, *Getting Smart: Feminist Research and Pedagogy with/in the Postmodern* (New York: Routledge, 1991); L. Weis and M. Fine, *Speed Bumps: A Student-Friendly Guide to Qualitative Research* (New York: Teachers College Press, 2000).

16. D. Tripp, *Critical Incidents in Teaching: Developing Professional Judgement* (London: Routledge, 1993), 8–9.

17. M. L. Griffin, "Using Critical Incidents to Promote and Assess Reflective Thinking in Preservice Teachers," *Reflective Practice* 4, no. 2 (June 2003): 207–20.

18. O'Hair and Blase, "Power and Politics in the Classroom."

19. Epstein and Less, *Educational Jewish Moments: The Training.*

20. E.g., Y. Debow, *Life Values and Intimacy Education: Health Education for the Jewish School* (New York: Ktav, 2008); I. Eliav, *Yad B'Yad: Working Hand in Hand to Create Healthy Relationships* (Seattle: FaithTrust Institute, 2005); S. D. Epstein, *Strong Girls, Healthy Relationships: A Conversation on Dating, Friendship, and Self Esteem* (Washington, DC: JWI, 2006); L. Novak-Winer, *Sacred Choices: Adolescent Relationships and Sexual Ethics (Middle School Module)* (New York: URJ Press, 2007); *Love Shouldn't Hurt: Building Healthy Relationships for Jewish Youth* (Oakland, CA: Shalom Bayit, 2007).

21. P. Orenstein, *Schoolgirls: Young Women, Self-Esteem, and the Confidence Gap* (New York: Anchor Books, 1994), 270.

22. M. Boler, *Feeling Power: Emotions and Education* (New York: Routledge, 1999); E. Ellsworth, *Teaching Positions: Difference, Pedagogy, and the Power of Address* (New York: Teachers College Press, 1997).

CHAPTER 10: FACILITATING CHANGE IN THE CULTURE OF PRAYER IN DAY SCHOOL

1. *Tanakh* refers to the Torah, Prophets, and Writings, which comprise the canonized Bible. *Mishnah* refers to the Oral Law, and *sifrut* refers to Jewish/Hebrew literature.

2. See Moshe Drelich's report that at a *t'filah* workshop he ran for teachers, "almost all of the twenty participants in the workshop identified *tefillah* as their least favorite part of the school day. One teacher commented that supervising *davening* was as enjoyable as covering lunch duty!" Moshe Drelich, "*Tefillah* Motivation through Relationship Building and Role Modeling: One Rabbi's Approach," *Jewish Educational Leadership* 5, no. 2 (Winter 2007): 40–43.

3. D. Lehmann, "Student and Teacher Responses to Prayer at a Modern Orthodox Jewish High School," *Religious Education* 105 (2010): 299–316.

4. M. Drelich, "*Tefillah* Motivation through Relationship Building and Role Modeling."

5. Typically, non-Orthodox day schools attract a very heterogeneous population.

6. A striking exception to this practice is the South Area Solomon Schechter Day School (Norwood, Massachusetts), where, under the leadership of Jane Cohen, its longtime head, the school decided to engage teachers who were models of its religious philosophy. In that situation, it was not unusual for pupils to encounter their teachers in the synagogue on Shabbat and *Yom Tov*.

7. The three sections of the morning prayer service: the Morning Blessings, the Chapters of Praise, and the *Sh'ma* and Its Blessings.

8. R. A. Eammons and M. E. McCullough, "Counting Blessings versus Burdens: Experimental Studies of Gratitude and Subjective Well-Being," *Journal of Personality and Social Psychology* 84 (2003): 377–89.

9. J. Froh, W. J. Sefick, and R. A. Eammons, "Counting Blessings in Early Adolescents," *Journal of School Psychology* 46 (2008): 213–33.

10. M. E. McCullough, R. A. Eammons, and J. Tsang, "The Grateful Disposition: A Conceptual and Empirical Topography," *Journal of Personality and Social Psychology* 82 (2002): 112–17.

11. Ibid. The authors point out that while religious faith is not required in order for someone to feel gratitude, faith does enhance that ability.

12. It can be argued that the Jewish people introduced the organized concept of hope to the world in the image of the Messiah. *G'ulah* (redemption) is the dominant idea in the *Amidah*, the most important prayer in the liturgy, and is frequently encountered elsewhere in Rabbinic prayers, such as the *Kaddish* and *Aleinu*, which climax most services throughout the year.

13. It is probably relevant that many of these teachers were themselves also raising children and teenagers at home. In the case of Israelis, there was also some overlay of anxiety due to the decision to remain in the Diaspora, despite initial plans to make the move a temporary one.

14. Mezirow, 75–117.

15. J. Vella, *Professional Development as Transformative Learning* (San Francisco: Jossey-Bass, 1994).
16. Wachs.
17. The examples in this section are excerpted from material collected by the researcher.
18. Part of the morning prayers, based on Numbers 24:5. This prayer contains several different Hebrew terms for "dwelling."

Chapter 11: Kesher v'K'hilah

1. J. Woocher, "The Virtues of Knowing Oneself," *Torah at the Center* 11, no. 2 (2008):14, http://urj.org//learning/teacheducate/publications/tatc//?syspage=document&item_id=11190.
2. L. Novak Winer, "NFTY Isn't Just about Bowling," *Torah at the Center* 11, no. 2 (2008): 20–21, http://urj.org//learning/teacheducate/publications/tatc//?syspage=document&item_id=11190.
3. M. Ben-Avie and R. L. Goodman, "Learning about Youth Development from the NFTY Survey: An Interpretive Essay," Yale Child Study Center and Jewish Educational Change Team, 2007.
4. Ben-Avie and Goodman, "Learning about Youth Development," 5.
5. Ibid., 17.
6. Ibid., 12.
7. Ari Vared, conversation with Laura N. Winer, 2010.
8. Novak Winer, "NFTY Isn't Just about Bowling," 21.
9. North American Federation of Temple Youth, "Survey Results and Analysis for 2010 NFTY Survey" (unpublished raw data, 2010), 2.
10. D. Siroka, 6.
11. Bobby Harris, conversation with Laura N. Winer, 2010.
12. Literally, "repairing the world," the term *tikkun olam* often refers to social action/justice and/or service learning.
13. Ben-Avie and Goodman, "Learning about Youth Development," 28.
14. Alison Kur, "*K'hilah K'doshah*—If Not for Our Teens, When?" *Torah at the Center* 13, no. 1 (2009): 8, http://urj.org/learning/teacheducate/publications/tatc/?syspage=document&item_id=22580.
15. B. Pomerantz, "A Jump Start for a Small Congregation," *Torah at the Center* 13, no. 1 (2009): 10, http://urj.org/learning/teacheducate/publications/tatc/?syspage=document&item_id=22580.
16. James and James, cited in R. Kessler, *The Soul of Education: Helping Learners Find Connection, Compassion, and Character at School* (Alexandria, VA: Association for Supervision and Curriculum Development, 2000), 23.

CHAPTER 12: ASK JETHRO

1. Council of Jewish Federations, *NJPS 1990*, North American Jewish Data Bank, http://www.jewishdatabank.org/NJPS1990.asp.
2. B. Cousens, *Hillel's Journey: Distinctly Jewish, Universally Human* (Washington, DC: Hillel—The Foundation for Jewish Campus Life, 2007).
3. J. Zwilling, *Emerging Adulthood: The Hillel Model for Jewish Engagement* (Washington DC: Hillel—The Foundation for Jewish Campus Life, 2010).
4. P. M. King, "Principles of Development and Developmental Theory Underlying Theories of Cognitive and Moral Change," *Journal of College Student Development* 50, no. 6 (2009): 597–620; V. Torres, S. R. Jones, and K. A. Renn, "Identity Develoment Theories in Student Affairs: Origins, Current Status and New Approaches," *Journal of College Student Development* 50, no. 6 (2009): 577–96.
5. J. J. Arnett, "Emerging Adulthood: A Theory of Development from the Late Teens through the Twenties," *American Psychologist* 55, no. 5 (2000): 469.
6. The term "experiential education" is often used as interchangeable with "informal education," though this is the subject of much discussion. There is ongoing debate in the Jewish education field about whether or not there is a clear distinction between formal and informal education as separate disciplines, but that goes beyond the scope of this chapter. The authors do subscribe to the separate field theory, though, and have treated it in this chapter in that context.
7. B. Chazan, "What Is Informal Jewish Education?" *Journal of Jewish Communal Service* 67, no. 4 (1991): 300–308.
8. B. Chazan, "The Philosophy of Informal Jewish Education" (2003), in *Encyclopaedia of Informal Education*, http://www.infed.org/informaljew-isheducation/informal_jewish_education.htm.
9. Ibid., 15–16.
10. L. Saxe et al., *Jewish Futures Project: The Impact of Taglit Birthright Israel: 2010 Update* (Waltham, MA: Brandeis University, 2011).
11. E. Kopelowitz and A. Engelberg, *A Framework for Strategic Thinking about Jewish Peoplehood* (Tel Aviv: Nadav Foundation for the Advancement of Jewish Heritage, 2007), 3–4.
12. Ibid., 9.
13. S. Daloz Parks, *Big Questions, Worthy Dreams: Mentoring Young Adults in their Search for Meaning, Purpose and Faith* (San Francisco: Jossey-Bass, 2000), 6.
14. CEI is described below in greater detail in the section discussing programming at the University of Chicago Hillel.
15. Arnett, "Emerging Adulthood," 473.

REFERENCES

Pew Research Center for People and the Press, *How Young People View Their Lives, Futures and Politics: A Portrait of Generation Next* (Washington D.C.: Pew Research Center, 2007).

CHAPTER 13: CARRYING THE BURDEN OF THE OTHER

The authors wish to thank Jeffrey Kress for his thoughtful feedback on earlier drafts of this chapter.

1. Claussen, 2010; Michaelson, 2008.
2. Ira F. Stone, *A Responsible Life: The Spiritual Path of Mussar* (New York: Aviv Press, 2006); Moses Hayyim Luzzatto, *Mesillat Yesharim: The Path of the Upright*, introduction and commentary by Ira F. Stone (Philadelphia: Jewish Publication Society, 2010).
3. Grant, Schuster, Woocher, & Cohen (2004).
4. Diane Tickton Schuster, "Adult Jewish Learners: Entering the Conversation," *Journal of Jewish Education* 71 (2005): 246.
5. Bethamie Horowitz, "Reframing the Study of Contemporary American Jewish Identity," *Contemporary Jewry* 23, no. 1 (2002): 20.
6. See, e.g., Orit Kent, "A Theory of 'Havruta' Learning," *Journal of Jewish Education* 76, no. 3 (2010): 215–45; Miriam Raider-Roth and Elie Holzer, "Learning to Be Present: How 'Hevruta' Learning Can Activate Teachers' Relationships to Self, Other and Text," *Journal of Jewish Education* 75, no. 3 (2009): 216–39.
7. John Dewey, *Experience and Education*, 60th anniversary ed. (West Lafayette, IN: Kappa Delta Pi, 1998; L. S. Vygotsky, *Mind in Society: The Development of Higher Psychological Processes* (Cambridge, MA: Harvard University Press, 1978).
8. P. Fonagy et al., "Attachment, the Reflective Self, and Borderline States: The Predictive Specificity of the Adult Attachment Interview and Pathological Emotional Development," in *Attachment Theory: Social, Developmental, and Clinical Perspectives*, eds. S. Goldberg, R. Muir, and J. Kerr (New York: Analytic Press, 1995), 233–78.
9. A. Slade, "Reflective Parenting Programs: Theory and Development," *Psychoanalytic Inquiry* 26, no. 4 (2007): 641.
10. P. Fonagy and M. Target, "Bridging the Transmission Gap: An End to an Important Mystery of Attachment Research?" *Attachment & Human Development* 7 (2005): 3, 333–43; H. Steele and M. Steele, "On the Origins of Reflective Functioning," in Fredric N. Busch, *Mentalization: Theoretical Considerations, Research Findings, and Clinical Implications,*

Psychoanalytic Inquiry Book Series 29 (New York: Analytic Press, 2008), 133–58).

11. The MLP *madrich* (facilitator) training has been standardized into a two-year program that addresses this issue and as well as other questions pertaining to facilitating a *musar vaad*.

12. Bellah, 1985; Wuthnow, 1998.

13. Robert Wuthnow, *Sharing the Journey: Support Groups and America's New Quest for Community* (New York: Free Press, 1994), 4.

14. Ibid., 7.

15. Cohen and Eisen, 2000.

16. Joseph Reimer, "Beyond More Jews Doing Jewish: Clarifying the Goals of Informal Jewish Education," *Journal of Jewish Education* 73, no. 1 (2007): 16.

17. M. Donovan, "Ethics and Reflecting Processes: A Systemic Perspective," *Journal of Social Work Practice* 21, no. 2 (2007): 225–33.

18. E. Gantt and R. N. Williams, eds., *Psychology for the Other: Levinas, Ethics and the Practice of Psychology* (Pittsburgh: Duquesne University Press, 2002).

19. J. Grienenberger, "Group Process as a Holding Environment Facilitating the Development of the Parental Reflective Function: Commentary on the Article by Arietta Slade," *Psychoanalytic Inquiry* 26, no. 4 (2007): 668–75.

20. Andrew Heinze, "The Americanization of Mussar: Abraham Twerski's Twelve Steps," *Judaism* 48, no. 4 (1999): 450–69.

21. N. Jecker, "Adult Moral Development: Ancient, Medieval, Modern Paths," *Generations* 14, no. 4 (1990): 19–24.

22. M. Leicester, "Cognitive Development, Self Knowledge and Moral Education," *Journal of Moral Education* 26, no. 4 (1997): 455–72.

23. A. Leonard, "Educational Communities: The Future of Experiential Education," *Journal of Experiential Education* 3, no. 1 (1980): 13–16.

24. M. Levenson, "Three Models of Adult Development," *Human Development* 39, no. 3 (1996): 135–49.

25. J. Marcia, "Identity and Psychosocial Development in Adulthood," *Identity* 2, no. 1 (2002): 7–28.

26. M. Nakkula, "Transforming Self-Control through Peer Relationships," *Reclaiming Children and Youth* 17, no. 4 (2009): 35–40.

27. D. Reynolds, "Mindful Parenting: A Group Approach to Enhancing Reflective Capacity in Parents and Infants," *Journal of Child Psychotherapy* 29, no. 3 (2003): 357–74.

CHAPTER 14: SOCIAL-EMOTIONAL AND CHARACTER DEVELOPMENT AND JEWISH
PARENTING

1. H. G. Ginott, *Between Parent and Teenager* (New York: Macmillan, 1967),
   243.
2. R. Kessler, *The Soul of Education* (Alexandria, VA: ASCD, 2000); P.
   Palmer, "Evoking the Spirit in Public Education," *Educational Leadership*
   56, no. 4 (1999): 6–11; J. Zins et al., eds., *Building Academic Success on
   Social and Emotional Learning: What Does the Research Say?* (New York:
   Teachers College Press, 2004).
3. W. Damon, J. Menon, and K. Bronk, "The Development of Purpose during Adolescence," *Applied Developmental Science* 7, no. 3 (2003): 119–28.
4. R. Staton and H. Cobb, "Religion and Spirituality," in *Children's Needs
   III: Development, Prevention, and Intervention*, eds. G. Bear and K. Minke
   (Bethesda, MD: National Association of School Psychologists, 2006),
   369–78.
5. S. B. Sarason, "American Psychology, and the Needs for Transcendence
   and Community," *American Journal of Community Psychology* 21 (1993):
   188.
6. J. Fowler, *Stages of Faith* (New York: Harper and Row, 1981).
7. R. Staton and H. Cobb, "Religion and Spirituality."
8. D. Gordis, *Becoming a Jewish Parent* (New York: Three Rivers Press,
   1999); H. Gardner, *Intelligence Reframed: Multiple Intelligences for the 21st
   Century* (New York: Basic Books, 1999).
9. Gordis, *Becoming a Jewish Parent*, 95.
10. D. McAdams, *The Redemptive Self: Stories Americans Live By* (New
    York: Oxford University Press, 2006); J. W. Pennebaker, "Writing about
    Emotional Experiences as a Therapeutic Process," *Psychological Science* 8
    (1997): 162–66.
11. Y. Buxbaum, *Storytelling and Spirituality in Judaism* (Northvale, NJ: Jason
    Aronson, 1994.
12. N. Gillman, "Judaism and the Search for Spirituality," *Conservative
    Judaism* 38, no. 2 (1986): 5–18.
13. S. Wachs, *Teenagers, Spirituality, and Prayer in the Jewish Community
    Secondary School* (Merion Station, PA: Akiba Hebrew Academy Press,
    1999).
14. Gardner, *Intelligence Reframed*.
15. D. Goleman, *Social Intelligence: The New Science of Human Relationships*
    (New York: Bantam, 2007).
16. M. Elias et al., *Promoting Social and Emotional Learning: Guidelines for
    Educators* (Alexandria, VA: ASCD, 1997).
17. R. Brandt, "How New Knowledge about the Brain Applies to Social and
    Emotional Learning," in *EQ + IQ: Best Practices in Leadership for Caring*

and Successful Schools, ed. M. J. Elias, H. Arnold, and C. Steiger Hussey (Thousand Oaks, CA: Corwin Press, 2003), 57–70.

18. Zins et al., *Building Academic Success*.
19. M. J. Elias, S. E. Tobias, and B. S. Friedlander, *Emotionally Intelligent Parenting* (New York: Three Rivers Press/Random House, 2000).
20. I. E. Sigel, J. S. Kress, and M. J. Elias, "Beyond Questioning: Inquiry Strategies and Cognitive and Affective Elements of Jewish Education, *Journal of Jewish Education* 73, no. 1 (2007): 51–66.
21. M. J. Elias and M. Gootman, *The J(oy) of Parenting: Everyday Insights from Jewish Wisdom* (in press).
22. M. Eisenberg et al., "Correlations between Family Meals and Psychosocial Well-Being among Adolescents," *Archives of Pediatric Adolescent Medicine* 158 (2004): 792–96; http://family.samhsa.gov/get/mealtime.aspx.
23. Goleman, *Social Intelligence*.
24. R. A. Emmons and M. E. McCullough, *The Psychology of Gratitude* (New York: Oxford University Press, 2004).
25. J. Wertheimer, ed., *Family Matters: Jewish Education in an Age of Choice* (Waltham, MA: Brandeis University Press, 2007).
26. Cf. Elias and Gootman, *The J(oy) of Parenting*.

CONCLUSION: SETTING THE STAGE FOR SPIRITUAL, SOCIAL, AND EMOTIONAL GROWTH

1. E.g., U. Bronfenbrenner, *The Ecology of Human Development: Experiments by Nature and Design* (Cambridge, MA: Harvard University Press, 1979).
2. S. H. Billig, "Research on K–12 School-Based Service Learning: The Evidence Builds," *Phi Delta Kappan* 81 (2000): 658–64.
3. B. Novick, J. S. Kress, and M. J. Elias, *Building Learning Communities with Character: How to Integrate Academic, Social, and Emotional Learning* (Alexandria, VA: Association for Supervision and Curriculum Development, 2002).
4. J. S. Kress and J. Reimer, "Shabbatonim as Experiential Education in North American Community Day High Schools," in *Jewish Day Schools, Jewish Communities*, eds. A. Pomson and H. Deitcher (Oxford: Littman Library of Jewish Studies, 2009), 341–60.
5. J. Wertheimer, *Linking the Silos: How to Accelerate the Momentum in Jewish Education Today* (New York: AVI CHAI Foundation, 2005).
6. Smith and Denton (2005).
7. Ibid., 269.
8. P. L. Berger, *The Sacred Canopy: Elements of a Sociological Theory of Religion* (New York: Anchor Books, 1967), 16–17.

9. C. Cherniss, "Teacher Empowerment, Consultation, and the Creation of New Programs in Schools," *Journal of Educational & Psychological Consultation* 8, no. 2 (1997): 135; R. Evans, *The Human Side of School Change: Reform, Resistance, and the Real-Life Problems of Innovation* (San Francisco: Jossey-Bass, 1996).

10. J. Reimer and D. Bryfman, "Experiential Jewish Education," in *What We Now Know about Jewish Education: Perspectives on Research for Practice*, eds. R. L. Goodman, P. A. Flexner, and L. D. Bloomberg (Los Angeles: Torah Aura Productions, 2008), 343–52.

11. J. S. Kress, *Development, Learning, and Community: Educating for Identity in Pluralistic Jewish High Schools* (Brighton, MA: Academic Studies Press, in press).

12. M. Csikszentmihalyi, *Flow: The Psychology of Optimal Experience* (New York: Harper and Row, 1990).

13. J. S. Kress, "Reflection and Connections: The Other Side of Integration," *Journal of Jewish Education* 76 (2010): 164–88.

14. J. Reimer, "A Response to Barry Chazan: The Philosophy of Informal Jewish Education," *Encyclopedia of Informal Education*, 2003, http://www.infed.org/informaljewisheducation/informal_jewish_education_reply.htm.

15. Z. Schachter-Shalomi and H. Smith, "Spirituality in Education: A Dialogue," in *The Heart of Learning: Spirituality in Education*, ed. S. Glazer (New York: Tarcher/Penguin, 1999), 230.

16. B. Chazan, "The Philosopy of Informal Jewish Education," *Encyclopedia of Informal Education*, 2003, http://www.infed.org/informaljewisheducation/informal_jewish_education.htm.

17. D. A. Drubach, "Judaism, Brain Plasticity, and the Making of the Self," *Journal of Religion and Health* 41, no. 4 (2002): 311–322; E. Jensen, *Teaching with the Brain in Mind* (Alexandria, VA: Association for Supervision and Curriculum Development, 1998).

Permissions

Every attempt has been made to obtain permission to reprint previously published material. The publisher gratefully acknowledges the following for permissions obtained.

Anna Fuchs, Executive Director, Jewish Kids Groups (in Atlanta).